OUT ON A LIMB

"This book is about the experience of getting in touch with myself when I was in my early forties. It's about the connection between mind, body, and spirit. And what I learned as a result has enabled me to get on with the rest of my life as an almost transformed human being. So this book is about a quest for myself—a quest which took me on a long journey that was gradually revealing and at all times amazing. I tried to keep an open mind as I went because I found myself gently but firmly exposed to dimensions of time and space that heretofore, for me, belonged to science fiction or what I would describe as the occult. But it happened to me. It happened slowly. It happened at a pace that apparently was peculiarly my own, as I believe all people experience such events. People progress according to what they're ready for. I must have been ready for what I learned because it was the right time. . . ."

—Shirley MacLaine

"A woman of considerable intelligence and charm."
—*The Washington Post*

"More startling than any of her celebrated films . . . *Out on a Limb* is out of this world."
—*The Toronto Sun*

Bantam Books by Shirley MacLaine

DANCING IN THE LIGHT
"DON'T FALL OFF THE MOUNTAIN"
OUT ON A LIMB
YOU CAN GET THERE FROM HERE

Out
on a
Limb

Shirley MacLaine

BANTAM BOOKS
TORONTO · NEW YORK · LONDON · SYDNEY · AUCKLAND

OUT ON A LIMB

A Bantam hardcover edition / July 1983
13 printings through December 1983
Bantam rack-size edition / April 1984
31 printings through August 1987

Grateful acknowledgment is made to the publishers named below for
permission to reprint the following material:

Excerpt from The Forgotten Language by Erich Fromm. Copyright
1951, © 1979 by Erich Fromm. Reprinted by permission of Holt, Rinehart
and Winston, Publishers.
Excerpt from Albert Einstein: Philosopher-Scientist. Copyright ©
1959 by the Library of Living Philosophers, Inc. All rights reserved.
Excerpt from C. G. Jung, Letters, ed. Gerhard Adler and Aniela
Jaffe, trans. R. F. C. Hull, Bollingen Series XCV, Vol. 1.: 1906–1950.
Copyright © 1971, 1973 by Princeton University Press. Excerpt, page
343, reprinted by permission of Princeton University Press.
Excerpt from A. Eddington, The Nature of the Physical World.
Reprinted with the kind permission of Cambridge University Press. All
rights reserved.
Excerpt from Albert Einstein, The World As I See It. Reprinted with
the kind permission of the Philosophical Library, Inc. All rights reserved.
Excerpt from Joseph Wood Krutch, More Lives Than One. Copyright
© 1962 by Joseph Wood Krutch. By permission of William Morrow &
Company.
Note: Every effort has been made to locate the copyright owner of
material reproduced in this book. Omissions brought to our attention
will be corrected in subsequent editions.

Library of Congress Cataloging in Publication Data
MacLaine, Shirley, 1934–
Out on a limb.
1. MacLaine, Shirley, 1934–   . 2. Entertainers—
United States—Biography. 3. Spiritualists—United
States—Biography. 1. Title.
PN2287.M18A83 1938   791.43'028'0924 [B]   82-45955
ISBN 0-553-26352-8

Published simultaneously in the United States and Canada

PRINTED IN THE UNITED STATES OF AMERICA

O   40 39 38 37 36 35 34 33 32 31

Dear Reader,

From the time I was very small, I remember having the impulse to "express" myself. At the age of three I attended dance classes because I wanted to express myself physically. As a teenager, I went from dancing to singing, which seemed a natural and logical extension of that self-expression. Later, as an adult, I carried that impulse for expression even further, into acting, and experienced a greater form of expression. I loved the intricate mystery of being another character, sorting out background and motivation and meaning, exploring my own feelings and thoughts in relation to another person.

Then I found writing—an outlet that enabled me to express more intricately and specifically my experiences. I wrote to know what I was thinking. I wrote to understand my profession, my travels, my relationships, and, in fact, my life. Writing helped to whet an already insatiable appetite to understand the *why* and *how* of everything.

I like to think of each of my books as a kind of map depicting where I've been and where I'm going. *"Don't Fall off the Mountain"* described how I learned to spread my wings as a young artist and began to take charge of my personal destiny. In a series of expeditions to Africa, India, the Himalayan Kingdom of Bhutan, and to the land of my daughter Sachi's namesake, Japan, I first reached out to touch the unknown—and was changed by it. The personal period profiled in *You Can Get There From Here* was one of great internal, intellectual, and political growth for me. The star system had come to an end in Hollywood, so I ventured into the quicksands of television. The result was disastrous and the impact on me profound. It drove me to test myself in the political arena during the presidential election of 1972, when I campaigned for George McGovern against Richard Nixon. That experience motivated me to pursue a desire few Westerners had been allowed to fulfill in the early 1970s. I led the first women's delegation to China to study the remarkable evolution of a brand-new culture from the ashes of an ancient and little-known land. The experience of adjusting to an alien culture brought us smack-up against ourselves. We learned about our own evolution as well, and even more about what the human will, properly directed, can accomplish even against great odds. All of this prepared me to return to my performing career with a greater enthusiasm and appreciation for the craft by which I earned my living, and to explore what new levels of creativity I could bring to it. I believe this experience also helped to drive home another lesson: Anything is possible if you believe you deserve it.

I thought for a long time before I published *Out on a Limb* because it is the written expression of a spiritual odyssey that took me further than I ever expected to go, into an astonishing and moving world of psychic phenomena where past lives, the existence of spirit guides, and the genuine immortality of the soul became more than concepts to me—they became real, true parts of my life. I think of this book as my spiritual diary opened to the eyes of those who also seek an inner understanding, and as my statement to those who taught me and opened my eyes that I accept their gifts with gratitude and humility.

I like to think of *Dancing in the Light* as a celebration of all my "selves." It was a fulfilling and satisfying exploration of the promises I made to myself in *Out on a Limb*. In it I look with pleasure, humor, and some contentment upon my experiences as a daughter, a mother, a lover, a friend, a seeker of spiritual destiny, and a voice calling for peace in the world. I think it expresses my great personal joy at reaching this important point in my life, as well as the strengthening of my sense of purpose. But the story is not yet finished, for I am still a woman in search of myself, the lives I might have lived and the inner heart of my being.

If my search for inner truth helps give you, the reader, the gift of insight, then I am rewarded. But my first reward has been the journey through myself, the only journey worth taking. Through it all I have learned one deep and meaningful lesson: LIFE, LIVES, and REALITY are only what we each *perceive* them to be. Life doesn't happen to us. We make it happen. Reality isn't separate from us. We are creating our reality every moment of the day. For me that truth is the ultimate freedom and the ultimate responsibility.

Love and Light,

Shirley MacLaine

Some of the people who appear in this book are presented as composite characters in order to protect their privacy, and the sequence of some of the events is adapted accordingly. But all the events are real.

*To my Mother
and
my Father*

"Never utter these words: 'I do not know this, therefore it is false.' One must study to know; know to understand; understand to judge."

—Apothegm of Narada

"There are more things in heaven and earth, Horatio, than are dreamt of in your philosophy."

—Hamlet

Chapter 1

"The dreams of ancient and modern man are written in the same language as the myths whose authors lived in the dawn of history. . . . I believe that symbolic language is the one foreign language that each of us must learn. Its understanding brings us in touch with one of the most significant sources of wisdom. . . . Indeed, both dreams and myths are important communications from ourselves to ourselves."

—ERICH FROMM
The Forgotten Language

The sand was cold and soft as I jogged along the beach. The tide came in steadily and by sundown it would reach the pilings that supported the houses along Malibu Road. I loved to jog just before the sun set because watching the magenta clouds above the surf helped divert my attention from how much my legs hurt. Some health instructor had once told me that jogging three miles in soft sand was the same as jogging six miles on a hard surface. And I wanted to stay healthy no matter how painful it was. When I wasn't dancing, running kept me in shape.

But what was the story I had heard the day before—about the two brothers? One was a health nut who jogged along the boulevard five miles early every morning of his life regardless of how he felt. The other never

1

did any exercise. One morning the health nut brother was out jogging along the road and turned around to shake a finger at his lazy brother when—bam! He just didn't see the truck...

Maybe it didn't really matter what we did to preserve ourselves. There was always some truck somewhere. The thing was not to let that stop you, not to let it direct your life.

I remembered sitting at the dinner table with my mother and father in Virginia, where I grew up. I was about twelve and the thought struck me that regardless of how much happiness I might feel at any given moment, I was *aware* of the struggle underneath. The "trouble" I called it then... everything had some brand of trouble attached to it. I remembered my Dad had said I had inadvertently struck on an old Greek principle— Pythagorean, I think he said. Dad was a kind of country philosopher and had almost gotten his degree in philosophy at Johns Hopkins University. He loved to speculate on philosophical meaning. I guess I inherited the same trait. I remembered he said my thought had a deep and principled meaning which was true of all life. No matter how good something might seem to be, there was always the negative compensating factor to consider. Vice versa was true too, of course—he said—but Dad seemed to focus on the negative. For me, it made me aware of the duality in life. In a blinding flash over the Birdseye peas, I had felt I understood *some*thing, without knowing quite what I understood.

❧ The wind came up sloshing the waves into white-caps further out to sea. Sandpipers scurried in and out of the ripples, savoring what food might be washed up with the tide while their graceful wide-winged pelican brothers swooped and then dove, like mad kamikaze pilots, headlong into schools of fish swimming further out in deeper water.

I wondered what it would feel like to be a bird with nothing on my mind but flying and eating. I remembered reading that the smallest bird could travel thousands of miles across the Pacific unencumbered and alone, needing only one piece of baggage; one possession . . . a twig. He could carry the twig in his beak and when he got tired he simply descended to the sea and floated on it until he was ready to move on again. He fished from the twig, ate from the twig, and slept on the twig. Who needed the *Queen Mary*? He flapped his wings, clamped his life raft in his mouth and set out to see more of the world.

What a life. I wondered if that bird ever got lonely. But even if he was alone he seemed to perceive the proper direction for his life. Birds seemed to have innate compasses that guided them wherever they wanted to go. They seemed to know just exactly what they were, how to live, why they were alive. But did they have feelings? Did they fall in love? Did they cocoon themselves off with only one other bird as though it was the two of them against everything? Birds seemed *part* of everything. Space, time, air. No, how could they shut out the world if they wanted to fly over it?

I remembered an experience I had had once. I call it an experience and not a dream, even though it happened when I was asleep, because it felt more real than a dream. I felt I was suspended over the Earth and I dipped and flowed with the air currents just like the birds. I floated over countries and mountains and streams and trees. As I drifted, the tops of trees brushed gently across me. I was careful not to pluck even one loose leaf from the branch to which it belonged because I, too, belonged to everything there was. I wanted to go further and faster and higher and wider—and the higher I went the more I became connected, my being concentrated and expanded at the same time. I had the sensation that this was actually happening, that my body was irrelevant and that *that* was part of the experience. The real me was floating free and clear, filled with the peace of connection to everything that was.

It was not the usual sexually oriented flying dream which psychologists describe. This was more. There was another dimension to it. The word I'm looking for, I thought to myself as I ran, is "extra." That was why I had remembered it so vividly, and whenever I felt displeased or lonely or out of sorts or strung up and nervous, I thought of that experience and of how peaceful I had felt when I floated outside of my physical body feeling *involved* with all there was above and below me.

That feeling of belonging to "everything" gave me more pleasure than anything. More pleasure than working, than simply making love, than being successful or any of the other human endeavors people devoted themselves to in order to achieve happiness. I loved to *think*. I loved to concentrate. I loved to be *involved* with concerns outside myself because, to be honest, I believed that was actually my path to understanding myself. Somewhere way underneath *me* were the answers to everything that caused anxiety and confusion in the *world*. What an arrogant thought! But, if I could touch *me*, really touch *me*, I could touch the world... maybe even the universe. That was why I was a political activist, a feminist, a traveler, a kind of curious human reporter; and probably it was why I was an actress and performer. I needed to reach inside and touch me if I was going to understand the world and also if I was going to be any good in my work. That was probably why I began my life as a dancer. When I moved, I was in touch with who I was. Whatever... to me the journey most worthwhile taking was the journey through myself.

A chill wind scattered sand around my legs as I ran. I slowed down to a walk, remembering that after hard exercise it's good to ease off gradually so the lactic acid in the muscles doesn't congeal. "That's what makes your muscles sore," the gym instructor had said. "Never stop cold after hard exercise. Come down slowly. You'll hurt less later."

I listened with attentiveness to anything to do with physical culture because I understood that it put me more in touch with myself. I respected my body because it was the only one I had. I wanted to make it last. But, my God, it could be painful, especially when I had let fifteen years pass with no exercise at all to speak of. That was really dumb, I thought as I walked. All those years of acting, I thought my body wasn't that important. I had had good formal training as a dancer when I was young; that would be enough, I thought. I was wrong. People have to take care of their bodies every day or they can wake up one morning and find it won't do what they want it to. Then they'll say they are old. I always felt old when I was not in touch with my body. And the process of connecting with my body put me more in touch with the real me inside of that body. And what was the real me? What was it that made me question and search and think and feel? Was it just the physical brain, the little gray cells, or was it the mind which was something more than brain? Did "mind," or perhaps "personality," include what people called the soul"? Were they all separate, or was being human a recognition that one was the sum of all these parts, and if so, how did they fit together?

That is what this book is about . . . it's about the experience of getting in touch with myself when I was in my early forties; it's about what the experience did to my mind, to my forbearance, to my spirit, and *for* my patience and belief. It's about the connection between mind, body, and spirit. And what I learned as a result has enabled me to get on with the rest of my life as an almost transformed human being.

So this book is about a quest for my self—a quest which took me on a long journey that was gradually revealing and at all times simply amazing. I tried to keep an open mind as I went because I found myself gently but firmly exposed to dimensions of time and space that heretofore, for me, belonged in science fiction or what I would describe as the occult. But it happened to me. It happened slowly. It happened at a pace that apparently was peculiarly my own, as I believe all people experience such events. People progress according to what they're ready for. I must have been ready for what I learned because it was the right time.

❧ I had made about thirty-five movies—some good, some bad, and from each I think I learned, although, not surprisingly, more from the bad ones than the good ones. I had traveled all over the world, sometimes as a private person, usually unrecognizable (because I wanted it that way), and sometimes as an entertainer (where I wanted to be recognized), either publicizing one of my films, shooting a television special, or touring with my live show. I loved performing live because it enabled me to *feel* the audiences; what they were thinking, where their interests lay, their differing senses of humor. But mostly I loved meeting new people and crashing head-on into foreign cultures until I learned to meld into them comfortably.

I developed a kind of home-away-from-home circle of friends. They were people in the arts—performers, movie people from every country that made films, writers (I had written two books myself about my travels and adventures in life and they had been translated nearly everywhere), heads of state, prime ministers, kings and queens (my political activism had been duly reported, pro and con, all over the world too). I was a privileged person, there was no doubt about that. I had worked hard for my success but still I felt lucky and as I said, *privileged* to be able to meet and converse with anyone I wanted to, from Castro, the Pope, the Queen of England, and other dignitaries, to India's sick and dying, or revolutionary peasants in the barrios of the Philippines, or Sherpas in the Himalayas, just to name a few.

And the more I traveled and met people, the more my social and political conscience became activated. And the more it became activated, the more I found myself identifying with the "underdogs" as my father defined them. But as I pointed out to him, most of the world could be classified as underdogs. Anyway, I found myself thinking a great deal about what was going wrong in the world. You can't avoid it when you actually *see* the destitution, the starvation, the hatred. I began traveling when I was nineteen, and now, at mid-forty, I could objectively say things had steadily progressed downhill. To me, democratic idealism seemed to be no longer possible because people who were part of the democratic way of life were apparently more concerned with serving their own interests and were therefore abusing their basic philosophy of the well-being of the majority. Not many people were addressing themselves to international ethics. "Political thinking" in the world seemed to be based on the dual fields of power politics and material economics, with solutions expressed in terms of graphs, charts, polls, and industrial programs that ignored the individual human being.

Somewhere on the planet at all times there was war, violence, crime, oppression, dictatorship, starvation, genocide—a global spectacle of human desperation and misery. Meanwhile, leaders worldwide continued to examine the problems solely in terms of the *problems themselves* without recognizing their true relationship to a larger and more universal necessity—the deep-seated need to achieve an enduringly peaceful state of mind on an individual basis, with all the broad implications that that would entail. They had temporary solutions for permanent problems. Or, as Dad would say, "they are putting Band-Aids on cancer."

I found myself in endless discussions all over the world about whether mankind was fundamentally selfish, self-serving, and concerned primarily with the attainment of more luxurious creature comforts and personal gain. I found myself saying that maybe personal selfishness and competition were detrimental not only to happiness but even to personal success. It seemed to me that even though the world powers recognized the need for a unity of human interest, they always recommended more highly competitive economic policies to achieve that end, which could only lead to human conflict, discord, and inevitably larger wars. Something was surely missing.

Then, as I continued to travel, I noticed that something was changing. People I talked to began to speculate on what it was that was missing. The tone of

our conversations shifted from dismay and confusion to
a consideration that the answers might lie within ourselves,
as though the self-created plight of mankind had nothing whatever to do with economic solutions. We began
to speculate on the inner search for what we as humans
really meant. What were we here for? Did we have a
purpose or were we simply a passing accident? That we
were *physical* was obvious. Our physical needs were, in
theory at least, the priority concern of governments and
leaders. That we were *mental* creatures was clear too.
The world of the mind, the mental dimension, was
attended to by education, arts, sciences and the halls of
learning.

But were we all not also *spiritual*? I found that
more and more people were focusing on the question of
our inner spirituality which had for so long been starved
for recognition. Did confusion stem from the fact that
spirituality was not only obvious, but invisible? The
religions of the world didn't seem to explain or satisfy
our spiritual needs. In fact, the Church seemed to
divide people more than it unified them, whether one
followed Christianity, Islam, Judaism, or Buddhism.
Indeed, the world seemed to be moving into an era of
Holy Conflict, what with the violent rise of Islamic
pride in the Arab world, of self-righteous Christian
fundamentalism among the so-called moral majority in
America, and of militant Zionism in Israel.

I found myself in touch with a network of friends
all over the world who were involved with their own
spiritual search. We asked questions about human purpose and meaning in relation not only to our physical
perspective of life on earth, but also to our metaphysical perspective in relation to time and space. It began
to seem possible that this life was not all there was.
Perhaps the physical plane of existence was not the only
plane of existence. The marvellous possibility existed
that the *real* reality was much more.

In other words, perhaps Buckminster Fuller was
right when he claimed that ninety-nine percent of
reality was *invisible,* and our inability to acknowledge

that invisible reality was due to what was now common-
ly being referred to as our low conscious awareness.

When I began to ask myself these questions and
found a real kinship with others who were also involved
in the same inner search, my life changed and so did
my perspective. It was thrilling, at times frightening,
and always mind-boggling because it caused me to
reevaluate what being alive was all about. Perhaps we,
as human beings, were actually part of an ongoing
experience that continued long after we thought we
died. Perhaps there was no such thing as death.

But I'm getting ahead of myself.

The sun was setting chilled and shimmering beyond
the hills of Point Dume. I remembered standing on
those hills looking into the crashing waves of the Pacific
below, wondering if the human race really did get its
start in the sea. The Pacific always reminded me of my
friend David. Or perhaps he was much on my mind
these days simply because I seemed to be arriving at
some kind of turning point in my life and he was easy to
talk to. What was it he had said? Something about the
spiritual need for respecting both the positive and the
negative in life equally.

"It's impossible to have one without the other," he
said. "Life is the *combustion* of the two. You just try to
overwhelm the negative with the positive and you'll be
much happier."

"Sure," I had said, "you don't have to be a rocket
scientist to know that . . . but living it is something
else."

David was an interesting man. About thirty-five
years old, he was a sweet, very gentle person, with
chiseled cheekbones and a kind of soft, sad smile. I had
met him at an art gallery in the Village in New York.
We struck up a friendship because I found it comfortable being with him. He was a painter and a poet and
very much at home anywhere because he was an observer of life. In Manhattan we'd walk for hours watching

people and wondering what they thought. When he was in California, which was often, we'd walk the beach in Malibu. David loved to travel too, and he'd done a lot of it, from Africa and India to the Far East and back again to Europe and South America. He painted and wrote along the way. It didn't cost him much because he worked his way around the world doing all sorts of odd jobs. He had been married once. He didn't talk about it but he did volunteer one day that he used to be a "fast liver." When I asked him what that meant he just waved his hand and said, "That's in the past. I'm finished with the fast cars, high living—kid stuff. Now I'm alone, and happy." I didn't talk much about my personal life either. That was not the nature of our relationship. He was also into a whole lot of stuff I had no time for—reincarnation, past life recall, cosmic justice, vibrational frequencies, food-combining, spiritual enlightenment, meditation, self-realization, and God knows what else. He talked seriously about all that and seemingly with deep knowledge. But most of it went right by me because I was caught up in my movie scripts, my television specials, new numbers for my club act, losing weight, and Gerry. I wanted to talk to David about Gerry, but because of the circumstances, I couldn't talk to anyone, not even David, about Gerry.

❷ Now, in the chill breeze, I felt perspiration dripping down the back of my hair onto my neck. My legs hurt, but it was a good feeling. I had jogged hard. It was a satisfied kind of hurt. Maybe, as David said, that was the price for everything in life. And when you reached the proper place after struggle it wouldn't hurt anymore.

I took a last look at the setting sun and made my way up the wooden stairs that led to the beach. I loved those wooden stairs, scarred and broken from high tides and storms. For twenty years I had used those stairs, since I built the apartment building with the paycheck I had received from my first picture, *The Trouble with Harry,* for Alfred Hitchcock. The first thing I did was get a loan so I could put up a building where I could rent out apartments and live rent-free myself . . . just in case I got hit by a truck and couldn't work. My middle-class upbringing, I guess. Always protect against the future. You never know.

I washed the sand from my feet under a shower at the top of the wooden stairs . . . mustn't track sand into the apartment. It lodges in the carpet that the builder told me I shouldn't install in a beach place anyway.

I climbed the last set of stairs leading to the patio, where I stopped and looked at the Japanese garden I had landscaped myself, complete with a bonsai tree from Kyoto and a trickling stream of water that flowed constantly up and over itself. The years I had traveled in the Far East, particularly Japan, had influenced me deeply. Their Spartan sense of respect for nature moved me. Since the Japanese were so buffeted by nature, they had no choice but to harmonize with it. They didn't believe in conquering it as we did in the West. They used it and became part of it . . . that is, until they forfeited their respect for nature in favor of their respect for business and profit. And when Japan became polluted, I stopped going there. I wondered how long it would be before the whole world would industrialize nature just so it could make more money. Simplistic, I suppose, but that's how it seemed to me.

I heard the phone ring in my apartment. I nearly tripped over myself in a lurching jolt to get there before it stopped. Phones did that to me. I'd answer someone else's phone if it rang when I was there. Something about being efficient and prompt and tidy. I was annoyed by people who let a phone ring four times before they picked it up. Sloppy it was to me—just plain lazy and sloppy.

I bolted through the door into the living room and dove for the phone on the floor. I had to laugh at myself. Who the hell could be that important? And if they were, they'd call back.

"Hello," I said breathlessly, wondering what the person on the other end would think I'd been doing.

"Hellooo . . ." It was Gerry. "How are you?"

I could hear the long-distance operator in the background. Gerry's face, tumbling hair on his forehead, soft black eyes, swept through my mind.

"I'm great," I said, glad he couldn't see how happy I was to hear his voice. "How's it going with Her Majesty?"

"We are declining in England with grace," he joked with a twinge of serious concern I had learned to detect.

"Well," I cleared my throat, "grace is a quality everyone admires."

"Yes. Well, I'm doing what I can to prevent the ship from sinking completely."

I could feel him reach for a cigarette and inhale with a soft whistling sound.

"Gerry?"

"Yes."

"How's your campaign going? Are you making headway?"

"Oh, fine," he said. But there was a slight depression in his voice. "It's a long, slow process. People need to be taught and educated with velvet-firm strokes. The balance isn't easy. But we'll talk about that when we're together."

"Oh?" I said. "Will that be soon?"

"Yes, I hope so. Can you meet me this weekend in Honolulu? I have a conference on North-South Economics."

"Oh, Jesus. Yes," I said. "Will there be many journalists?"

"Yes."

"Is that all right?"

"Yes."

"You are willing to take that risk?"

"Yes."

"Okay. I'll be there. When?"

"Friday."

"Where?"

"Kahala Hilton. I have to go now. I have a meeting with my Deputy Secretary. He's waiting."

"Okay. Great. See you this weekend."

"Goodbye." He hung up. There were never prolonged telephonic goodbyes with Gerry. His professional demeanor and habit precluded that kind of sloppiness. His personal life was another matter.

I hung up, took a shower and drove, more slowly than usual, to my big house in Encino.

I loved to sit behind the wheel in a California car, mosey along the wide open highways, and think. I loved to think in California. New York was so live-wired there was time only to act on instinct and for survival, which I found creative and exciting, but in California I could reflect. Of course, California wasn't called the Big Orange for nothing. You could turn into one if you weren't careful. So the Big Apple, for me, was a place where I could act on things that I had thought through in the Big Orange. Gerry had not been able to come to California since I'd known him.

I remembered our first night in New York together. Actually, I had been introduced to him several times before, when I was in London and once again when he had come to an anti-Vietnam rally in New York. I had been impressed by his self-assured soft-spokenness, and his mind of quick brilliance. He was in Parliament, a Socialist, and he believed he could make England work again.

He wasn't pompous like so many well-educated English people I knew. In fact, he was the opposite: a big man, well over six feet, with such shoulders and arms that he reminded me of a bear who needed to hug the world. Loose and freewheeling. His body moved in a careless way and his shirt fell open when his tie was slung around his neck. When he was excited about something a thick shock of hair tumbled into his eyes. And when he paced with long strides across a room, searching for the best way to make a point, one had the impression that the room tilted with his weight. He seemed unaware of how imposing he was. Often he had a hole in his sock. His eyes were moist and black. They made me think of olives.

When I had first been introduced to him in London I was playing the Palladium. He came backstage and I liked him. I didn't know much about English politics but he seemed open, penetratingly intelligent, and involuntarily funny. When he left my dressing room he walked so deliberately that he fell over a chair, but not until he had first walked into my closet.

So when he happened to be in New York a year later and called me I said yes, I'd love to have dinner.

We went to an Indian restaurant on Fifty-eighth Street. He didn't eat much. He was hardly aware the food was there. And he had a habit of resting his eyes on my mouth when he needed to think through a point he was making. I thought he liked my lips but he was really only thinking about what he was going to say next.

After dinner we walked all the way to Elaine's on Eighty-eighth and Second. He wanted to see where my crowd hung out. I was wearing spike heels, felt uncomfortable, and couldn't keep up with his long strides. I had a blister.

When we walked into Elaine's people looked up. But I wasn't the only one they noticed despite Gerry's rumpled suit and scuffed shoes. Anyway, no one bothered us. We had squid salad and a few drinks. We talked about New York and London and when we were ready to leave I told him I was coming to London in a week to talk about a new script and I'd call him.

A limousine was supposed to pick him up and drive him to some political conference upstate, but the car never came. So there he was in my apartment looking at my shelves full of books on China, show business, American politics, Marxist theory, and ballet dancers. He was rattling on about the need for freedom in a Socialist society, towering over my low coffee table when his thick shock of hair fell into his eyes. And that's how it all started. I reached up to touch his hair. I needed to know how it felt, and as simply and easily as though we had known each other for a lifetime he looked away from the biography of Marx he was holding, stared into my eyes and pulled me close to him. We held each other for a moment and I was lost. That had never happened to me before, at least not the same way. I didn't understand it then but it was part of the puzzle I would put together later.

❧ When we got up in the morning I fixed him some tea and biscuits. We were sitting in my sunny kitchen. From the window you can see the Fifty-ninth Street Bridge.

"You're coming to London next week?" he asked. I said yes.

"Can I see you there?" I said yes.

"Will you be able to come with me to Paris the week after?" I said yes again. With great determination he got up, headed for what he thought was my front door. It wasn't. He ended up back in the bedroom. Then he pointed himself in the right direction and was gone. He hadn't said goodbye or even looked back.

I arranged to have the script conferences in London and meet with Gerry at the same time. In the film business, a great deal of time is spent poring over scripts that never develop into pictures. Such was the case with this one. I was glad to have Gerry, so the time in London wasn't a complete waste. Sometimes I wonder if the script wouldn't have been better if I hadn't had Gerry to divert my attention. Anyway, all of London seemed to be on strike when I arrived. Gerry was right. The ship was sinking, but I wasn't sure it was gracefully, flowered cups at tea time and the misty morning walks in Hyde Park notwithstanding. But all that really mattered to me was the smell of his tweed jacket and his thick hair falling across my face: the softness of his fingers on my cheeks and the way he swayed me in his huge arms seemed to close out the reality that not only England, and my script, but also the world was in big trouble.

We were careful not to be seen when we were together (I stayed in the apartment of a friend) and anyway Gerry was known for enjoying his privacy while walking the streets of the city he grew up in.

Then, after a few days, I went on to Paris and he met me there a day later. We watched the rooftops of St. Germain from my hotel room, and after we made

love we never talked about our relationship or what we
meant to each other. Gerry and I never discussed his
wife or my personal life. It wasn't necessary or anything
we needed to get into . . . not, that is, until the night he
took me to dinner and a table full of English journalists
recognized us. They smiled and waved. Gerry froze and
couldn't eat. He talked of how this would hurt his
wife—how she couldn't accept it and how we should
progress more slowly. I said of course, but hadn't he
thought of all this when we began? He was so terrified
that my heart turned over. That night he couldn't sleep.
His mind, he said, was tumbling in confusion. I offered
to leave so he could collect himself. We stayed away
from each other for a day while he attended conferences
and meetings. I planned to leave anyway, when, in
lonely desperation, he called me.

He said he couldn't bear to see me go. He had a
terrible longing for me and could we be together again.

We met outside of Paris in St. Germain en Laye.
He fell on me, showering me with kisses and touches,
holding me so tightly I felt *he* couldn't breathe. He
seemed abandoned and considerate, pleading and demanding all at the same time. It was rare and real and
open and direct and a little bit frightening.

He said he had never done anything like this
before in his life. He said he was confused and terribly
guilty. He talked about the state of the world and how
he wanted to make a contribution to improve it. He
talked about Democratic-Socialist principles and how it
was possible to have them both at the same time, if the
rich would only share their wealth more.

He was soft and whispering and challengingly loud
and hard driving, almost as though he was experimenting
with the many facets of his personality. He never asked
me about myself or whether there were other men I
might know or be involved with.

It seemed to be an emotional purge for him. And
when the time came to leave each other, he was eco-
nomical and not at all sentimental.

He wondered if I'd be all right getting back to
America. I said I had found my way back from wilder

places than the French countryside. He apologized for his behavior in Paris and said he'd call me soon. With no superfluous motions, he simply said goodbye in his Spartan English manner, opened the door and walked through it. The trouble was—he was in the closet. He laughed and, saying nothing, he walked out the right way.

The room we had brought to life for two days came to a silent halt. The walls closed in on me. And neither one of us had mentioned the word "love." I felt I had somehow been compelled to involve myself in this relationship that I knew could offer little more than irreconcilable obstacles. The question was, *why*?

Chapter 2

*"Pure logical thinking cannot yield us any knowl-
edge of the empirical world; all knowledge of reality
starts from experience and ends in it. Propositions
arrived at by purely logical means are completely
empty of reality."*

—ALBERT EINSTEIN
Albert Einstein: Philosopher-Scientist

❀ I drove through Malibu Canyon and onto the
Ventura Freeway. There wasn't much traffic. The San
Fernando Valley stretched out in front of me, household
lights beginning to twinkle, like a giant jewel box in the
night. I remembered how they had taken Khrushchev
to the Valley when he came to California. It was America
in progress, they said. It *was* beautiful if you looked at
it from the right perspective. But otherwise everybody
made jokes about the Valley—like saying a person was
so bad off, the only thing he had going for him was he
didn't live in the Valley.

I turned off the freeway to my street. Climbing my
long driveway I felt the low-hanging cherry trees brush
the top of my car. I loved those trees. They reminded
me of the cherry trees my former husband Steve and I
had had in his house in Japan before our divorce. Steve
had planted them there when he lived in a residential
section of Tokyo called Shibuya. He wanted to stay and

live and work in and around Asia. I wanted to live and work in America, not because I grew up there, but because my work was there. We discussed the dilemma and decided to try to make the globe a golf ball and do both.

For a while it worked. But gradually we each developed separate lives. We remained friends as we raised our daughter Sachi, who spent the first seven years of her life with me in America, the next six in an international school in Japan, and her remaining school years in Switzerland and England. She learned to speak and read and write fluent Japanese (which meant she could read most any Oriental language) and she began to *think* and *perceive* like an Oriental, which was sometimes amusing because Sachi is a freckle-faced blonde with the map of Ireland written on her face and the loping arms and legs of a Westerner, which she somehow manages to orchestrate as though she's wearing a restrictive kimono and obi when she walks and sits. She still kneels in a living room and looks up adoringly at whoever is speaking, and her Alice-in-Wonderland countenance can be quite confusing even when I think I understand her. What I'm really getting is a combination of straightforward, direct Western thinking tempered with circuitous Asian ambiguity usually employed to rescue what might be an embarrassing, impolite or insensitive remark.

I learned a lot about Asia from Sachi, which she didn't even mean to teach me. She is one of that new breed of people whose blood and ancestry is Western, but whose psychology and thought processes are half Asian. With Sachi this was a result of the "golf ball" belief that Steve and I had had in the beginning. As with everything, it has its duality—its drawbacks and its assets. In the long run, though, I would say the assets outweigh the liabilities, if for no other reason than the fact that Sachi is a combination of two worlds—and if she can handle it, she will help each understand the other. She has lived and studied French in Paris, where she says it was most difficult for her to make the sociological and cultural adjustment. Apropos of Parisian rudeness and cynicism, she said, "Mom, it's really hard to bow with Japanese politeness and say 'up your ass' at the same time!"

My house sat warm and homey at the top of the hill. "MacLaine Mountain" one of my friends called it, and wondered if I ever fell off it. If they only knew how often I had wondered the same thing.

My friend David had joked that the tallest mountain I was climbing was myself. He didn't have much time for small talk, yet he could make the smallest moment seem important. Like the time he peeled an orange into a flower and the juice of the luscious fruit gently dribbled down his chin as he ate it. He said there were no accidents in life and we all basically meant something important to each other if we'd just open our hearts and our feelings and not be afraid of the consequences. When he was in California we took walks on the beach and had lunch in a health food restaurant after yoga class. So many times he had suggested that I stop "climbing" myself and journey "into" myself instead.

"That's where all you are searching for resides," he said. "What's the matter with you? Why don't you take the time to look?" He hadn't said it angrily, really, but more impatiently.

He gave me books about spiritual teachings to read. He told me I should get more in touch with my true identity. I really didn't understand what he meant. I had always thought that was what I'd been doing, but apparently he was talking on a different level. When I asked him, he would never elaborate. He said I should just think about it and it would come. I thought about what he said, skimmed through the books, but continued to happily approach everything from a head-on, open-minded point of view. Not totally satisfying, really, but certainly functional.

I was not an unhappy person—not at all. And I always thought I had a pretty good sense of my identity. That's what everybody said about me. "She knows who she is," they'd say. In fact, it was sometimes difficult for me to relate to the complaint of the women's movement that they had been colonized away from their female identities. I had never really had that experience in my life. I sometimes felt to the contrary. I seemed to be so sure of what I felt and what I wanted that some others complained I was *too* liberated, that I didn't *need* anyone.

But I wasn't so sure of that anymore. Maybe David was right. Possibly he was seeing something much deeper in me that I was missing *because* I was already so liberated. Maybe *because* of that I should realize that I had a long way to go. It's hard to know something really deep is missing inside yourself when you feel successful and busy and responsible and creative.

I could smell Marie's good French cooking waft across the driveway. Mine was the best restaurant in town, only I hardly ever invited anyone to eat. I liked being alone and I was uncomfortable entertaining anyway, especially when I could be spending the time reading or writing.

Slamming the front door shut so Marie would know I was home, I yelled that I was going to take a bath and relax a little before dinner.

Two steps at a time when there was no need to rush, I broke a nail as I opened my bedroom door. Damn, I thought, that will take a repair job. But there was the bedroom I loved—spread out, blue and cool and refreshing—waiting for me.

I loved my ice-blue colored bedroom and its adjacent sitting room-office, as much as a person could love a room. I spent hours there alone. I knew I could lock the door and without seeming impolite or unsociable I could shut out the world. I could have lived in those rooms and never wanted anything more. I never felt detached or abstract in those rooms. I designed the bedroom myself. The blue was pale enough yet vibrant enough to keep both the morning and the evening alive. The drapes were filmy and flowing and stretched across a solid glass sliding wall which overlooked a view of the San Fernando Valley and the mountains beyond—mountains which always took me by surprise on a clear evening. The furniture was covered in crushed blue velvet and the bed with a band-brocaded blue satin spread.

I remembered hearing about a movie star once who slid out of bed because she slept on satin sheets. I liked being stuck to my regular sheets because I usually read in bed and wrote in bed whenever I didn't want to feel professional. I had books and notebooks strewn all around me, and whenever I was stuck on a transition or a story point, I would turn the electric blanket up very warm, take a little nap underneath all my research, and by the time I woke, usually had figured out whatever was bothering me. I loved to feel alone in my beautiful bedroom, with nothing but me and whatever I wanted to think about. It was such a fulfilling feeling to know I had concentrated on something deeply and had forgotten all about myself. Maybe David was right. Maybe I should actually learn to meditate . . . to meditate deeply. Maybe what I would find was what he was talking about.

I walked into my dressing room and changed. It was a room of mirrors. Mirrors on all four walls and the ceiling . . . a monument to vanity, I thought—which embarrassed me, because unless I was working on a film I didn't much care about how I looked.

I opened one of the mirrored closet doors to change into a robe. I wondered what Gerry would think of my movie star's closet indulgently crammed with clothes left over from pictures I had made or that I had bought in nearly every big city in the world. I wondered what he'd think if I told him that I loved the feeling of beautiful pearls around my neck at the same time that I felt ostentatious and out of place wearing them. I wondered what he'd think if I told him I loved to snuggle into the deep fur of a soft sable coat, but hardly ever wore it, even though I did get it just for posing for an ad. I wondered how he'd feel about how I loved to travel on the Concorde even though he had campaigned against it.

I wanted to talk to him about how I had made a lot of money and that it made me feel elite in a world that was broke to know I could buy just about anything I wished for. I wanted to ask him what he would do if he could demand large sums for his services. I had seen him eye my expensive luggage in the hotel room in Paris. Did he think physical manifestations of earned wealth violated socialist principles? Did being born poor automatically make one a good guy? I had wanted to talk to him about it all, but couldn't because once I had asked him if his wife had nice clothes and luggage that would last a lifetime. "No," he had said, "my wife is a Marxist. She doesn't even like it if I wear fur gloves in the winter."

I took out a robe and looked around. One of the mirrored walls was a sliding door which led to a terrace with a tumbling rock waterfall and tropical plants and flowers. They were cared for by a Japanese gardener who loved them like children and believed that Peter Tomkins was correct, that plants had emotions. I remembered how silly Gerry thought I was when I first mentioned such a concept to him.

"Plants can feel?" he laughed. "Well, I'm just glad they can't talk back." I had wanted to pursue the conversation but his sardonic laughter nipped it in the bud, so to speak. So often I had longed to pursue some crazy metaphysical idea that might just be a recognized scientific fact in twenty years, but Gerry was the kind of man who dealt only with what he had proof of, what he could see, and what he could therefore parody or comment on sociologically in his occasional fits of black humor. It left out so many possibilities.

The bathroom was my favorite room. It was just adjacent to the dressing room on the other side of the terrace garden. A sunken square marble tub overlooked the rock waterfall where indirect light now played on the falling, dancing water in the evening light. There were two toilets and two sinks in pink marble and a shower head above the tub in brass. I loved the fact that the sunken tub was so large I didn't need a shower curtain to protect the carpeting from the spray of the shower.

I leaned over and turned on the tub faucet. Warm water always made me feel better. Often, no matter where I was in the world, a tub of warm water could change my spirits into happiness.

Now as I simply held my hands under the warm flow I began to feel more relaxed.

I sighed to myself, climbing into the hot VitaBath soap suds. I thought of my mother. She loved hot baths too. I remembered how she'd sit in the tub and just think. I always wondered if she might be thinking about how to get out . . . how to get out of her life. It seemed as though everything Mother did, she did for Dad. And after him, for her children. It was the same story with everyone else's mother, I guess. Her cooking was punctuated by deep sighs. Often she would manage to burn something, and then she would have to wring her hands. Her lovely hands were the most expressive part of her. I always knew how she felt by watching her long, slim fingers, for they never stopped twisting or being busy with something around her neck or wrists. She was either fiddling with a high-necked sweater (wool against her skin bothered her) or toying with her silver chains. I understood that she enjoyed the sensuality of the chains slipping through her fingers. But there was a contradiction because I sometimes felt she would choke herself out of frustration. I wanted to understand the contradiction, scream for her to clarify what she was feeling—but when she reached a certain pitch of desperation, before I could sort out my own thinking, she'd launch into another project like peeling potatoes or making scotch cakes.

Dad knew that Mother had wanted to be an actress, so he said that most of what she was doing was a performance. The two of them, in fact, were like a pair of vaudevillians. I thought I remembered Dad saying something about wanting to run away with a circus when he was fourteen. He loved railway cars and traveling and said that he felt he wouldn't even have needed make-up to play a clown. And he had a way of commanding attention like no one I've seen before or since. He usually did it with his pipe. Regardless of where he sat in a room, it became the center. His chair would become a stage and his friends or family, the audience. He'd crook one leg over the other, pick up his pipe and knock it against the heel of his shoe, as though he were bringing a meeting to order. A tiny hunk of ash would spill from the bowl of his pipe onto the carpet beneath him.

The roomful of people would by now be uneasily watchful. Then he'd sigh deeply, uncrook his leg, grunt a little and proceed to bend over to determine what to do about the ash. This was the master attention-getter. Would he pick it up? Would he gently squeeze the hunk of ash between his fingers so he wouldn't crush it into powder? Or would he rifle for a matchbook cover in the top drawer of his little pipe stand beside his chair and scoop it up? It never occurred to anyone watching to go to his rescue. This was a scientifically manipulated exercise of such commanding expertise that it would have been like rushing to the stage to help Laurence Olivier recover a prop he had purposely dropped.

Usually Dad picked the ash up with the matchbook cover. However, in mid-bend, out of the corner of his eye, he would spot a piece of lint on the shoulder of his jacket. With the pipe in one hand, matchbook cover in the other, the focus of attention on the ashes, he would slowly but surely proceed to flick any discernible flecks of lint he could find while everyone in the room waited on the fate of the ashes. His complete capture of attention accomplished, he was a happy man. If, however, no one paid any attention, Dad would get unmercifully drunk.

Mother would usually get up and go to the bathroom, returning after she sensed that Dad's act had run its course, to suggest a nice hot piece of apple pie that she had baked herself. In striding toward the kitchen maybe she'd bump into a piece of furniture which would produce a startled gesture of sympathy from whoever was closest. Meanwhile Dad would suck on his pipe, drink slowly from a glass of scotch and milk, not moving, knowing that Mother had successfully stolen his thunder, trying to understand that every play must have more than one central character. No wonder Warren and I became actors: we learned from the best.

Mother had done a Little Theater play once, all about a mother who went slowly bananas. Rehearsals took her away from the house at least four nights a week. So Dad began to complain that he never had hot meals waiting for him anymore and that there was dust on the mantelpiece. He teased Mother, said that she was becoming a replica of that "bitch" she was playing in that "damn fool play" and warned her that conditions at home were slowly deteriorating. Little by little Mother began to succumb to his pressure. Her gracefully chiseled nose pinched up when she tried to express herself and her speech patterns became erratic. Soon she agreed that she *had* become the character and therefore it wasn't worth it. So she quit the play. She had bought Dad's propaganda, and came back home to tend her family.

Growing up, I too did what was expected of me. I wore standard white blouses, unscuffed saddle oxford shoes, bobby sox rolled down over nylon stockings, and pleated skirts that I neatly tucked under me when I sat down. I brushed my hair one hundred strokes every night and I finished my homework and I might have been Football Queen if my boyfriend hadn't gotten sick the day the team made their nominations and screwed up my chances. I had a bright-new-penny smile for everyone and never allowed myself to get overtly angry at anybody, because you could never tell where the crucial popularity vote might come from during the next election for Prom Queen. I went on hayrides but wouldn't do more than kiss. I was a good student but only because I learned how to cheat well. I had real "school spirit," wore the school colors at all times and when I heard the roll of the school drums before a ballgame my heart would pop with pride. I spent a lot of time after school smoking and carousing in cars with boys . . . always teasing but never going all the way because Mother had said I should be a virgin when I got married, since my husband would know if I wasn't. Still, I had to sneak around, because Mom and Dad were more worried about my reputation than about what I might actually be doing.

I laughed a lot, mostly out of tenseness, as a kind of outlet for suppressed feelings that often bordered on hysteria. Laughter was a life saver to me. But apparently it upset people too. My friends took to calling me "Silly Squirrely" because I laughed at most anything. They thought I was happy-go-lucky and my "carefreeness" was a topic of conversation. They said I was "such a nut" which I accepted as a compliment at first until I began to realize there was really something wrong. One day in the hallway I was holding hands with Dick McNulty. He told me a joke and I began to laugh. But I couldn't stop and with a kind of theatrical glee that I didn't want to control I began to scream with laughter. I laughed and laughed until the principal came and ordered the nurse to take me home. Dad and Mom only wanted to know why I had been holding hands in the hall. They didn't seem to be interested in why I was laughing so hard.

Dick McNulty was the first boy I ever loved. Three years later he was killed in Korea.

🐿 I sat in the tub until the water was lukewarm. What clothes would I take to Honolulu? I had met Gerry in so many places in the world . . . in snow and in the tropics. I would go anywhere and at any time he suggested it . . . but oh, the clandestine trips to London! It had become so suffocating for me.

It wasn't easy to find an apartment for a week at a time. And it was doubly difficult to stay unrecognized by the press. But the most difficult emotional conflict was our being together in his home territory.

Once I found a place that was two or three tube stops from his office and another ten minutes walk from there.

So when I arrived we began a ten-day sojourn, he making subway trips, and I waiting in the dark apartment for him to visit me whenever he could. Why were all the apartments dark?

I would stand at the front window watching him amble up the road. Now and then he was stopped by well-wishers who wondered what he was doing in that part of London.

He walked in. I hugged him.

"I used to live in this area when I was first married," he said, as he released me and walked around the apartment surveying the bookshelves and the pottery on the tables. He didn't say much about the books or the prints on the walls but he spotted a magazine that had arrived in the mail. It was *Penthouse*.

"How can people subscribe to junk like that?" he said as he led me into the bedroom.

"I don't know; pornography is only a question of geography or upbringing, isn't it?" I said. "A lot of people would think we were pornographic with what we're doing with each other."

He looked at me for a moment and smiled. His glasses looked incongruous perched on the bridge of such a proud nose.

We made love, but he was preoccupied. We lay together for a while and then he said he had to get back to work. A chill scribbled through me. But I let it pass. When he left I called a writer friend and was gone for the rest of the day and out to dinner at night.

The next day Gerry was freer and seemed more abandoned. He told me that he carried the joy of our meeting with him so intensely that he had not been able to sleep all night. He said it was an exquisite way to feel exhausted. He said he had feelings he had never had in his life before.

Around about the fourth day he walked in and sat down with a sheepish smile on his face.

"What's wrong?" I asked.

He breathed deeply. "My daughter went into my closet looking for something in my coat and asked why my clothes smelled of perfume. It caught me so off guard that I acted guilty. I rushed to the closet instead of brushing it off. My wife noticed and I could feel her eyeing me. I said I couldn't smell any perfume and then she came to the closet. She said she smelled it too. I said I didn't know what they were talking about and I walked away. I didn't handle it well. I was as bad as I was in Paris."

He walked into the kitchen, tripped over a waste bin and made himself some tea.

"Well, how was it left?" I asked.

"Oh. It's all right, I guess. Everybody forgot about it. I just hate this hypocrisy. I don't like to lie."

From that day on I never wore perfume. I didn't even wear it when I wasn't with him. I was afraid it would cling to my clothes. But whenever we had been together he took a shower and washed his hair too. And he always smiled shyly and shrugged at the absurdity of it.

❷ I put on glasses, a scarf, a hat over the scarf, and went to the English Parliament where Gerry was participating along with the Prime Minister and various opposition leaders in a debate on the economy. I sat in the last row of the balcony. It was the first time I had seen Gerry at work.

He paced aggressively around the floor as if he were the Prime Minister already. He was so sure of himself that he mingled challenging and aggressive jokes into his speeches and rebuttals. He seemed to toy with what he believed to be the inferior intelligence of his colleagues and his political superiors.

He didn't sit in his seat when it was another member's turn to speak, and when he did sit, he crossed one leg over the other and bounced his foot, his blue socks creeping down over his ankles. He leapt up impatiently, energetically calling for attention. Then he strode the floor of Parliament as though the place belonged to him. He spread his legs apart, stuffed his hands in his pockets and counted the house as though the number of people watching him from the gallery was more important than what anybody else might have to say. And when he asked for time to speak himself, he called one of his opponents half a man, said he was a hypocrite unable to follow through on an unpopular point of view, whether it dealt with the trade unions, nuclear energy, or tax revision. He took his glasses on and off to make his points. He never used notes. He jabbed at the air. But beneath the podium his feet curled over and under each other like the feet of a school boy. As I sat there I wondered whether he would ever lead his party to victory. He was aggressive, and brilliant. But if the voters ever saw his feet moving and stepping on each other, they'd also know why he knocked all the contents of his briefcase to the floor with his elbow when he finally sat down. It was a good thing he knew the exits in the House of Commons.

That night he walked into the apartment and asked me what I thought. With my glasses, hat and scarf I didn't think he'd known I was there that afternoon.

"You knew I was there from the beginning?"

"Yes," he said, "certainly, for me you would be hard to miss."

I hesitated. Maybe he had been performing for me then. Maybe he didn't always act that way.

"Well," he said, "what did you think?"

"Were you performing for me or do you always act like that?"

He looked surprised. "Like what?"

"Well, aside from a little Jacques Tati number you acted as though *you* were the Prime Minister, like you owned the place."

He laughed and put down his coffee and leaned forward. "Yes?" he said with an interested gleam.

"Well, you just seemed so insensitive to your colleagues . . . calling them half a man and stuff. Is that how you're supposed to do it over here?"

He brushed his hair out of his eyes.

"Well, it's a game, you see? That's half the fun of it for me. In fact that's half of politics for me. I love to make them squirm at their own inconsistencies. It's part of the game. Otherwise why am I in it?"

I saw a flicker of doubt cross his face but it disappeared quickly.

"Would you," I asked, "have acted that way if you knew television cameras were recording you?"

He blanched slightly but went immediately to the point that interested him.

"Why? Do you think I'm too intense for television? Do you think I should soften my approach from that point of view?"

I couldn't believe he was discussing technique. I thought it was clear I wanted to know *why* he acted the way he did.

"Why were you so combative with the people you were trying to change?"

"I told you," he said. "I hate their hypocrisy. I hate how they pussyfoot around. And they are liars. Besides, I represent working people who never have an opportunity to talk out strongly like that and this kind of approach appeals to them."

I listened carefully, trying to understand. Perhaps he wasn't really interested in changing the minds of the Parliamentarians he was addressing. I asked if he was combative so that his working class constituency could identify with what they wished to be like, or did he himself really mean it?

"Both," he said. "Anyway they are consistent with one another."

As he talked he seemed to be aware that he could be outsmarting himself. I wondered if I should press my criticism, or even if my feelings were accurate. His smile had that same sheepish quality to it. I couldn't figure out why. He was open-minded about the criticism while defending his strong approach, but there was something else underneath it that eluded me. Something like shame almost, as though he was aggressive because he was ashamed.

"You know," he said, "no one else will tell me these things. I mean they tell me not to move around so much. They tell me not to pace when others are speaking. But they don't talk to me about what you're talking about."

"I'm not even sure *what* I'm talking about. I only know your smile and something you're feeling right now doesn't jibe with how you defend yourself."

"Yes. I see what you mean."

"I wonder what it is."

"I don't know." He was uncomfortable but he didn't back away. I was uncomfortable discussing his political attitudes so candidly. I had known many politicians and they were rarely capable of such self-scrutiny. But I had introduced the discussion and felt it should go further.

"Maybe, you know, you could be too smart for your own good," I said. "Maybe you sense that that's what people sense about you. And whether it's true or whether it could translate into no votes, it's the same thing, isn't it?"

"No," he said. "I don't know. Maybe."

"Maybe you're so aggressive about other people's inconsistencies because you have them yourself."

"What do you mean? I'm consistent with my political beliefs. I'll tell the truth even if it's damaging to me."

I thought a moment. I believed him but that's not what I meant. I didn't know whether to go further. "I know you are consistent politically but you were attacking them on a personal level and on that level I'm not so sure you are as pure as you come on."

He got up and as he paced around the room he ran his hands through his hair.

"You mean," he said, "that I accuse others of personal hypocrisy *because* I recognize the same thing in myself?"

"Well, we all do that, don't we? In fact we usually accuse others of the things we're most apt to be guilty of in ourselves."

"So what am I guilty about?"

"Probably me."

"Well, we both know that, don't we? What has that got to do with politics?"

"What about all those phone calls you make to me?"

He stopped pacing. "What about them?"

"Well, don't you make those calls from your office?"

"Yes," he said. "Of course."

"So who pays for the calls?"

"It's a government phone."

"And who pays for the government?"

He stared at me.

"You're making about seven long-distance calls a week on the taxpayers' tab. That must have added up by now."

"What are you trying to do?" he said.

"I'm trying to see the truth. You called somebody half a man today and expect to get away with it. What if that guy looks up your telephone log and discovers your phone calls to Reno and Las Vegas are to me?" Gerry's face froze.

He quickly looked at his watch.

"Christ," he said, "I'm late for my party meeting. I'll call you later."

He went toward the door, hair falling in his eyes, put on the trench coat that I hoped would have a lining for the winter and as usual left without saying goodbye. His glasses were on the table.

I sipped the rest of his coffee. Self-confrontation was not one of Gerry's strong points. And diplomacy was not one of mine.

That night I went out with friends and stayed out until five in the morning.

Gerry called early the next day. "I thought you came to London to see me," he said.

I was taken aback. "Yes," I said, "I did."

"Where were you last night?"

"Oh. I went out."

"What was so interesting about what you did all night?" he said. "Couldn't you find better things to do with your time?"

"What do you mean?"

"Where did you go?" he asked.

"I went to dinner at the White Elephant with some friends and we talked for a long time. Then we stopped at Annabelle's and danced."

"And whom did you dance with?"

"Gerry. Wait a minute, what's going on?"

"Nothing," he said. "I'll be over later."

"I can hardly wait." I hoped he would hear the sarcasm.

❧ When he walked in I didn't hug him and he noticed it. He took off his trench coat and headed for the bedroom where he lay on the bed staring up at the ceiling. I made him a scotch and soda. He put it on the night table and I sat on the bed next to him. I didn't say anything.

"I'm not a deceptive man, you know."

"No," I said. "I know."

"But I'm acting like one. *I am being deceitful.*"

"So what else is new?"

He sighed. "I don't know. But it's tearing me up."

"Then tell your wife."

"I can't."

"Then don't tell her about me. Leave me out of it. Talk about what's wrong with the two of you."

He stared at my face. "There's nothing wrong with the two of us."

"Nothing wrong with the two of *you*? How can you say that?"

"There isn't. We don't have a stormy or passionate love but it's satisfactory."

I wondered what I'd feel like if someone said that about me. I wondered what his wife would say if someone asked *her* the same question.

"Does she ever complain about feeling lonely?"

"Oh, yes. Well, she used to. I'm gone so much, you know. But she got used to that a long time ago."

"Are you sure she's used to it?"

"I don't know," he said.

"Are you *sure* she's not lonely?"

"She's never said so."

He sipped his scotch for a while.

"Okay," I said, "we know you're lonely, right?"

"Yes." He put his arm under his head and said, "But I had gotten used to it."

"What do you mean *had*?"

"Just what I said. I *had* become used to it until you came along. I'm not as lonely now."

"Then why don't you see if you can't help her not to be so lonely . . . not so unhappy."

"What do you mean? I'd be lying to her. How could that possibly make her happy?"

"Well, you're lying to her because telling her the truth would be worse, right?"

"Yes."

"So, we're back to hypocrisy again. Maybe sometimes it's necessary. Maybe it's the price you pay."

He looked at me strangely. He concentrated on the ice in his drink as though he didn't want to talk anymore.

"Will you tell me something? Honestly?" I asked.
"Yes."

"Do you feel as though you are living alone? I mean deep down where you *really* live, are you living there alone?"

The question seemed to be new to him; as though he had never thought about it.

"Yes," he said, "I do."

"Then she must feel that way too."

He turned over on his side.

"Maybe she needs another relationship just like you did."

He stared out the window. "No," he said, "she's happy raising the children. She knows what my work requires." He put his arm over his face.

I put a blanket over him and lay under it beside him.

"You know," he said, "I sound like one of your male chauvinist pigs, don't I?"

I didn't say anything. Then he said, ". . . and besides, if I told her she wouldn't believe me."

"Oh, Gerry," I said, and soon we fell asleep together.

A while later he woke up and said, "I'm very clear about what you are to me."

"And what is that?" I asked.

Gerry didn't say anything.

"Gerry?"

"Yes?"

"Come on. Don't freeze up on me. What do you mean, you're very clear about what I am to you? Tell me, so I'll know too."

He cleared his throat and said, "Well, I've told one of my aides that we met. I've told him you are in town. I asked him to take over my speech for tonight so I could be with you."

"Oh? And what did he say?"

"Well, he asked if there was anything else he should know, and I said she's in town and I want to be with her and that's that."

I sat up in the bed. "I see," I said. "And that's what you mean by being clear about me?"

"Look," he said, "I have to go now. The speech would be over by now. I must go for the questions and answers."

The familiar chill went through me.

He took a shower, washed his hair and dressed.

"You didn't need a shower tonight, you know. Not tonight."

"No," he said, placing his glass on the sink in the kitchen. "I didn't, did I?"

He put on his coat and walked out of the door. For his sake I was glad it was the right one.

The next day I went back to California.

Chapter 3

"What happens after death is so unspeakably glorious that our imagination and our feelings do not
suffice to form even an approximate conception of
it....The dissolution of our time-bound form in
eternity brings no loss of meaning."

—CARL G. JUNG
Letters, Vol. 1

I got up from the tub, dried my prune-wrinkled
skin, put on a pair of fuchsia colored slacks and an
orange sweater and went down to see Marie and have
dinner.

I walked into my kitchen. It was modern, fully
equipped, and not really mine. Marie, being French
and a cuisinière of exquisite ability, ruled her domain
with possessive authority and wouldn't let me fix even a
glass of Tab for myself. She was tiny and fragile, with
legs the circumference of most people's wrists. Her
fingers were twisted from arthritis and her hands and
arms shook when she served. She wore slippers with
toes cut out because her feet were deformed as a result
of injuries sustained during World War Two running
guns for the Free French against the Nazis. Her sister
Louise, who had been in America twenty years and
spoke not one word of English, was Marie's shadow,

taking orders from her and clucking in desperation that nothing much ever went right.

Some six years before, about three in the morning, Marie had awakened me, excitedly knocking at my bedroom door and exclaiming that something was wrong with her husband John. I went downstairs to their room and saw he was stretched out on his bed. He was the color of oatmeal. His eyes were closed and he shuddered as though he was gagging for breath. I didn't know what to do. I was truly horrified and didn't want to touch him. I lifted his head to apply mouth-to-mouth resuscitation. An awful sound came out of him, a deep guttural rattle. It sounded like an animal I didn't recognize. It frightened me deeply. At first I didn't know it was a death rattle and Marie didn't understand either. She kept insisting that he had just collapsed. I shook him, afraid that the rattle sound would come louder. It did. And finally it stopped. He died abruptly in my arms.

It was the first time I had ever seen a dead person. I wondered at what exact moment he had died, and I think it was at that moment that I began to seriously consider if there was such a thing as a soul. It seemed so impossible that what I held in my arms was all there could be that was left of a man. Did something that was John—his "soul"—live on? Did death hurt? If the soul survived the body, where did it go? To what purpose?

I couldn't sleep the rest of that night or for three nights after that, and I was working hard on shooting *Sweet Charity*. I seemed to be groping with the actual metaphysical meaning of death. I say metaphysical because it wasn't anything I could see, or touch, or hear, or smell, or taste. All I knew was that John, as I knew him, was gone. Or was he? I had been fond of him, but aside from the initial shock, I felt no great grief, no desperate gap. Yet I couldn't seem to accept his death as simply the end of his life. I knew somehow that there was more to it, and I knew I couldn't stop thinking about it. Every time I walked into the kitchen I thought about it and now was no different.

Marie and Louise and I talked awhile in broken French and English. I told her I was leaving for a long weekend, and she served me dinner in front of the television set in the living room. I watched the news and with the wine and a kind of exhaustion that I didn't understand, I went back upstairs and lay down on my bed. I was depressed and didn't know why.

What a world; we all seemed to be sleepwalking like cruel, friendly strangers—bumping into each other but never really making contact with what was true . . . talking past and over and around each other . . . afraid of our own words as much as we were of those we might hear from others. There was such a communication breakdown that we were starving for trust, groping for handles and lifeboats and touching and niceness. We focused so much on big desperations and disciplined, quiet patience so as not to rock anybody's boat—much less our own. Always hoping maybe things would get better, always wondering what we could do—on and on until our futility became institutionalized, almost as though it had become safer not to know what our lives really meant.

I tried to feel sleepy. The glass in my hand dripped sweat from the warmth of my holding it. Little things, I thought. I should focus on the pleasure of little things. The soft green of the palm tree leaves just outside my window, the squashed black olives fallen on the cement driveway from the companion tree I had planted myself, wondering if I could actually be responsible for something growing . . . warm water and soap bubbles, the jog I would take tomorrow morning that would make me feel good all day because I had worked hard for it— small, but strung together, small stuff made me feel better.

❦ I remembered sitting on Clifford Odets' bed just before he died. I had loved and respected his plays very much. He could really write about human hope and triumph over adversity . . . especially in people with small and unrecognized lives. The cancer had made his head look like that of a shriveled bird. His massive mane of hair had fallen out; his stomach was swollen

with the disease and tubes hung from his nose. He
sipped milk from a plastic container and asked me to
open the windows so cool air would blow across the
chilled container.

"I want to live," he said, "so that I can write for
large bunches of people about how much pleasure there
is in things no bigger than a fly's eye."

🐿 About two o'clock I felt sleepy. In London it was
ten in the morning.

Images of my life drifted in and out of my mind . . . a
long stretch of the Sahara Desert I wished I had crossed
once just to see if I could do it . . . dancing with a
handkerchief and a Russian peasant in a restaurant in
Leningrad while the patrons clapped . . . a Masai mother in Africa dying of syphilis while giving birth . . . a
squadron of birds flying as one, on a film location in
Mexico, while I wondered how they kept together . . .
wide, vast spaces through the countryside of China
where I took the first American women's delegation,
dressed in the same unisex Chinese clothing . . . Gerry's
face when I told him I loved to travel alone . . . a big but
compact trunk with drawers and closets that I wished
could be my mobile home so I would never have to live
anywhere permanently . . . dancers, choreographers, flying
sweat, tinny pianos, flashbulbs, standing ovations, hot
television lights, quiet movie sets, press conferences,
difficult questions, political campaigns, bumbling but
well-meaning candidates . . . George McGovern's crum-
pled face the night Richard Nixon won by a landslide . . .
Academy Awards and my anxiety that I would *win* one
for *Irma La Douce* when I thought my performance
didn't deserve it . . . my disappointment when I *didn't*
win one for *The Apartment* because that was the year
Elizabeth Taylor had almost died with her tracheotomy . . .
the four other times I was nominated and really didn't
care . . . long rehearsals, professional arguments, painful
muscles and stage fright, dumb studio executives, disciplined hours of writing which revolved around the

personal and ever-present feeling of a long search for
who I really was.

What was it that was missing? And was I, like so
many other women, continually searching for the shape
of my own identity in a relationship with a man? Did I
believe the other half of me was to be found in loving
someone, regardless of the frustration and futility involved?

Hong Kong and Gerry flooded my mind. I had met
him there on another of his conferences. Another hope
that this time it would be different, more fulfilling.

"It's wonderful how you love to pick up and go on a
moment's notice," he had said. "How do you do that?
How can you be so flexible? And you see so much. I
never have time."

He never noticed that I didn't answer . . . that I
wasn't sure whether I was running *toward* something or
away from myself. I wondered if Gerry would really
have taken the time if he had it. I didn't think he would
see what he looked at . . . not really. He had traveled
through Africa as a young man. But when he spoke of
it, I suddenly realized that he never once mentioned
what he ate, what he touched, what he saw, what he
smelled, how he felt. He spoke mainly about Africa as a
sociological trip, not as a human trip. He spoke of how
the "masses" were exploited and poor and colonized,
but never how they really lived and felt about it.

He had never been to Hong Kong before, and
when we sat in his hotel room I had to interpret the
surroundings for him. He didn't seem to feel the mill-
ing paradisiacal mess that was Hong Kong—the rick-
shaw coolies mingled with taxis; the teeming millions
(5,500,000) swollen and spilling into the bay; the shoppers'
paradise of Chinese silks, Japanese brocades, Indian
cottons, and Swiss laces; goods and watches, and food
and jewelry and dope and perfume and designs and
jade and ivory and trinkets from all over the world
brought to this free port for profit—none of it seemed
to dazzle Gerry or cause his mouth to drop open. In
fact, he said he hadn't even had a Chinese meal since
he'd arrived.

He was concerned that the guards patrolling his floor would recognize us and think ill of him. I told him that in Asia everyone always knows everything we foreigners do anyway and it doesn't matter to them. They just need to know.

He listened as though I were telling him a fairy tale when I described how I had walked to the bottom of Kowloon; past the silk shops, the jade factories, the watches from Switzerland and the residential district where his countrymen, the British, lived. I told him about the Star Ferry and the Bay itself where the crimson-sailed Chinese junks glided from the mainland. I told him about Cat's Street where shopping stalls spilled over with anything your imagination could conjure up. I told him how I had climbed to the top of Victoria Peak and watched the boats below in the harbor. He sat entranced at my dizzying description of diamonds, pearls, antiques, luxurious food, hand-woven materials, and intricate artistry done by children as young as twelve who were doing grown-up business before they realized what it was doing to them. I described the throngs of tourists . . . European, African, Japanese, Malay, Indian, American . . . on and on, all looking for bargains.

I described to Gerry how the spices hung in the air, how rock and roll music mingled with Chinese opera. How hawkers of plastic necklaces stooped and squatted to shovel rice into their mouths from delicate china bowls with hand carved ivory chopsticks. Tourists rushed, merchants rushed, children rushed, buses rushed, coolies rushed . . . a rush to cram as much buying and selling into the smallest amount of time.

And somehow it all worked. Everybody there was dedicated to making money, with no illusions, no pretensions about why Hong Kong existed. It was like Las Vegas. No self-righteousness about it. It was what it was. If you got taken it was part of the game. And somehow you expected it because all anybody wanted was a bargain anyway. Hong Kong was a place where you went broke saving money.

Gerry's eyes sparkled and gleamed as I talked

every night of what I had done during the day while he was attending meetings. It was true that he didn't get out as much as he wanted, but when he did it was as though he had never left his room.

And on our last day I had arranged for a small boat to take us to the New Territories where I knew a spot for a picnic. I packed lemon squash and sandwiches and tarts.

But on the boat he talked again of the squalid conditions he saw the Chinese living in. He spoke again of the disparity between rich and poor. He talked of how the wealthy must find a way to willingly share their profits with those who were less fortunate. It never occurred to him that the poverty stricken might have a richness of spirit the wealthy would envy if they knew of it. It never occurred to him that a rich person might be miserable in another more isolated and alienated way. He never thought "a rich person." It was "the rich," "the poor," an amorphous whole.

I remembered how a dear friend of mine had caught me in my sometimes knee-jerk liberalism by accusing me of having absolutely no compassion for the wealthy while I lavished my bleeding heart completely on only the poor. The truth of it had shocked me deeply.

"Gerry?" I stopped him. "What about those hills over there that look like jade that even the poor can enjoy?"

He looked up.

"And look at those sampans gliding by with the crimson sails. How about the way those people are waving at us?"

He stood up. "I guess I sound like the *Sunday Observer*, don't I?" Gerry smiled shyly. "I'm sorry," he said, "I can get tedious, can't I?"

We put into port at an inlet in the New Territories and went ashore. The crew remained aboard. Gerry carried the picnic boxes and I carried the thermos and a blanket.

Overhanging trees rustled in the sea breeze at the edge of the water as we began to walk into the lush hills

above. We breathed the fragrant air. He took off his
shoes and sank his feet into the earth. He sighed and
spread out his arms into the warm sun. He stopped at
every tree and wild flower. He stuck a daisy behind his
ear.

We came to a stream sparkling in the sun with
birds swooping through the flowering bushes on either
side. No one was around. He took off his shirt and
trousers and with a movement like liquid he sprawled
on his back in the gushing water. He reached up for
me. I took off my summer dress and waded in and lay
next to him. We felt the slippery rocks under us and
didn't care when the stream began to gently glide us
downstream. Birds chirped at us above from the trees.
We locked arms and stood up at the same time dripping
sparkling drops from our hair. Gerry circled his arm
around my head and rolled me into his chest. Silently
we walked back to our clothes.

I stood beside him.

"Oh shit," he said, resting his arms on my shoulders and looking into my eyes. "How am I going to
reconcile you with the rest of my life?"

"I don't know," I said. "I don't know."

He unfolded the blanket and spread it out on the
ground. We lay on it and looked up through the big
tree at the sky.

About an hour later we walked back to the boat. I
wondered how he would reconcile *himself* with the rest
of his life.

❧ The next morning Marie fixed me breakfast as I sat
on the patio. I wasn't sure what I was thinking—my
thoughts were too jumbled, clanking against one another.
Certainly I was frustrated with Gerry, but it was much
more than that. I was in between pictures, but my work
was going fine. And I had another date to play Vegas
and Tahoe soon which I knew I'd be prepared for. So I
can only say that I was a reasonably happy person by all
comparative standards but I was not particularly peaceful.

David called. He had just gotten into town and asked if I was going to yoga class. I said I'd meet him there.

I loved hatha yoga because it was physical, not meditational, although it did require concentration and a sense of relaxation. But with the sun streaming through the window and the sound of the instructor's voice acting as accompaniment, I loved it as I strained every muscle and sinew in my body to feel activated. The physical struggle cleared my brain.

"Have respect for your body and it will be nice to you," said my teacher (he was Hindu), "and go slow. Yoga requires common sense. Don't take your body by surprise. You must warm up before you stretch. Don't ambush your muscles. Muscles are like people; they need preparation, otherwise they get frightened and tighten up. You must have respect for their pace. Think of it like an explorer going into new territory. A wise explorer goes slow, for he never knows what may be around the bend. Only when you go slow can you feel it before you reach it. You see, yoga gives you self-esteem because it puts you in touch with yourself. It is very peaceful inside yourself. Learn to live there. You will like it."

I listened to his words in between postures.

"Yoga achievement requires four attitudes," he said, "faith, determination, patience, and love. It is like life. And if you are good and faithful in your struggle in this life, the next one will be easier."

My leotard was damp with sweat. "Struggle in this life and the next one will be easier?" I guessed he really believed that stuff. He was, after all, a Hindu. I put on a skirt and T-shirt, and David and I left class.

Walking out into the drenching California sunshine, David said, "I'm going over to the Bodhi Tree bookstore. Want to come?"

"The Bodhi Tree?" I asked. "Isn't that the tree Buddha meditated under for forty days or something?"

"That's right," he said.

"So what kind of a bookshop is it—Indian?"

"Oh, a little," he answered. "They have all sorts of occult and metaphysical stuff there. Haven't you ever heard of it?"

I felt shy but admitted I hadn't.

"Well, I think you'll like it," he said gently. "If you relate so well to your yoga, you'll love some of the writing of the ancient mystics. I'm surprised you spent so much time in India without getting into the spiritualization of the place. Anyway, it's on Melrose near La Cienega. I'll meet you there."

"Sure, why not," I said. Looking back, I can say that making that simple, lazy-afternoon decision to visit an unusual bookstore was one of the most important decisions of my life. And again, I am reminded that we make important small moves when we are prepared. Earlier in my life such a suggestion would have seemed a waste of an afternoon when I had so many scripts to read and so many phone calls to answer. I was too busy being successful to understand that there were other dimensions to life.

David was already at the Bodhi Tree when I arrived, waiting for me outside, leaning against a tree. He smiled as I fitted my big Lincoln into a parking space meant for a Volkswagen.

"I rent this car," I said. "I don't own one. They're a pain in the ass and I don't understand them. As long as I have four wheels and some gas I'm satisfied. Do you know what I mean?"

"Yes," he answered. "Probably better than you realize." He took me by the arm and led me inside. As we walked in, I smelled sandalwood incense filtering faintly through the rooms of the cluttered bookstore. I looked around. Posters of Buddha and of yogis I had never heard of smiled down from the walls. Customers with books in their hands stood about drinking herb teas and talking in soft voices. I began to study the bookshelves. Lined up along the walls were books and books on subjects ranging from life after death to how to eat on Earth while alive. I smiled faintly at David. I felt out of place and a little silly.

"This is fascinating," I said, wishing that I hadn't found it necessary to say anything at all.

A young woman in sandals and a gauze skirt came over to us handing us tea.

"Can I help you?" she asked in a voice that was calm and peaceful. She matched the atmosphere in the shop—or maybe I was being theatrical. When I turned to look at her, she recognized me and suggested that she introduce me to the owner who was in his office having tea. David smiled and we followed.

The office was creaking with books. The owner was young, in his mid-thirties, and wore a beard. He was pleased to see me and said he was honored. He said he had read my books and was especially interested in what I had to say about my time in the Himalayas.

"How deeply are you into meditational technique?" he asked. "Do you use Kampalbhati breathing? It's difficult but effective, don't you think?"

I didn't know what he was talking about and just at that moment a young man with a crew cut and a football T-shirt sauntered in. He looked at me, at David, at the owner (whose name was John) and had a kind of smirk on his face.

"Listen, man," he said, "what's all this shit about if you think right you get happy? I mean, man, how *can* a dude be happy in this world and why are you people conning folks into thinking they can?"

David touched my arm when he felt how startled I was. John asked if he could help the guy, but he went right on. "I mean, what is this?" he said, "with the incense and the herb teas and the flashy posters—you guys are full of shit."

John gently took David and me by the arm and led us out of the office and back into the shop.

"I'm sorry," he said.

"No problem," said David. "He's got to find his own way like we all do." I nodded that it didn't matter, and David suggested we could find what we wanted by ourselves—not to be concerned.

"Jesus," I said, "why does he find this place so threatening?"

"I don't know," said David. "Maybe he's got a big emotional investment in hostility. It's hard to believe that peace is possible."

Then he led me over to a huge bookshelf marked "Reincarnation and Immortality." On it were books from the Bhagavad Gita to the Egyptian Books of the Dead to interpretations of the Holy Bible and the Kabala. I didn't know what I was looking at.

I looked at David closely. "Do you believe all this?" I asked.

"All what?" he asked.

"I don't know," I said. "Do you really believe in reincarnation?"

"Well," he said, "when you've studied the occult as long as I have you learn that it's not a question of whether it's true but more a question of how it works."

"You mean you believe it's that firmly established as a fact?"

He shrugged his shoulders and said, "Why yeah, I do. It's the only thing that makes sense. If we don't each have a soul—then why are we alive? Who knows if it's true? It's true if you believe it and that goes for anything, right? Besides, there must be something to the fact that the belief in the soul is the one thing *all* religions have in common."

"Yes," I said. "But maybe all religions are phony too."

He went on looking through the books not as though the conversation was uninteresting to him, but more as though he was simply and directly looking for a book.

I hadn't thought much about religion since I was twelve years old and played tic-tac-toe in Sunday school class.

David reached up for a book. "You should read some of the works not only on this shelf but also of Pythagoras, Plato, Ralph Waldo Emerson, Walt Whitman, Goethe, and Voltaire."

"Did those guys believe in reincarnation?"

"Sure, and they wrote extensively about it. But it always ends up on the occult bookshelf like it's black magic or something."

"Voltaire believed in reincarnation?"

"Sure," said David, "he said he didn't find it any more surprising to be born lots of times than to be born once. I feel the same way."

I looked at him. His blue eyes were steady and clear.

"Listen," he said. "Do you know what the definition of occult means?"

"No," I answered.

"Well, it means 'hidden.' So just because something is hidden doesn't mean it's not there."

I looked more closely at David's bony-cheeked, sad face. He spoke in a peaceful tone, with no hesitancy except when he realized I was trying to comprehend what he was saying.

"Do you want me to compile a kind of reading list for you?" he asked with down-to-earth practicality.

I hesitated slightly, remembering five scripts I had to read and also wondering what Gerry would think if he saw me reading books like these.

"Sure," I said. "Why not? People thought the world was flat too until someone proved otherwise. I guess I should be curious about all kinds of 'hidden' possibilities. Whoever thought there were bugs crawling all over our skin until someone came up with the microscope?"

"Great," said David. "For me, real intelligence is open-mindedness. If you feel you're looking for something, why not give it a shot?"

"Okay." I found myself smiling.

David said, "Make yourself comfortable browsing around and I'll get you a bunch of stuff to read." He wiped the corners of his mouth and with an intense squint he began to survey the bookshelves. I thumbed through books on food-combining, yoga exercises, meditation and other healthful subjects I understood.

After about half an hour, David had an armful of books and I wondered as I thanked him and we walked out into the California sunlight if I'd ever crack one of them.

I was leaving for Honolulu the next day so I said goodbye to David and went home to think, rest, pack, and if I had time, to read.

❷ That night I found myself looking up reincarnation in the encyclopedia.

Let me say that I was not brought up to be a religious person. My parents sent me to church and Sunday school, but it was because it was the accepted place to be on Sundays. I wore crinoline petticoats and tried not to glance too often at the lyrics in the hymnal I was supposed to have memorized. I wondered where the money went after the collection plate was passed, but I really never had any feeling one way or the other whether there was a God or not.

Jesus Christ seemed like a smart, wise, and certainly a good man, but I viewed what I learned about him in the Bible as philosophical, mythological, and somehow detached. What he preached and did didn't really touch *me, so* I didn't believe or disbelieve. He just happened . . . like all of us . . . and he did some good things a long time ago. I took his being the Son of God with a grain of salt and, in fact, by the time I was in my late teens, had decided for myself that God and religion were definitely mythological and if people needed to believe in it that was okay with me, but I couldn't.

I couldn't believe in anything that had no proof and besides, I wasn't all that agonized by the need for a purpose in life or something to believe in besides myself. In short, where religion, faith in God, or the immortality of the soul were concerned, I didn't think much about them. No one insisted and I found the subject boring—not nearly so stimulating as something real and humorous like people. Every now and then as I grew older I would engage in a bemused argument over the pitfalls of such mythological beliefs and how they detracted from the real plight of the human race. I didn't much like the authoritarianism of the church— any church—and I considered it dangerous because it made people afraid they would burn in hell if they didn't believe in heaven.

But as much as I was disinterested in God and religion and the hereafter, there was something I was extremely interested in. From the time I was very young I *was* interested in identity. My identity and that of everyone I met. Identity seemed real to me. Who was I? Who was anyone? Why did I do the things I did? Why did they? Why did I care about some people and not others? The analysis of relationships became a favorite subject of mine—the relationship I had with myself as well as with others.

So maybe because I was interested in the origin of my own identity it intrigued me that there might be more to me than what I was aware of in my conscious mind. Perhaps there were other identities buried deep in my subconscious that I only needed to search for and find. Indeed many times in my work with self-expression, whether dancing, writing, or acting, I would be amazed at myself, baffled as to where a feeling or a memory or an inspiration had come from. I had put it down to a hazy concept called the creative process, as did most of my fellow artists, but I have to admit that at the bottom of whoever I was I felt a flame that I was not able to understand, to touch. What was the origin of that flame? Where did it come from? And what had come before it?

I was always more interested in what went *before* than what might come after. So for that reason, I suppose I wasn't so interested in what would happen to me after I died as I was in what made me the way I was. Therefore when the notion of *life before birth* first struck me I guess you might say I was curious to explore it.

The encyclopedia said that the doctrine of reincarnation went back as far as recorded history. It consisted of belief in the connection of all living things and the gradual purification of the soul, or spirit, of man until it returned to the common source and origin of all life which was God. It was the belief that the soul was immortal and embodied itself time and time again until it morally worked out the purification of itself. It said that the companion subjects of karma—that is, working out one's inner burdens—and reincarnation—the physical opportunity to live through one's karma—were two of the oldest beliefs in the history of mankind and more widely accepted than almost any religious concepts on earth. This was news to me—I had always vaguely connected reincarnation with disembodied spirits, hence ghosts, the occult and things that go bump in the night. I had never connected it with any major, serious religion.

Then I looked up religion. Although it was impossible to give a conclusive definition, several characteristics were common to most religions. One was belief in the existence of the soul, another the acceptance of supernatural revelation, and finally, among others, the repeated quest for salvation of the soul. From the Egyptians to the Greeks, to the Buddhists and Hindus, the soul was considered a pre-existent entity which took up residence in a succession of bodies, becoming incarnate for a period, then spending time in the astral form as a disembodied entity, but reincarnating time and time again. Each religion had its own belief for the origin of the soul, but no religion was without the belief that the soul existed as a part of man and was immortal. And somewhere between Judaism and Christianity, the West had lost the ancient concept of reincarnation.

I closed the encyclopedias and thought for a while.

Hundreds of millions of people believed in the theory of reincarnation (or whatever the term might be) but I, coming from a Christian background, hadn't even known what it actually meant.

I prepared to leave to meet Gerry wondering what else might be going on in this world that I had never thought about before. ❧

Chapter 4

*"It is the secret of the world that all things subsist
and do not die, but only retire a little from sight and
afterward return again.... Jesus is not dead: he is
very well alive; nor John, nor Paul, nor Mahomet,
nor Aristotle; at times we believe we have seen them
all, and could easily tell the names under which they
go."*

—RALPH WALDO EMERSON
Nominalist and Realist

The flight from L.A. to Hawaii was blue and
smooth. I slept and thought of Gerry most of the way. I
thought of my friendship with David and wondered
how many other people I had walked and eaten and
hung out with and had never *really* known. I checked
into the Kahala Hilton under another name. No one
noticed. Then I went to my room to wait.

There I was... standing out on the balcony of yet
another hotel room overlooking the lilting, lulling Pacific,
the red sun nestling on the water... waiting. Waiting for
a man. Waiting for a man I loved or thought I loved,
whatever that meant. I knew that what I felt for him
was powerful and I knew that I'd go anywhere I had to
to be with him. We were both busy and had creative
work to fill our lives, but I guess we needed more. I
know I did. As long as I could remember, I needed to

be in love. A man seemed the most obvious object of such a feeling and desire. But maybe not, maybe I just needed to *feel love*, and a deeper objective was what seemed to be eluding me. I don't know.

Honolulu is one of my favorite places, especially at sunset, even though now it was crammed with muumuu-clad, camera-toting tourists on conventions. And the Kahala Hilton is one of the prettiest hotels in the world, with its indoor-outdoor landscaping, the underwater bar, and the dolphins that leap playfully in the seawater pool below. I listened quietly to the lull of the water slapping the beach. I heard the coconut pines rustle. Then I heard a thud. A coconut had fallen ripe and ready to crack. I looked at my watch. Gerry said he would arrive by six-thirty. It was already seven-thirty. The weather was good so there were no planes delayed. And airport control had said there was no weather problem out of London. So he must have taken off on time. Well, the world was only a golf ball. He'd be here soon. But I resented the tardiness because I knew we'd only have thirty-six hours. Jesus, how time seemed to be my enemy. No matter what I was involved with I never had enough of it. So much did I want to use and enjoy whatever there was of it that I was continually frustrated at the time I didn't have, and somehow the past and the future were always getting in the way; the past with its consequences, the future with its mystery. I wanted the present to be all there was.

I breathed the soft twilight air, walked inside the room and turned on the television set.

Carter was upset with Begin. Teddy Kennedy was upset with Carter. The dollar was still falling. Pierre Trudeau had called someone a dirty name in the Canadian Parliament. The world was funny or falling apart, depending on how you looked at it. Nobody had it together.

I looked around the hotel room. I hadn't wanted to attract attention so I had asked for a room, not a suite. But it was plenty for the time Gerry and I would have together. I knew he would love Honolulu. He had never been here. I hoped he would be able to *feel* it. The first thing he would do would be to walk out on the balcony and survey what surrounded him. He needed to do that. He would look out at Diamond Head and he would talk about the palm trees. He calmed down when he was surrounded by nature. His mind could actually idle in neutral over a rain-drenched tree with a bird quivering its wings in the wet. He could actually stop fretting over the state of the world and the prospects of his reelection when the sun rose flamingo-pink. His spirit seemed soothed by the idea that nature was beautiful, more powerful than anything else. But then he had grown up in the English countryside, endured the English winters. He had walked in English meadows and swum in the cold water of the English Channel. City life got him down. He needed space and natural challenge. I was glad we were meeting in Honolulu. He would enjoy the swaying peace of it. There I was thinking of Gerry again as though I were he.

Another fifteen minutes had gone by. Fifteen minutes we'd never get back. The carpet in the room was deep maroon, tufted. The bedspread was olive green with maroon flowers. Why did the draperies always have to match the spread? I wondered if Hilton would hack a hotel into the side of a mountain in China. How silly the Chinese looked dancing to "Staying Alive" from *Saturday Night Fever* at the Chinese-American reception. And how were one billion Chinese going to turn on a dime yet another time in their long struggle toward modernization? Was it really worth it? I didn't know what was worth anything anymore.

I lit another cigarette. Gerry had tried giving up smoking a year ago and now continually scolded me for not even trying. He said he smoked because he was always walking into rooms where someone else was smoking. I knew what he meant. I could give it up too. And had—lots of times. But whenever I had big decisions to make I needed a silent companion; anything that would sit there and smolder but not interfere. I didn't inhale so it never bothered me when I sang and danced, but it did hurt my throat and make me feel like coughing. Okay, so I'd give it up when Gerry arrived and see if he would too.

The moon was coming up over Waikiki now. Diamond Head was a black hulk in the reflection of the sea. Maybe he missed the plane from London. The meeting to discuss North-South problems could take place without him, I supposed. But I couldn't.

The phone rang beside the bed. It was nearly eight o'clock.

"Hi," said Gerry, as though we hadn't been apart for weeks.

I melted at his quiet voice. He talked differently when he was away from his office.

"We've been at the airport in a reception hall," he said. "We were there for an hour. Somebody was supposed to be attending to the luggage while they told us to wait. But nobody was. I finally collected it myself. When did you arrive?"

"A few hours ago," I said, not wanting to say how I'd counted each wasted minute.

"I have to get rid of some worthy women who want to have a drink with our delegation."

"Worthy women?" I asked.

"Yes, worthy women. They're silly but they mean well. So I'll take care of that and be down as fast as I can. I'm longing to see you."

I hung up, looked in the mirror again, swallowed my irritation at his chauvinistic remark about the worthy women and decided to change into my favorite green wool sweater.

I opened my door so Gerry wouldn't have to knock and wait for me to answer. The hallway was alive with Secret Service and visiting politicians from all over the world. I wondered how he'd get through without being recognized.

I had my sweater over my head when I heard him open the door and come into the room. I knew he was there but I couldn't see him because the wool got stuck on my earring. I felt his arms around my waist. My eyes were full of green wool. He kissed my neck. I could feel myself gasp both at the warmth of his mouth and also because the sweater was tearing at my pierced ear. I couldn't move. He ducked his hand under the sweater and through the wool found my face. "Don't ever move," he said. "I like you just like this. Let me help you," he offered. He released my earring, then kissed my ear.

He backed away from me, looked me over. "I like that color," he said. "It's nice." Then he walked around the room and said it was just like his. As I thought he would, he walked immediately onto the balcony and looked out toward Diamond Head.

"Look at those palm trees," he said. "They seem unreal, almost painted against that sky. Is that Diamond Head?"

"Yes," I answered. "It looks like a backdrop, but it's real."

"It's a paradise, isn't it?" He took my arm and wrapped it around his waist. "Are you hungry?" he said. "You must be. You always are."

"Yes."

"So am I. Let's eat."

So I went to the phone and ordered two Mai-Tais and some dinner. Gerry didn't know what Mai-Tais were. He was amused by my asking for extra pineapple and went to the bathroom to soak in the tub.

He was in there when the waiter arrived. I covered the dinner plates and took the Mai-Tais into the bathroom. I sat on the toilet seat while he soaked.

He sipped his Mai-Tai through a floating cherry in the glass. He swished the hot sudsy water around his legs. They were too long for the tub.

"So," I said, "how's it going? How've you been?"

"Fine," he said.

"What else? That's what you always say."

"Well, we've been having our problems in London. You've read about it. Never mind about me. How is your life?"

I told him about the new choreography for my show, about the exercise I did every day to keep in shape, about the health-food diets I was experimenting with, and about how hard it was to find good movie scripts for women. He asked why, and I said it must have something to do with a backlash reaction from militant feminism. Nobody seemed to know how to write women's roles anymore because they didn't know what women really wanted. At least, the men writers didn't know. And the women writers wrote about how unhappy and unfulfilled women were. So who cared? When it came to entertainment, who would pay to see that?

"I don't know," said Gerry. "I'm having enough trouble trying to decipher what *people* want . . . not what women want. I don't mean to sound arrogant," he said, "but we have an economy that's failing for everyone and I'm not sure we are going to be able to keep our chins up."

I said I could see what he meant, and then he questioned me about what was going on in America. I hesitated, then told him I wasn't sure. The American people were hard to figure out. Then I questioned him about what was going on in the world. We bantered back and forth, loving to savor one another as we talked and smiled and listened even if we were talking past each other. It wasn't *what* we were saying, it was *how* we were saying it. That's what we liked. We watched each other with a double fascination. We got something special from how our hands moved, our expressions, the way one would hold a head in a hand when trying to concentrate: one performer mesmerized by another.

We talked about Carter, inflation, the dollar, even about Idi Amin and solar energy, and as we talked it was like making love with our minds on a double level, each word setting off tiny sparks and explosions in our heads. It didn't matter whether the conversation was a new tax proposal or OPEC price hikes or women's roles in movies. Some kind of sensual dynamic was operating. A dynamic that was hard for me to explain, but we were both familiar with it. I would say something about the oil fields in Iran and the need for the workers to be unionized and behind Gerry's eyes he would melt over me like hot drawn butter. He was listening and heard my words, but I could feel a volcano slowly erupting inside of him spilling through his eyes. I didn't want to reach over and touch him or kiss him or even climb into the tub with him. I liked the feeling of holding back and communicating on the double level. I liked the feeling of using words to control what was underneath, because I felt it was almost too explosive. I wasn't sure why.

I gazed at his body in the warm water. VitaBath suds bubbled around the outline of his skin. I watched how his penis floated. I wondered what that felt like, yet in some way I felt I knew.

Gerry lay back in the tub and closed his eyes.

After a few moments, I said, "Gerry?"

He opened his eyes. "What?" he asked.

"Do you believe in reincarnation?"

"*Reincarnation?*" He was astonished. "My God," he said, "why do you ask that? Of course not."

"Why do you say, 'Of course not'?" I asked.

"Well, because," he laughed, "it's a fantasy. People who can't accept life as it is *here* and *now* on its own terms feel the need to believe such imaginings."

"Well, maybe," I said feeling somehow hurt that he would ridicule such a theory so resoundingly. "Maybe you're right, but more than a few million people do believe in it. Maybe they have a point."

"They *have* to," he said. "Those poor buggers don't have anything else in their lives. I can't blame them, of course, but if they believed a little more in the here and now it would make jobs like mine a great deal easier."

"What do you mean?" I asked.

"I mean, they don't tend to their lives as though they could improve them. I mean, they just exist as though it will be better the next time around, and this time isn't all that important. No, Shirl," he went on, his tone very determined, "I want to do something about the desperation of people's lives *now*. This is all we've got, and I respect that. Why? Do you believe in that gibberish?"

I felt put off by his put-down. I wished he would have been open-minded enough to discuss it at least.

"I don't know," I said. "Not really. But not Reilly either."

"Not Reilly?" he said. "What does that mean?"

"Just an Irish joke, Gerry. Just an Irish joke to an Englishman, if you get my meaning."

He flipped one hand over in the water and closed his eyes again.

Jesus, I thought, this metaphysical stuff certainly could get people upset. I wondered why. I didn't feel threatened by it at all. It seemed like a good dimension to explore. What harm could it do? I could see his point about people not taking responsibility for their own destinies here and now, but how *did* you reconcile the injustice of the accident of birth into poverty and deprivation when others were born into comfort? Was life really that cruel? Was life simply an accident? Accepting that seemed suddenly too easy, even lazy.

"This feels so good," said Gerry, lolling in the soapy tub. "This is a nice bathroom. This tub's too short, but it's nice. In fact this hotel is lovely, but especially this bathroom. It's just a bathroom, but it's nice because you're sitting here."

"Yes," I said, shifting my mind away from my thoughts. "Bathrooms are private places, aren't they? If you feel comfortable with somebody in a bathroom you've really got something important going with them."

Gerry smiled and nodded.

A bathroom *was* a private, primitive place, a place for basics. I thought of the time years ago a lover of mine had smashed up the bathroom in a hotel room in Washington. He had swept his arms violently through the drinking glasses on the sink and thrown my hair dryer into the mirror, shattering its pieces clear into the tub. We had been arguing in the bedroom about his jealousy but it was the bathroom where he went to be violent.

Then I thought of an incident in my childhood. I had lost the starring part in a school ballet I had dreamed for five years of doing. I remembered looking at myself in the mirror above the sink wondering what was wrong with me and before I realized what was happening I threw up in the sink.

I thought of the first dinner party I had given in California. I was so nervous and unable to cope as a hostess that I sat in my bathroom until dinner was over.

I thought of the bitter cold winter day that Warren and I had played in icy mud puddles. I was six and he was three. Mother was angry. She plunged Warren into the tub to wash him and I could hear his anguished cries coming from the bathroom. I remembered the day he fell on a broken milk bottle and Dad had rushed him to the bathroom to hold his gushing bleeding arm over the tub. I remembered his pleading face looking up at Dad's as he said, "Daddy, don't let it hurt."

I remembered a housekeeper I had had who retired to the bathroom every afternoon at six and lit a candle in the tub and prayed.

And I remembered how the most important, private, comfortable, relaxed and necessary place *I* could ever have wherever I was in the world was a well-lit room with a clean sparkling tub of warm, soft-flowing water. It helped me make transitions from depression, confusion and hard work. It helped me get in touch with myself. It put me to sleep. It soothed my aching legs. It woke me up. It coordinated my body and mind, gave me a burst of new ideas and hopes and wit. And whenever I was out during a day if I knew I had a nice bathtub that I could fill with liquid warmth in a nice bathroom to come home to I was happy.

Gerry finished his Mai-Tai and handed me the glass. He washed himself and asked me to wash his back.

"You know," he said, out of the tub and drying himself, "I'm glad there is such a thing as a telephone, taxpayers or not. By the way, you were quite right about that. I *am* paying the bills myself. It would have been difficult for me if I hadn't been able to talk to you all these weeks."

"Yes, I know," I said. "For me too," watching him swing the towel behind his back.

"But you know," he said, "I've been obsessed with your voice and I don't like feeling obsessed."

"What do you mean?" I asked, shivering a bit.

"Well, I find that my whole day revolves around the time when I can find the private time to talk to you. It just depletes my energy, that's all, and I don't like the feeling."

I stared at him. What was he saying? It made me apprehensive.

"Are you going to eat your cherry?" Standing there in his towel he looked at my empty glass.

"No, it's too sweet for me."

"May I have it?"

I handed it to him and took his hand as he led me into the bedroom. We sat down to the now cold seafood Newburg on the room service tray. The waiter had brought only one fork. I gave it to Gerry. He didn't notice that I was eating with a knife. I put my trench coat over him so he wouldn't be chilled and he looked like a clean, overgrown, rugged cherub as he began to eat.

"You know those scuffed shoes that you loved to see me wear all the time?" he asked. I nodded. "Well, my daughter threw them away into the dustbin. She thought I should have new shoes so she just threw them away."

"Your daughter threw away my favorite shoes?"

"Yes." He leaned forward in anticipation of what I would say with an almost lost smile on his face. I didn't know what he expected me to say. So I said, "Well, maybe they smelled of perfume."

He leapt up, throwing my coat from his shoulders. He lifted me above his shoulders and hugged me to him laughing, and tumbled me onto the bed. His soft warm hands were everywhere on me. His hair brushed against my face. His nose collided with mine and squashed it. His skin was creamy and warm, smelling of VitaBath. He trembled slightly and hugged me close to him.

I opened my eyes and looked at his face. It was astonished, ecstatic and abandoned all at the same

time. I sat up and held his hair in my hands and tugged
at it.

"How do you keep your nails so long?" he said.

"Do you think they're too long?"

"No. I think they're beautiful. But they must be
very strong."

He lifted his left hand in the air wiggling the little
finger from which almost all the top joint was missing,
lost in a freakish accident when he was very small. The
damage had healed so well that one seldom noticed the
finger, except when he himself drew attention to it.
Now he said, "I have arthritis in this finger and it hurts.
It's only developed recently. I wonder why."

"Probably not enough vitamin C," I said. "And no
exercise."

We lay together watching him work his finger up
and down.

"You know," he said, "I think I have this arthritis
because I'm depleting my energy. I'm too obsessed
with you. Yes," he went on, "you know how life is made
up of small but blinding insights?"

"Yes," I said, "I know what you mean."

"I think I have to cool my feelings. I have to get
back on an even keel."

"All right," I said. "Make it easy for yourself." I
could feel my heart stop, frozen.

"You know," he said, "I've never had this kind of
experience. Nothing anywhere near it. I don't know
what I think about it. And I don't know why I feel so
drawn to you. In spite of myself, I can't stop it."

I stared at my long fingernails. "Maybe we've had
another life together," I said. I turned my head quickly
toward him to see his reaction. "Maybe we left things
unresolved between us and need to work them out in
this lifetime."

A flush of confusion swept across his face. For one
brief instant he didn't ridicule my notion. Then his
expression cleared and he smiled at me.

"Sure," he said. "But seriously, I don't know what I
want to do about us. I want you to know that."

"I know," I said. "I know what you're saying. I

don't know what to do either. So, why don't we do nothing and for the time being just enjoy what we have?"

"But I want to be fair with you," he said. "I want to be fair with everybody. I've always put my work first. And if I dissipate my energy now, I'll lose what I've been working for. I have so much to do in the next eleven months and I'm reluctant to fragment myself."

I turned over and looked at him and sighed. "Yes, Gerry, I know all that. So have you considered giving us up? Just walking away from it?"

He answered immediately and with certainty. "No." And with genuine anxiety in his face he said, "Have you?"

"No," I lied. "Never. And I won't."

He took a deep breath and went on. "But you see I'm terribly bothered by the idea that I might be disappointing you. That is a real problem for me. I don't want to disappoint you."

"The way you don't want to disappoint the voters?" I asked.

"I have to ask you," he said. "What do you want from me?"

He caught me off guard. I thought a moment and said as if I had known it all along, "I want us to be happy when we're together. I don't understand why we are together either. But I don't want you to have to choose between me and anyone or anything else. I think you can have everything you already have and me, too. You can have it all, can't you? So you add one more dimension to your life. What's wrong with that? Maybe life should include all kinds of dimensions we haven't had the courage to embrace yet. I don't need a commitment of any kind from you. I don't even want one. I just want to know that you're happy when you're with me, and somehow we'll figure out what it's all about."

"But the more I have of you the more I want."

"Then take more of me. What's wrong with that?"

"That would mean giving up something else."

"Why?"

"Because I haven't got the time for you and for the rest of my life too."

"Maybe if you gave more time to feeling you deserved happiness it would not take so much."

"I can't. I think of what else I should be doing."

"Why don't you just think of what you *are* doing?"

"Because I always feel I should be doing something else."

"But what about yourself? What about enjoying yourself more when you can? What's wrong with enjoying yourself? Why do you think you don't deserve a good time?"

"Because I've got better things to do with my life than having a good time. I can't think of myself first."

"Maybe you should. Maybe if you figured out more of who you are you'd be able to help more people."

I remembered a reporter who interviewed me when I first returned from China. He was cynical about the enthusiasm I had for how the Chinese had struggled to win their new self-identity. Like most of the others, he thought I had been naive to be as moved as I was by the Chinese revolution. I explained how the Chinese had improved themselves compared to the recent past, and I said that the thing that moved me most was how they seemed to believe so deeply in themselves. That really angered the reporter.

"What do you mean, they believe in themselves? That's only propaganda and you bought it."

I asked, even if it was just propaganda, why was he so upset by the idea of believing you can do and have anything? And to my astonishment the anger turned to tears. He said nobody had the right to believe he could do or have anything—because in the end he'd be crushed. I realized he was talking about himself. *He* felt unworthy, couldn't trust himself. He left my apartment in New York and five hours later he called me.

"I've been driving around all night," he said. "What you said is exactly why my marriage is falling apart. My wife tells me the same thing. She says we'll never make a go of it unless I believe in myself more, unless I *believe* I can be happy. That's why I got so upset with you. I'm afraid I can't do it, not strong enough. In fact I've set up a set of eloquently cynical standards as a journalist so that I ridicule anyone who hopes or dreams or dares to be what they want. Myself included. And that's because I don't believe in myself. So how can I take seriously anyone else who does?"

I said I hoped he'd write a good article anyway and wished him well.

Suddenly I thought I understood why people had been so upset with the success of the Chinese revolution. Whatever their system was they had dared to believe in themselves alone, without the help of the rest of the world.

Gerry fell asleep holding me. In sleep he looked so vulnerable. My thoughts worried at the inner uncertainty of this otherwise very strong man. Did he somehow hold himself responsible for the tragedy of his first brief marriage because his wife had died in childbirth? Certainly the second marriage had been expedient for him and personally convenient in providing a mother for the baby. But did he now feel guilty because he sensed he had cheated *himself*? I thought of a conversation I had had recently with my father. With all his forceful command he had never believed in himself either. And he was one of the most talented people I had ever known. Aside from being a superb real-life performer he was an accomplished violinist, a good teacher, and a perceptive thinker.

Now he was reaching the end of his life—or so he thought. And he had always drunk too much. Lately my mother had been ill with a major hip operation. Dad was faced with what he would do without her, and began to drink so heavily from early in the morning that Mother called me, more deeply concerned than she had ever been that this time he was really killing himself. Dad was with her as she spoke to me openly and honestly on the phone. Neither of them minded. For years we had all been frightened of where his drinking was leading and the fear was culminating in this one phone call.

"I'm so worried about him, Shirl," she said, "and I

can't help him. You know what a talented good man he is but he doesn't believe that he is."

I asked her to let me speak to him.

"Hi, Monkey," he said, calling me by my nickname. I could see him sitting in that favorite chair of his, pipe rack beside him, the telephone tucked into his shoulder. I could feel him reach for his pipe and light it with the old antique lighter I had brought him from England.

"Daddy, let me be to the point, okay?"

"Okay," he said.

"Why are you drinking so much now?"

I had never asked him that question. I could never bring myself to ask him, I suppose because I was afraid he would tell me.

He began to cry. This was what I had been afraid of. I had never wanted to see Dad openly crack. Then he said, "Because I've wasted my life. I may have acted strong but that was because I never believed I could do anything. My mother taught me too well to be afraid and whenever I think about how afraid I am I can't stand it. So I have to drink." I could see his hands shaking as they used to whenever he wanted to detract from any emotion he might be displaying.

"I love you, Daddy," I said. And I started to cry too. I felt somehow that I had never really said that to him before. "Look what you did. You raised Warren and me. Doesn't that mean anything?"

"No, but I know you two didn't want to be like me. That's why you turned out like you did. You didn't want to be nothing. Like me." We were both crying and trying to talk through our tears. I wondered if any ashes had fallen to the floor.

"That's not altogether true," I said. "We just did more with the help you gave us than you did with the help *you* never got."

"But I feel so worthless when I realize what I haven't done with what I've got."

"Okay," I said. "But there's still time, you know."

"How?" he said. "What do you mean?" He tried to clear his throat. I wondered if Mother was watching him.

"Why don't you get out a pen and paper and every time you feel worthless put those feelings down on a piece of paper? I'll bet you could come up with some great notions on the feeling of feeling worthless."

He was really sobbing now. "Sometimes I think I can't stand it and if I just drink enough I won't have to bother waking up in the morning."

I swallowed. "Daddy," I said, "I've never asked you to promise me anything in my life, have I?"

"No, Monkey, you haven't."

"Well, will you promise me something now?"

"Yes, anything. What?"

"Will you promise me that instead of drinking, that every day you'll write at least one page of something you're feeling?"

"Me write? Christ, I'd be so ashamed if anybody read it."

"Okay, then don't let anybody read it. Just do it for yourself."

"But I don't have anything to say."

"How do you know if you haven't tried?" I could see him brush the lint from his left shoulder. I heard him cough.

"I can't write about myself. I can't even think about myself."

"Then write about me or Mother or Warren."

"You and Warren?"

"Sure."

"Lots of people would want to read that, wouldn't they?" he said sarcastically. I knew he was smiling.

"Well, only because it's from your point of view."

"You think so?"

"Yes, I do," I said. I could see him begin to rock in the chair.

"You know old Mrs. Hannah, my sophomore teacher, once told me I should write. In fact she told me I should talk less and write more."

"Really?" I remembered how he spoke of Mrs. Hannah when I was little. She had a broken-down car he loved to fix.

"Old Mrs. Hannah had the goddamdest car. She'd

have been better off with a horse and buggy. That damned car was like another person to her. Do you know that one day out in the hayfield. . . ."

"Hey, Daddy," I said, "why don't you start by writing about Mrs. Hannah's car out in the hayfield? Don't waste it by talking about it."

"Is that how it works?" he asked, clearing his throat and sounding funny and mischievous. "You mean all the times I've held court could have been a book?"

"Sure. Didn't Mrs. Hannah always say you talked too long and too much with nothing to show for it afterwards?"

"Yep," he said, "she sure did. She was a pisser. She burned down her barn to get the insurance money and then ran off with the guy who sold it to her."

"Well, she sounds like a good character to write about."

"Would you read something if I wrote it?"

"Sure. I can't wait. Send it to New York. It'll get to me wherever I am."

"You mean you really think I have something to say?"

"Well, I've been listening to you for over forty years and I think you're funny and touching. Why don't you write about your pipe?"

We had both stopped crying now.

"Will you do it? Will you try?"

"Well, Monkey, I guess I have to, don't I?"

"Yep."

"I promise then. I promise."

"I love you, Daddy."

"I love you, Monkey."

We hung up. I walked around the house crying for another hour. Then I went to the phone and called a florist. I ordered a rose a day for a month with a note attached. "A rose for a page. I love you."

Dad has been writing on and off ever since. I'm not sure if he's completely on the wagon. But then no writer I know is! But I do wish old Mrs. Hannah had mentioned his talent and her belief in him a little more often.

The notes that he sends me are short and each one tells a story, a story from the life of a man who influenced me deeply, because he inadvertently taught me to love brilliant and complicated men who needed someone to help unlock them.

Chapter 5

*"I very much doubt if anyone of us has the faintest
idea of what is meant by the reality of existence of
anything but our own egos."*

—A. EDDINGTON
The Nature of the Physical World

🐚 Gerry and I slept. Whenever we moved we adjusted
ourselves to fit, leaving no space between us. At some
point he murmured something about a wake-up call so
his delegation wouldn't wonder where he was in the
morning. I called the operator and waited for dawn
when he would have to leave. I felt forlorn as I watched
him sleep. He went away. His eyes were shut. He was
lost in his own unconscious. I watched his sleep until I
finally did the same. As I slept, double images of my
father and Gerry tumbled over each other in my dreams.

When the wake-up call came, Gerry sat straight up
in bed as though a bugle had called him to duty.
Quickly he kissed me, dressed, and said he'd be back
after he got rid of his press aide and reporters.

"I'll probably have breakfast with them," he said,
"so why don't you eat now? I'll tell everyone in the
delegation I have jet lag and we can spend the day
together."

He left, gone before I noticed he had forgotten one
of his socks. I ordered some papaya and toast and ate on

71

the balcony. Below me an attendant was feeding the dolphins. I remembered how Sachi used to ride the dolphins when she was a kid and we'd meet Steve in Hawaii as a halfway point to Japan. She used to say she understood the dolphins and they were her playmates.

Somewhere below me I could hear journalists talking about what would make good stories out of Hawaii. Interspersed in their professional kidding was speculation about Dr. Lilly's experiments with dolphins. I wondered if dolphins really were as highly intelligent as scientists said, or if they really could have their own evolved language. I remembered someone telling me once that residing in the great brains of the dolphins were all the secrets of some immense lost civilization called Lemuria. I had heard about Atlantis, but Lemuria was unknown to me.

I watched the Secret Service men and the journalists watching the dolphins. I wondered how Gerry and I would get through the day without being recognized.

About an hour later he called. "Look," he said, "meet me on the beach to the left of the hotel. Most everyone will be keeping close to these premises. I'll be there in fifteen minutes."

I dressed in jeans and a shirt and underneath I wore a bathing suit. I tied a scarf around my head and put on black-rimmed sunglasses.

Walking through the lobby and out the back entrance nobody noticed me, but I was afraid to stop and watch the dolphins because of the journalists. I walked quickly past the pool and out onto the warm sand where tourists were already lying on the beach with radios blaring rock and roll. The smell of coconut suntan oil hung in the air.

I walked along the edge of the beach where the clear blue waves lapped the shore, heading left. No one was swimming yet. The palm trees bent in a soft trade wind. I did a few bends in the shallow waves, not having done my exercises in the morning. My show seemed half a life away.

A few hundred yards up the empty beach I stopped, sat on the sand, lifted my head to the sun and waited for Gerry. It felt almost regular, almost human. More than anything, I hated the secrecy. I didn't like feeling furtive, clandestine, dishonest; it hurt. I hoped that Gerry didn't get a dangerous kick out of it like some people did.

He was wearing khaki slacks and a white, loose shirt as I watched him amble up the beach through the edge of the surf. His arms swung out from his body and he carried a pair of sandals in his hand. He didn't wave when he saw me. I got up and met him in the water so we could continue to walk.

"So I see you *do* have another pair of shoes," I said.

"My vacation shoes," he laughed and touched my face.

"Did your delegation buy your story about jet lag?"

"Oh sure. They will do a little of the same themselves. Having a conference in Honolulu is too tempting anyway."

He buckled his sandals together, slung them over his shoulder and took my hand when we were well out of range of the hotel. I leaned my head against his shoulder and we began to walk.

We found a coral reef that led way out into the ocean and felt as though we were walking on water. Gerry teased that everyone thought that's what he claimed to be able to do anyway. The coral was sharp. We stopped and looked out at the big surf breaking further out to sea.

"Can you ride the waves?" he asked.

"I used to when I was in my twenties," I said. "Before I got old enough to be afraid of it."

I remembered how carefree I used to be with my body. It never occurred to me that I might break something or that anything could go wrong at all. Now I had to think ahead even when I got out of a taxicab. If I turned an ankle or banged my knee it would interfere with my dancing. When I was younger I had danced more recklessly. In fact, I guess I had done most everything without thinking very much. And I had had a wonderful time at it too. With adulthood, I had become more and more aware of the consequences of everything I did, whether it was leaping into the waves or having a love affair.

Awareness didn't lessen the fun or the wonder. On the contrary, now I wanted to learn to live totally in the *now*—in the present, with a confirmed completeness that that was all there really was anyway. If I had in fact lived other lives in the past and would possibly live other lives in the future, belief in that would only serve to intensify my commitment with all my heart and soul to the *present*.

Reincarnation was a new concept to me, of course, but I found that each time I thought about it I derived great pleasure from its implications. Were time and space so overwhelmingly infinite that they served to make one realize the preciousness of each and every moment on Earth? Did my mind need to take quantum leaps of imagination into other possible realities in order to appreciate the joy of reality now? Or, were real joy and happiness the *inclusion* of all those other realities that in effect expanded one's awareness of the reality of now?

Expanded consciousness. That was the phrase so many people were using more and more. One needn't trade in an old consciousness for a new one. One could simply expand and raise the consciousness one already had—an expanded consciousness simply recognized the existence of previously unrecognized dimensions . . . dimensions of space, time, color, sound, taste, joy, and on and on. Was the conflict between Gerry and me simply a difference in movement toward expanded consciousness? Perhaps I was trying to force him to move at a pace that was mine instead of his. His pace wasn't to be judged either. It was just different. I knew I could be demandingly insistent, a result in part of intense curiosity and in part of impatience. I was impatient with others who didn't indulge in the same search. My life seemed to be devoted to a series of questions. Gerry's seemed to be devoted to answers.

We headed away from Diamond Head, Waikiki and

Kahala, walking toward the thick underbrush of the deserted side of the island. The further away we got from people, the more Gerry touched me. Soon we were walking with our bodies joined together. It was too lovely to talk. The sun fell behind the clouds and the coconut palms began to bend in the wind. It started to rain. We ran from the water into a grove of trees where ripe coconuts lay strewn on the ground. We stood under a tree and watched the rain fall on the fuchsia-colored azaleas around us. A blue bird shook its wings and flew further into the underbrush. Gerry put his arms around me and looked out to sea.

"This is so beautiful," he said.

He hugged me closer.

The rain fell harder now—one of those thick tropical rains that looked like a sparkling beaded sheet.

"Do you want to go swimming in this rain?" I asked.

Without answering Gerry pulled off his shirt and trousers. He too had a bathing suit underneath. He rolled his clothes into a ball, placed them under his sandals beneath the tree and ran into the ocean.

I took off my jeans and shirt and followed him.

The waves were higher now and whitecapped. We dove under them, feeling the salt spray mingle with the fresh rain. We laughed and splashed each other. I wiped the salt from my eyes, glad I hadn't worn mascara. Gerry swam out further, waving me to come with him. I was afraid to go, so floating in the rainy waves I watched him. He stopped and lay on his back past where the waves were breaking. Then he turned over on his stomach and waited for the right wave. It came, and he rode the crest of it until it subsided close to where I waited. He swam toward me and swept me up in his arms. I kissed his salty face and he smothered me in his big shoulder. We swam back to shore and lay together in the shallow breaking waves looking up at the rain, water soaking our faces.

"That . . . just then was the happiest I've ever been," he said, breathing hard and shouting slightly above the surf. "You know I've never done this before? That was the first wave I ever rode. I've missed a great deal, haven't I?"

I didn't say anything. I just turned over in the water and thought it was the happiest I had been in a long time too—only I wished I had had the abandonment to ride that wave with him.

We lay in the water until the sun came out. Then on our backs we inched our way out of the sea and onto the wet sand where we lay until we could feel the sun drying us off.

"Gerry?" I asked, "when you look back at your life, when were you happiest?"

He thought awhile and then with a kind of startled look said, "You know, now that you've asked me, I would have to say all my happiness has been connected with nature—sometimes with people—but never with my work. That's astonishing to me. *My happiest moments have never been connected to my work*. My God, why is that?"

"I don't know. Maybe because you felt work was duty."

"But even when I win I'm depressed. For example, the last time I was elected I fell into a depression for days." He looked up into the sky. "I must think about that, mustn't I?"

I got up to get dressed.

"It seems a shame that you should feel depressed when you win. What do you feel when you lose?"

He got up and walked to the tree where we had left our clothes. "When I lose I feel challenged. I feel a sense of struggle and that makes everything worth it. I think I need to spit against the wind."

❧ We walked further around the island and soon found a small food stand by the sea that sold pineapples and papayas. We squeezed lemon over the papayas and sat on the sand. The Hawaiian who owned the place was reading a Raymond Chandler novel and intermittently looking at the sea. Gerry and I talked about Asia, the

Middle East, and the time I had spent in Japan. He didn't ask me any personal questions and I didn't volunteer any information.

We continued walking until we found the directions to Sea World. We went in to see the dolphins and killer whales. It was feeding time. One of the dolphins got more to eat than the others. Gerry didn't think it was fair. He said survival of the fittest was cruel and there ought to be a way for man to restructure that basic fact of nature. He said that was what civilization was for . . . to make the world a kinder place. He felt sorry for those who couldn't fend for themselves.

At the large tank a killer whale was being fed. Seagulls circled overhead waiting for the whale to miss one of the fish that the attendant, who wore a wet suit, was dropping into the gigantic mouth. Then he missed one. A gull swooped down, scooped up the fish, and flew to the other side of the tank. The whale saw him and with a great lunge went after him. The gull sat on the rim where the whale couldn't get at him. The gull blinked at him. And the whale interrupted his feeding to glare at the gull for a full three minutes. Gerry laughed out loud, and the whale went back to his feeding.

We left the aquarium and walked into the hills above the sea. Birds of every color flitted and squawked through the lush tropical trees. We tried to open a dried coconut but we needed a machete. I told Gerry about the time I had gone to the big island of Hawaii once to be alone. I rented a little house on the Kona Coast and sat on the volcanic rocks for days thinking about competition, among other things.

I had been in Hollywood for five years and the way good friends would fight each other for good parts was getting me down. I had just been nominated for another Academy Award and I didn't like the false pressure that the nomination seemed to burden me with either. I didn't like the feeling that winning a little brass statue should be more rewarding than doing good work. It had confused me because everyone else thought it was what Hollywood was all about. But I didn't see why anybody should win or lose. I didn't like how crestfallen people felt when they lost. And I hated how much money was spent trying to influence votes by giving parties and taking ads in the trade papers. Gerry seemed interested in what I was saying but couldn't understand that I had genuinely not cared whether I won or not.

"Why didn't you care?" he asked.

"I don't know," I said, "but I didn't. And I don't care now. I think I didn't want to be embarrassed to win something that had no business being a contest in the first place. I wouldn't be depressed the way you say you are when you win—I would be embarrassed. *You need* to win because that's how democracy and majority rule work and there's no other way to be a successful politician. But artists shouldn't be involved with that kind of competition. I think we should only be concerned with competing against the best we have in ourselves."

He asked me if I really had gone there alone. I told him yes, I had; that I had done a lot of that in my life. I needed to be alone. I needed time to reflect. He said he had gathered that from my first book, *Don't Fall Off The Mountain*. He said that book was one of his daughter's favorite books.

He asked me if I ever got lonely. I said being alone was different from being lonely but that I believed I was a basically lonely person in any case. He never asked me about my divorce, or my relationships with other men. If it was going to come up it would have come up then. I assumed he wasn't ready to know.

We stopped, sat, and watched sand crabs dig their holes as late afternoon began to fall. One of them fell over on its back. With a twig Gerry turned it upright and smiled gently. I told him how I had watched a colony of ants outside that little house on Kona. They diligently spent their days carrying a stale bun, crumb by crumb, from one rock to a hiding place under another rock. They were so organized and determined. There were no individuals. No way to be one. They seemed selfless. I wondered if that was a good way to be, to submit your own interests to the good of the species. Was that what Gerry thought he was doing? Gerry asked me about China. Though he had never been there he knew a lot about it. We talked about the Chinese revolution and he said he wished there had been time when we were in Hong Kong to go across the border, if only for a few days.

We fell asleep in the afternoon sun, and when we woke a cool breeze had come up. We ran together on the edge of the surf laughing and pummeling each other. Gerry stopped to skim flat stones over the surf. Then we walked, holding hands, until we came in sight of the hotel, where we separated. Gerry walked ahead of me and disappeared into the throng at the pool area. I stood watching the sun set for a while. Then it struck me how free Gerry had seemed all day being outside and how inept he could be inside, with four walls around him. He was really a different person when he was unconstrained. I was sure that he'd be better at his work if he'd let himself go more, better at his marriage too probably, better with me.

Entering the hotel, Gerry was waylaid in the lobby by his delegation. "Where have you been? Are you feeling better?" I heard snatches of conversation as I walked unnoticed by him and everyone else. I felt like background music.

I got into the elevator, glad that I was alone in it, except for a porter.

I was taking a hot shower, washing the salt from my hair when the phone rang. Gerry said, "Why have you been away from me for so long?"

In five minutes he was in my room sitting on the floor. There was a TV special on from Las Vegas starring Sinatra, Sammy Davis, Jr., Paul Anka and Ann-Margret. He sat with his legs crossed, leaning forward, and asked me about musical comedy shows. Were the singers really singing or did they mouth to a playback? Did they have to memorize the lyrics or did they have cue cards? How much rehearsal did they have before they actually performed?

As we talked we decided to have dinner at an out-of-the-way Japanese restaurant I knew on the other side of Waikiki. If we could successfully negotiate getting a cab there would be no problem from then on.

I left the hotel room first. The down elevator took so long that he found himself going up just to avoid arriving in the lobby with me.

The lobby was full of journalists and Secret Service men. I put my head in a magazine and kept it there until I got outside. A cab was waiting in line. Photographers popped flashbulbs as famous delegates entered and left. I got in the cab and asked the driver to wait for just a moment. He said he couldn't wait long. I looked nervously into the lobby. Gerry was there but he had been stopped by a visiting delegation. I counted the seconds.

"My friend is coming," I said. "Hang on just a moment." The driver waited.

A few minutes later Gerry extricated himself, smiled into a camera that popped a bulb in his face and saw me wave to him. Nonchalantly he walked toward the cab and got in. No one noticed anything.

We drove to the Japanese restaurant. I knew the manager but she wasn't interested in whom I was with. I asked her in Japanese for a private tatami room and she showed us in, brought us some hot saki and went to prepare our sushi. Gerry wasn't sure about the raw fish but he ate it anyway.

The candle on the table flickered under his face.

"Oh, how I loved today," he said.

I smiled.

"And oh, how I love talking to you."

I smiled again.

"And, oh, how I love being with you."

I smiled and rolled my eyes in mock disgust. He knew what I meant.

"And oh, how I love you."

I began to cry.

He reached over and took my hand. I couldn't talk.

"I'm sorry that makes you unhappy," he said.

I pulled out a Kleenex and blew my nose.

"Oh, Gerry," I said finally. "Why is it so hard for you to say?"

His face went solemn. "Because I say it in ways other than words. I say it with my hands, with my body."

"Why?"

"I don't know. I think it's because I have to manipulate words all day long in my work and I don't want to feel that I'm manipulating words with you."

"You mean that's playing fair with me?"

"Yes."

"Well, I need to manipulate words to express my feelings. Is that *un*fair?"

"I don't know how it is for you."

"I'm not sure that love is fair anyway."

"I don't think I know anything about love," he said. "This is all new to me. I only know I feel comfortable expressing myself physically because I've never done that before and I use words all the time."

I tried to grasp what he was saying. Did he mean he couldn't really be trusted? Or did he mean he didn't want to commit himself in so many words because he didn't want the responsibility later?

"How," I asked, "will you express yourself when we're apart then?"

He shrugged. "I don't know. It's a contradiction, isn't it? I'll have to think about it."

We ate dinner talking about Japan and how it was sacrificing its culture for the sake of industrial development. After dinner we walked awhile before we took separate cabs back to the hotel.

There was a convention banquet in the hotel dining room. I went to my room and waited. The dolphins leapt gently in the aquarium below and the palm trees rustled drily in the trade winds.

Half an hour later we were in bed. Gerry said his work had piled up for the next two days and he needed to be up early in the morning. I was leaving in the late morning.

We turned out the light and tried to sleep.

Suddenly he got up and with that determined walk he crashed into a chair. I laughed. He went to the bathroom and came back and paced up and down at the foot of the bed.

"What's wrong?" I asked.

"I don't know what I'm thinking," he said. "I don't know what to do. And I'm not even ready to think about what I'm thinking."

I watched him quietly. He got an apple out of the fruit basket. He paced with the apple in his hand. Then he came back to bed and began to eat it. Deliberately and with great concentration he chewed each bite thoroughly without saying a word. It was as though he didn't know I was there. He didn't eat the apple like most people, leaving the two ends. He ate the apple from the top down and finally he devoured the whole thing, seeds, core and all.

I laughed and it startled him.

"I don't eat much," he said, "but once I do I eat it all." He leaned over on his elbow. "Remember that."

🐦 I tried to sleep. I didn't know when I'd see him again. I thought of what it would be like in the morning when he'd walk out the door and shut it behind him. I couldn't make myself comfortable. I turned from one side to the other. Each time I turned he touched me. On and off all night I tossed and slept, tossed and slept. Each time I moved he touched me. Soon daylight filtered through the curtains. He sat up, pulled the covers around me, and lifted my face.

"Listen," he said, "we've had thirty-six hours of something too extraordinary to describe. Most people never have that. Look at the positive side. I always assume I begin at zero . . . so anything above that is a plus."

I swallowed hard. "I don't. I assume I start wherever I want and I can go anywhere I want after that. I feel I can make anything happen if I want and I'm not *grateful* for our thirty-six hours. I want more. I want all I can get."

He laughed and threw up his hands. He got out of bed and I could feel him prepare himself for a day of work. He had had his time with me, considered himself lucky, and now had to contend with his English sense of obligation. It was simple for him. He had made a career out of denial.

"Gerry," I said, "wait a minute. Could you live without this now?"

He thought for a moment and his face was grave. "Life would be bleak, gray, empty. Now give me a nice long kiss," he said, taking my face in his hands. I reached up and held his hair, letting it fall through my fingers. Quickly he dressed, and before I knew it he was at the door.

"I'll call you when I get back to London."

He didn't say goodbye. He didn't turn around. He walked straight to the door, opened it and left.

The room changed. It was the moment I was so afraid of. The silence made my ears ring. I felt sick. I sat up and threw my legs over the side of the bed. I looked around for something he might have forgotten. No, I thought. This is ridiculous. I'm not going to allow myself to wallow around like this. I got up and took a cold shower, ordered breakfast, and packed. Then I sat down and wrote him a letter about how right he was that half a glass of water was half full, not half empty.

I slept restlessly on the plane back over the Pacific.

"What do you want from *me*?" I could hear him saying it again. He was right. Did I want him to shatter his personal life, risk his political work and in general give up everything he had dedicated his life to for me? Now *I* didn't want to think about it.

"I have to finish the job I started in my work a long time ago," he had said. Did I want to risk that for this? And what, anyway, was *this*? Was it really love? Was it what people gave up everything for? Would he ever do that? Would I? Could I live in London? What would the English voters do if they knew? Would it really ruin him? He claimed with absolute certainty that his wife wouldn't be able to take it, but what would the people think?

So he had said, "I have to calm down. I need to cool myself out. I've been too obsessed with you. I need to be objective now. I don't want to think about what I'm thinking about." He had said all these things to me and when I tried to be helpful by assuming a cooler attitude myself he had said, You're not going to get rid of me that easily." So I too was confused. . . . Bleak, empty, and gray, he had said. Would it be bleak, empty, and gray for me, too? Could I do without him? What was I really doing *with* him? What was I doing with myself?

Chapter 6

"It is very difficult to explain this feeling to anyone who is entirely without it, especially as there is no anthropomorphic conception of God corresponding to it. The individual feels the nothingness of human desires and aims and the sublimity and marvellous order which reveal themselves both in nature and in the world of thought. He looks upon individual existence as a sort of prison and wants to experience the universe as a single significant whole."

—ALBERT EINSTEIN
The World As I See It

When I got home I was irritated, frustrated, upset with myself, and more bugged than ever by something I couldn't touch. Yes, I was bothered by all the obvious problems relating to Gerry. But it was more than that.

I called David. He was still in California. He sensed immediately that something was wrong. He asked how my weekend had gone, knowing that I wouldn't say much but endeavoring to be my friend and lend support if he could. I asked him to meet me in Malibu.

He came right out with a bag of fresh peaches. We took them down to the beach. The peaches were juicy and sticky and sweet.

"What's wrong?" asked David, knowing that he

could come right to the point because I had invited him.

I swallowed a huge bite of juicy peach sweetness and didn't know how to begin to tell him what I was feeling. "I don't know," I said. "I'm hung up . . . well, not exactly hung up. I just feel that there's something about why I'm alive that I'm not getting. I'm a happy person and getting plenty out of life—I don't mean I'm hung up with all that middle-aged crisis stuff. It's something I can't explain. In fact age has nothing to do with it except maybe that after awhile you finally get around to asking the right questions." I hesitated, hoping David would say something that would trigger me into more clarity. He didn't. He just waited for me to say more. I went on. "I mean, maybe I'm not even talking about me. I mean, well . . . maybe it's the world. Why doesn't the world work? And why should that get to me? I mean, how come *you* never seem bugged? Do you know something I don't know?"

"You mean, like why are we alive and what is our purpose?"

"Yeah," I said. "I guess that's about it. I mean, when you have as much as I do and have lived as much as I have you finally have to ask yourself very seriously, 'What's it all about?' And I'm not asking out of any unhappiness. I'm successful, I think, personally and professionally, and I'm certainly happy with it. I'm not into drugs or booze. I love my work and I love my friends. I have a great personal life even with some complicated problems. No—that's not what I mean. I mean, I think there must be more going on about our real purpose in life than I'm able to see."

David wiped peach juice from his chin. It was fascinating to me that I had even felt comfortable asking him such a question, almost as though he could answer it. It was a question I wouldn't even have asked Einstein had I known him well enough to sit on the beach slurping peaches with him.

David brushed sand from his sticky fingers. "Well," he said, "I think happiness is in our own back yard, to quote Al Jolson."

"You're a big help," I laughed. "Look at my back yard—it's the Pacific Ocean. Sooo?"

"Sooo, I mean, *you*. I mean, happiness and purpose and meaning is *you*."

"Look," I said, "you're really a nice polite person, but could you be a little less nice and polite and instead be a little more specific?"

"Okay," he went on undaunted by my irritability. "*You* are everything. Everything you want to know is inside of you. You are the universe."

Jesus, I thought, hippy-dippy jargon. He's going to use phrases that are simply not part of my realistic vocabulary. And as much as I might feel drawn to what he is saying, it is going to put me off because it's not part of my philosophic or intellectual lexicon of understanding. But then, I thought, my words and phrases and ideas have been limited to my own conceptions, my own frames of reference. Don't get bugged by words. Keep the mind open.

"David," I said, "please tell me what you mean. What you said then sounds so big and ponderous and hokey. I have enough trouble understanding what I'm doing day by day. Now I'm supposed to understand that *I* am the universe?"

"Okay," he said chuckling gently at my frustrated honesty. "Let's go at it another way. When you were in India and Bhutan, did you think much about the spiritual aspect of your own life? I mean, did it occur to you that your body and your mind might not be the only dimensions there were in your life?"

I thought for a moment. Yes, of course I had. I remembered how fascinated I had been when I saw a Bhutanese lama levitate in the lotus position (with his knees crossed under each other) three feet off the ground. Or to be possibly more accurate, I *thought* I had seen him levitate. It was explained to me that he had accomplished such a feat by reversing his polarities (whatever that was) and thereby had defied gravity. To me, it had made some kind of scientific sense, and also appealed to the metaphysical side of my nature. So I left it at that. For some reason, I had no trouble

accepting that it had happened, but I really couldn't
honestly say that I understood why. As another lama
told me later, "You wouldn't have seen the levitation if
you hadn't been prepared to see it." That's when I
began to think maybe I just *thought* I had seen it. I
remembered how, when living with the Masai in Kenya
and traveling to Tanzania, I was met by other Masai
who knew my name and the fact that I had been made a
Masai blood sister without anyone telling them. I accepted the safari white hunters' explanations that they
believed the Masai had perfected thought transference.
They said that the Masai had no other form of communication with each other throughout Africa so, out of
necessity and also because they were communal thinkers,
they could do what the white and civilized world was
too competitive to do—communicate through clear mental telepathy and thought transference to their brothers.

Again, I had accepted what the white hunters told
me. First, they had had a great deal of experience and
years of observing the Masai and their habits and
behavior patterns and second, it just made sense to me.
I had no problem understanding that the energy of
human thought could live and travel outside of the
human brain. It didn't seem outlandish or preposterous
to me at all. Nor to the white hunters, for that matter,
and they were certainly practical students with down-
to-earth experience of primitive tribes.

I thought of many moments in my life when I *knew*
something was going to happen, and it did. When I
knew someone was in trouble, and they were. When I
knew someone was trying to reach me, and they did. I
had often had such flashes about people I knew well. I
would, for example, *know* that a close friend had just
checked into the International Hotel in Seoul, Korea. I
would call on a lark and he'd be there; wondering
himself how I knew he was there. Those flashes happened
to me often. And if common or garden stories are to be
believed, these were experiences many, many people
had had, and almost all had heard about.

As for me, I never really questioned such things.
They just *were*. That was all. But no, I never really

related to any of that stuff spiritually. Yes, I was interested in mind over matter, in metaphysical phenomena, in meditational isolation, and certainly in expanded consciousness. But how could I find it for myself? Or was I already aware without recognizing it?

For instance, I met a lama in the Himalayas who had been meditating in near isolation for twenty years. I climbed 14,000 feet to his mountainside cave and when I arrived, he gave me some tea and a piece of saffron scarf that he had blessed to protect me, which he said would be necessary because I was soon going to run into trouble. He was right. On the way down the mountain, a man-eating leopard stalked me and my Sherpa guide. And one day later I found myself caught in a bizarre Himalayan coup d'état; I was arrested and held at bayonet point for two days while my captors tried to take away my guide and throw him in the *dzong* (a Himalayan dungeon where people usually died). The experience was like a bad grade-B movie—unbelievable to anyone who hadn't been there. To me, it was real— and the meditating lama had been right. About the danger, anyway. Even if the scarf only provided moral support.

But was his premonition or foreknowledge spiritual? I hadn't ever really thought in those terms. I was more of a pragmatist. I had respect for things I didn't understand, but I was more comfortable relating to those things on an intellectual or scientific level, which seemed more *real* to me.

"Yes," I said to David. "I'm thinking more and more about the spiritual aspect of myself or the world or whatever you want to call it."

David shifted his position around the bag of peaches and the sandy peach pits which were piling up between us.

"You mean," he said, "that the spiritual aspect of your life seems real to you?"

"Yeah," I answered, "I guess you could say that. But it doesn't seem to be a *real* part of the realistic life we lead. Maybe because I can't see it. I guess I'm saying that I believe what I have proof of."

"Sure," he said, "most Westerners feel that way. In fact, that's probably the basic difference between East and West—and never the twain shall meet."

"So what about you?" I asked. "How come you seem to have this spiritual understanding in such a pragmatic world? You're a Westerner. How did you come by your beliefs?"

He cleared his throat almost as though he wanted to avoid answering me, but knew he couldn't. "I've just traveled and wandered around a lot," he said. "I wasn't always like this. But something happened to me once. I'll tell you about it some time. But believe me, I used to be a regular Charlie Crass with fast cars, fast girls— just living in the fast lane. It wasn't getting me anywhere but I have to admit I dug it while it lasted." David's eyes had grown misty as he talked, remembering. I wondered what it was that had happened but didn't want to press it since he'd said he would tell me in his own time.

"So," I said. "You traveled around a lot?"

"Yeah."

"So have I. And I love it. I love flying to new places, seeing new faces. I don't think I could ever stay still in one spot."

David looked at me sidewise.

"I hitchhiked," he said, "and worked my way across the oceans on tramp steamers. I don't think it matters *how* we do those things, but instead *why* is what counts. We were probably both looking for the same thing, but from different vantage points."

"Yeah," I said, "but I've always thought I was looking for myself whenever I traveled. Like a journey anywhere was really a journey through myself."

"Sure," he said, "so was I. That's what I meant a few minutes ago when I said the answers are in *you*. *You* are the universe."

"Jesus," I said, "we both could have saved a lot of plane fares if we had known that in the beginning, couldn't we? We could have just sat in the back yard and meditated."

"You're joking, but I think it's true. That's why

everyone is essentially equal. *Everyone* has *themselves* regardless of what station of life they're born into. Actually a person considered stupid might be a lot more spiritual than someone who is a genius in Earth terms. The village idiot might be closer to God than Einstein although even Einstein said he believed there was a greater force at work than he could prove."

"But being a genius and being spiritual—whatever that means—are not mutually exclusive?"

"No."

I remembered a story someone at Princeton had told me. Einstein had been attempting to prove the theory of why those little mechanical birds you put on the edge of a glass would fill up with water and when they became unbalanced, would spill all the water out and begin again. He couldn't seem to explain how the little mechanical bird worked in mathematical terms and out of frustration, one day he went into town for a double dip strawberry ice cream cone. Strawberry was apparently Einstein's favorite flavor. He was licking the ice cream cone and walking along a curb in the road thinking about the mechanical bird when he tripped slightly and the top dip of the ice cream toppled off into the gutter. Einstein was so crushed he broke down and cried. . . . Here was one of the great geniuses of the world, but he couldn't handle his anxiety over what he didn't understand any better than the next guy.

I remembered reading that Einstein was an avid reader of the Bible. I never knew what he really thought of it other than the fact that he respected it. I wondered what he would have thought of the supposed imprint of Christ left on the Shroud of Turin. Some scientists said the imprint was caused by high-level radioactive energy, which spiritualists explained was an expression of the high level of spiritual energy Christ had acquired.

"So what about Christ?" I found myself asking David. "Who do you think he really was?"

"Okay," he said, straightening his posture as though he had finally found a thread to unravel. "Christ was the most advanced human ever to walk this planet. He was a highly evolved spiritual soul whose purpose on Earth was to impart the teachings of a Higher Order."

"What do you mean, 'A Higher Order'?" I asked.

"A higher spiritual order," said David. "He obviously knew more than the rest of us about life and death and God. I think his resurrection proved that."

"But how do we know it really happened?"

David shrugged his shoulders. "First of all," he said, "a lot of people saw it, and reported that they were awestruck and even terrified. And second, the remains of his body were never found, and third, a legend of that magnitude would be hard to make up. Besides, how do we *know* anything in history ever happened if we weren't witnesses to it ourselves? So, somewhere along the line education and knowledge of history require an act of faith that events are true, or we shouldn't bother learning anything about the past at all."

"In other words," I said, "why *not* believe it?"

"Sure," said David, "but first, take a hard look, *listen*, really listen, to what the man said. Everything Christ taught had to do with understanding the knowledge of mind, body *and spirit*. In fact, the First Commandment given to Moses, even long before Christ, was the recognition of the Divine Unity: Mind, Body, and Spirit. Christ said the First Commandment was the chief commandment and to misunderstand it would be to misunderstand all the other universal laws following it. But, he said to understand it fully we had to understand that the soul and spirit of man had everlasting life and the soul's quest was to rise higher and higher toward perfection until we were free."

I looked at David, trying to absorb what he was saying. A few years before I think I would have called him a Jesus freak, and launched into a dialogue accusing him of espousing beliefs that diverted attention from what was really wrong with the world.

"So how does all of this square with this world we're living in?" I asked instead. "I mean, how can belief in the soul and keeping the First Commandment and all that clean up the mess we've made of this world?" I didn't want to get upset, but it wouldn't have been difficult.

"Well," said David, "all our 'isms' and self-righteous wars and industrial technology and intellectual masturbation and socially compassionate programs have only made it worse, it seems to me. And the longer we disregard the spiritual aspect of life, the worse it will get. . . ." He folded his legs under him and used his hands to make points in the air. "See," he went on, "Christ and the Bible and spiritual teachings don't concern themselves with social or political questions. Instead, spirituality goes right to the *root* of the question—the individual. If each of us set ourselves right individually, we would be on the right path socially and politically. See what I mean?"

"Yes," I said, "I guess so."

"In other words, if we understood our own *individual purpose* and meaning in relation to God, or even to mankind and leave God out of it for the moment, it would automatically lead to social harmony and peace. There'd be no need for war and conflict and poverty and stuff, because we'd all know there was no need to be greedy or competitive or afraid and violent."

Well, it wasn't a new idea. Ultimate responsibility of the individual was basic to Quaker thought, for one thing, and—leaving God out of it as David suggested—the concept was also basic to Kropotkin's political philosophy of anarchism.

"Why are you saying we need to understand our individual purpose and meaning in relation to God?" I asked. "Why couldn't we just understand it in relation to our fellow men?"

David smiled and nodded. "You could," he said. "That would be a good beginning because in fact, in caring about mankind you *are* relating to God, to the divine spark in all of us." He paused. "But it's easier," he said, "if you first learn who *you* are. Because that's where cosmic justice comes in. We can't just relate to our lives here and now as though this has been the only life we've lived. All our previous lives are what have molded us. We are the product of all the lives we have led."

I thought of Gerry and his politics. Had such spiritual concepts in a political context ever occurred to him? Or to any politician for that matter? The voters would think our political leaders crazy if they voiced such ideas. Jimmy Carter came as close as anyone but most of the "smart" people I knew liked to think he was doing a "media-grope with God" and didn't really mean it. They didn't know what to make of him if he *really* meant all that stuff about being born again, and in fact, they just laughed, let him have his idiosyncrasies but wished he'd get the hell on with being a better administrator and a stronger leader. In fact, they were pissed off at his God talk while the economy was falling apart. And as far as reincarnation was concerned, any born-again Christian would freak out at the idea. And, where Gerry was concerned, if he believed in either God or reincarnation I could just see the English cartoons. . . . The British Isles sinking slowly into the sea while God smiled down from above, with a caption saying, "Cheer up! Next time around you'll do it right!" Guaranteed to lose Gerry the election—even if our affair didn't.

My mind began to tumble with the ideas implicit in our conversation. I wasn't sure I liked them. On the one hand, it sounded plausible in an idealistic sort of way. On the other, it just sounded outrageously impossible and flat flaky.

"Cosmic justice?" I questioned sarcastically, dripping peach juice from my chin in the ocean breeze. "Is this where your reincarnation comes in?"

"Sure," he answered.

"You mean, you believe our souls keep coming back physically until we finally get it right?"

"Well, it makes sense, doesn't it?" he asked. "It certainly makes as much sense as anything else going."

"I don't know. Maybe."

"Big truths are hidden, but that doesn't mean they're not true."

"But if I really let myself believe that every one of my actions has a consequence, I'd be paralyzed."

"But that's already happening," he said. "You just aren't aware of it. That's what Christ was trying to tell us. Everything we do or say in our lives every day has a consequence and where we find ourselves today is the result of what we've done before. If everyone felt that, understood it in their gut, the world would be a better place. We shall reap what we sow, bad *or good*, and we should be aware of it."

"And you believe if we took our actions more seriously in this cosmic sense, we'd be kinder and more responsible people?"

"Sure. That's the point. We are all part of a universal truth and plan. Like I said before, it's really very simple. And you *should* be more aware of it because you will ultimately then reduce how much you hurt yourself."

"You mean you really believe we all create our own karma like the hippy-dippies say?"

"Sure. That's not so hard to understand. The Indians said that thousands of years ago. They knew it long before your hippy-dippies. It's *how* we lead our lives that counts. And when we live by that, we will all be kinder to one another. And if we don't, each of us pays the consequences in terms of the universal plan. We don't live by accident—you know there are no accidents. There is a higher purpose going on."

"Well, maybe you believe that, but I'm just asking. I wonder how six million dead Jews feel about being part of a higher conscious cosmic design."

"Why stop at six million Jews? What about twenty-five million Russians? Or the kids in the Children's Crusade? Or God knows how many so-called heretics burned at the stake? If you're asking me to answer for every apparent injustice and horror the world has seen, I'll tell you flatly—I can't. And I doubt very much that you'll ever be able to either."

"Then what the hell is all this about for Christ's sake?"

"Shirley, I can only tell you what I believe." He paused. "Cause and effect..."

"Oh, come *on!*"

"Now wait! Science believes in cause and effect. Most reasonable people believe in cause and effect, right? Say to the average person, 'You reap what you sow,' and they won't give you an argument. But *think that through*—if you *don't* reap in this life, then *when?* In heaven? In hell? Even religion believes in cause and effect—that's why, when they threw out reincarnation, they dreamt up heaven and hell to take care of all the unfulfilled effects. But why, for God's sake, are a hypothetical heaven or hell easier to believe in than the justice of reincarnation on Earth? I mean, on the face of it, what seems more reasonable to you?"

"Oh, God," I said. Then I thought a moment. "Maybe I don't happen to believe in either. It could be life is just a meaningless accident."

"Then nobody's responsible for anything. And as far as I'm concerned, that's a dead end. I can't live with a dead end, and I don't think you can. But it's up to you. It all comes back to the individual, the person. Shirley, *that's* what karma means. Whatever action one takes will ultimately return to that person—good and bad—maybe not in this life embodiment, but sometime in the future. And no one is exempt."

I stood up and stretched. I needed to move. Maybe I'd think better. I felt like a person caught in a real life version of *The Twilight Zone*. I had been conditioned to believe in only what I could see... not what I could *sense* or *feel*. What David was saying made a kind of sense, at least in terms of individual responsibility. But I had always needed proof—something I could see, touch, or hear. It certainly was the Western way. We were trained to respect the physical and psychological sciences. But then even we in the Western World were learning that just because something didn't fit our concepts didn't mean it wasn't to be respected. Suppose the spiritual dimension of mankind *was* recognized as a possibility? Would it act as a kind of connective glue to bind together the purpose of each of our other sciences from chemistry to medicine to mathematics to politics? Weren't all of our sciences part of the search for harmony and understanding of the meaning and purpose of life? Maybe the science of the spirit was what was missing.

"Anyway," said David, "even Western scientists agree that matter never dies. It just changes form. That's all physical death means."

"I don't understand," I said. "What's the connection?"

"I mean," said David, "that when we die only our bodies die. Our souls simply leave them and take up residence in the astral form. Our souls, regardless of what form they assume, are what is permanent. Our bodies are only temporary houses for our souls. But what we've done with ourselves while we're alive is what counts. And it doesn't matter *who* we are. If we hurt someone in this life, we'll be hurt the next time around. Or the time after that. And it's like Pythagoras said, 'It's all necessary for the development of the soul.' He also said, 'Whoever fathomed *that* truth fathomed *the* very heart of the Great Mystery!'"

"Pythagoras, the great mathematician?"

"Yes," said David.

"You mean, *he* believed in all this stuff?"

"Sure," said David. "And he wrote a lot about it. So did Plato and a whole mess of other Westerners."

He smiled at me and gathered up the sandy peach pits. He put them into the bag, placed them under the house, and we slowly began to walk.

Jesus, I thought. I wished I could talk about this stuff with Gerry. But when you are *involved* with someone, you settle. You settle for whatever there is . . . because you are afraid of jeopardizing the blind illusion of love. And the blind illusion is sometimes so necessary, we can even allow it to obfuscate our real identities. I put Gerry firmly out of my mind. My personal search right now was more important.

Suppose humanity (and this human in particular) *could* solve the riddle of its identity?—its origin? . . . and end? Would such knowledge lead to greater moral responsibility? What if I could bring myself to understand that I was not merely a body with a mind, but that body and mind were inhabited by a soul, and furthermore, that my soul existed before my birth in this life and would continue to exist after the death of this body. Suppose for a moment that the behavior of a soul would determine not only what was inherited in this life, but also explain our fortunes or misfortunes? Would I, in that case, have an attitude of deeper résponsibility and a feeling for justice and participation in whatever I did? If I understood that my "actions" would require dues to be paid, both good and bad, would I finally understand that my life had a reason beyond what I could see?

Would I act more responsibly or more kindly toward myself, and toward others, recognizing that if I didn't I would prolong the struggle in the fundamental quest for perfection which I was apparently compelled to achieve one way or another because that was the real meaning and purpose of life? And was all this true whether one was an Arab sheik increasing oil prices, or a Jew who had been marched to the gas chamber? Whether one was a mafia godfather or a PLO terrorist or simply a beggar on the streets of Calcutta?

My mind spun and tumbled and recoiled and boggled at the possibilities of what I was thinking. Again, I wasn't sure whether I liked it or not. It was too new—too preposterous and, finally, maybe too simple.

"Belief in reincarnation would make the world a more moral place?" I said. "Not necessarily. I could imagine plenty of people who would manipulate that belief to aggrandize their own lives, acquire power, enhance their lifestyle—whatever."

"Sure," said David. "But this life is not the only one to be reckoned with. That's the whole point!"

"Okay, suppose for a minute the whole thing _is_ that honest and simple? Suppose life, like nature, is simply a question of getting back what we put into it, and suppose with every instant and every second of each of our days we are creating and dictating the terms of our futures by our own positive and negative actions?" I took a deep breath as I began to realize the implications.

"Well, my God," I went on, "how long would it take to be a 'good' person in relation to your cosmic justice?"

"Time doesn't really matter," said David calmly, "not when you're speaking in an overall sense, with the knowledge that you already have lived and will continue to lead many lives. Remember, all of the great religions speak of patience being the great virtue. That means patience with ourselves as well as our fellow humans."

"You mean we should just be patient with the Hitlers of this world?"

"I mean that six million Jews did not really die. Only their bodies died."

"Beautiful," I said. "That's really great. Tell the families of those six million lucky people that only their bodies died."

David winced as though I had hit him. Sadness bathed his face as he looked out across the ocean.

After a long while he finally said, very quietly, "I know it's hard to fathom. But so is turning the other cheek."

"Well," I said, "if I could have, I would have nailed Hitler to the cross!"

David turned and looked deep into my eyes. "Yes," he said. "I see."

Then I realized what I had said. "Well hell, what would you have done with Hitler?" I asked, hearing the defensiveness in my own voice. "Shit, there are a lot of people who believe that if the British had not disarmed, had developed weapons instead, Hitler could have been stopped before he really got started. Was it *wrong* to disarm? I mean you can really get into a can of worms this way."

"I know," said David. "That's why you have to start just with yourself. Think a minute—if Hitler had felt moral responsibility as a person, he would have stopped himself, wouldn't he? You have to make it personal. I don't believe in killing anyone. That's where your question about God and the grand design comes in because only God can judge in that context. An individual can only judge of his *own* behavior. Ultimately no one can judge another. Besides you know, Hitler is not the only monster that ever lived. What about Idi Amin or the guys in the Khmer Rouge, or Stalin? Genocide is an old human problem. Or how about the pilots who dropped bombs on hospitals in North Vietnam with no feeling that humans were under there?"

"So what are you saying? That humans are cruel to each other?"

"Right. And if they understood the consequences of their actions *for themselves* they would think twice."

"That would make reincarnation a form of deterrent."

"Of course. But an individual, a self-deterrent if you like. And that's only the negative aspect, remember. There are also positive consequences."

"How can you be so sure there are consequences? What proof do you have?"

"None. What proof do you have that there aren't?"

"None."

"Well, then. Why not give what I'm saying a shot? You might as well. What's going on in the world now certainly isn't working too well."

"Give what a shot? How?"

"I don't know," he said. "Just think about it, I guess. You're saying nothing has any meaningful purpose and I'm saying everything does. You say you're not peaceful and you want to know why I am. Well, this is why. I believe in that phrase you hate—Cosmic Justice. I believe that what we put in, good or bad, balances out somewhere, sometime. That's why I'm peaceful. Maybe you have a better idea."

David kissed me on the cheek and said he'd call me.

I stared out at the waves. I had a headache. On the whole, I thought, maybe I'd rather be a fish.

Chapter 7

"I lived in Judea eighteen hundred years ago, but I never knew that there was such a one as Christ among my contemporaries."

—HENRY DAVID THOREAU
Letters

When I woke up the next morning, I found myself wondering whether my daughter was some other reincarnated adult. Who might be living in the body of a person I thought of as my daughter?

There had been so many moments during our mother-daughter relationship when I had had the feeling that she knew me better than I knew her. And, of course, every mother feels she *learns* from her children. That was the miracle of child-rearing. But, if I let my mind wander and then focus on the possibility of reincarnation, I looked at Sachi with a totally different perspective. When the doctor brought her to me in the hospital bed on that afternoon in 1956, had she already lived many many times before, with other mothers? Had she, in fact, been one herself? Had she, in fact, ever been *my* mother? Was her one-hour-old face housing a soul perhaps millions of years old? And as she grew, did she gradually forget her spiritual dimension in an attempt to adjust to the physical world she found herself living in? Was *that* what they called the "veil of forgetfulness"? Was that what happened to all of us as we found ourselves encased in physical bodies?

When she went to live with her father in Japan, maybe she had actually planned it before she was born, and her talent for languages was based on having actually spoken them in previous lives. Perhaps she *became* Japanese when she spoke Japanese because she had actually *been* Japanese in another lifetime. And when, later on in her adult life, she argued with us to allow her more independence and self-identity, was she responding to a legitimate inner voice that murmured that she already knew who she was? Maybe parents were merely ancient friends, rather than authority figures who felt they knew better than their children. And too, maybe the unresolved conflicts of previous lifetimes contributed to the all-too-frequent antagonisms that erupted between parents and children today.

❷ I had some breakfast and drove into town and back to the Bodhi Tree bookstore.

John, the owner, was in his office having his herb tea and reading.

"Oh, hello," he said formally but sweetly. "Did you get some good reading in?"

Jesus, I thought, so many of these people into metaphysics were formal . . . formal and sort of awesomely patient. I mean, almost irritatingly patient.

I said I had been reading and thinking and talking to David, and now I'd like to talk to him for a few minutes.

"Certainly," he said, "along what lines?"

"Well," I said, "about reincarnation I guess, about reincarnation in relation to our children. I mean, who are our children if every soul has already lived many lives?"

John smiled and took off his glasses.

"Well," he began in a gentle tone, "from the teachings it says that we shouldn't treat our children as our possessions anyway. They are, as you say, just small bodies inhabited by souls that have already had many experiences. So, reincarnation principles help explain some of the crazy contradictions in parent-child relationships."

I thought of the news documentary I had seen on grown-up children beating and abusing their parents. Were these children doing that because *they* had been beaten in some previous life? Or because the parent had beaten someone else in a previous life? Who was working out whose karma? But John was continuing, "I can tell you," he said, "from some of my past-life recall, that I'm sure that my eight-year-old son was once my father."

I laughed out loud because of what I had been thinking about Sachi that morning. John put his fingers to his lips and smiled.

"I'm sorry," I said. "Did you ever tell your son that?"

"Sure. He laughed and said I should watch myself! See how Cosmic Justice works?"

Here we go again, I thought. The only way I'll get to hear about this is to listen to the "astral" jargon. Well, okay. The occult has as much right to its own verbiage as any science, or religion, or philosophy.

I sat down on a bench. "I'm not sure," I said, "if I see how anything works. How does a person find out who they were in a past life?"

"You go to the right person."

"Like who?"

"Like a psychic. That's what they're into."

"You mean fortune tellers?"

"Well, there's lots of cranks, but there have been some very well respected psychics, like Edgar Cayce. Have you ever read any of Edgar Cayce's stuff?"

"I've heard of him, but I've never read him," I said, knowing that, really, I had never heard of him either.

"Okay, that's what you'll read next."

John reached up on the bookshelf and pulled down some of Edgar Cayce's books.

"He was an uneducated man, essentially—in fact most psychics are. Cayce was actually a trance medium.

But they are all very spiritually and psychically attuned to the Akashic Records. Do you know what the Akashic Records are?"

I bent over and cracked my back into place.

"Listen," I said under my breath, "I'm really in over my head."

"You what?" asked John.

"What kind of records?" I asked, not even able to remember the name he had just mentioned.

"Oh," he answered. "The Akashic Records?"

"Yes. What are they?"

"Oh, okay," he said, "okay, it's hard to find much written about the Akashic Records, but let me try to explain. They are referred to as 'The Universe Memory of Nature,' or 'The Book of Life.' Akasha is a Sanskrit word meaning 'fundamental etheric substance of the universe.' Okay?"

"Jesus," I said, "I guess so. What's etheric?"

"Okay, all the universe is supposedly composed of ethers—that is, gaseous energies which have varying electromagnetic vibrational properties. As you know, everything we do, see, think, say, react to—everything we are—emits, or creates, energy charges. These energy charges are called 'vibrations.' So every sound, thought, light, movement, or action vibrationally reacts in those electromagnetic ethers. They are a kind of magnetic plate that attracts all vibrations. In fact, *everything* is electromagnetic vibrations. So the Akashic Records are a kind of panoramic record of everything that's ever been thought or felt or done. And if you are really sensitively attuned physically, you can plug in to those vibrations and, in fact, 'see' the past in the cosmic sense. So a good psychic can tell you what your previous lives were like."

"God," I said, "do you believe all that?"

"Oh sure," he said simply, "and furthermore, I think, and all the books say, that the inherent ability to see these records is in all of us. It's just a question of developing the ability, which really means getting more in tune with ourselves first. If our spiritual and mental powers are developed enough, we can. It's nothing more than developing our ESP, which now even science regards as a fact pretty much. See?"

"You mean," I said, "that it's just a question of expanding our consciousness?" I was grateful that I understood what I said.

"Sure," said John.

"And if we become more consciously aware of these other dimensions, we'll know more about who we are and what our lives are about?"

"Look," he said, "it's no more fantastic than sound waves or light waves, only these are thought waves. Science certainly knows they are there because no energy ever dies. So, if you are sensitive enough to get on the right thought wave lengths which plug into the Akashic vibrational waves, you can see lots of stuff that's already happened. And, if you are aware of what pain you've suffered in the past and also what pain you might have caused someone else to suffer, it all acts as an educative process. See what I mean?"

"Yeah, sure," I lied.

"You've read the ancient psychics, haven't you?"

"The ancient psychics?" I asked. "Like who?"

"Well," said John, feeling, I'm sure, that he was in *under* his head, "like Plato, Pythagoras, Buddha, Moses."

"Oh, they were psychics, too?" I said as impartially as possible.

"Why sure," said John. "How do you think they could write all that stuff they wrote? For example, how do you think Moses wrote of the creation of the world if he hadn't been plugged in psychically? And the same with Christ. I mean, those guys were highly developed spiritual people who felt their mission in life was to impart their knowledge. That's why the Bible is so valuable. It's a storehouse of knowledge. And most all of their writings jibe too. There's hardly any discrepancy in what any of them was saying."

"Did they talk about reincarnation?"

"Well, not all of them used that word. But they all spoke at length about the relationship between the *eternal* soul of man and the Divine. They *all* spoke of the universal laws of morality. They didn't always use the words karma or reincarnation, but the meaning was the same. Am I talking too much?"

I shook my head and coughed and smiled and cleared my throat.

"Well," I asked, "what did they say about *not* remembering your previous lives?"

"They talk about a kind of 'veil of forgetfulness' that exists in the conscious mind so that we aren't continually traumatized by what might have occurred before. They all say that the *present* lifetime is the important one, only sparked now and then by those déjà-vu feelings that you have experienced something before or know someone that you know you've never consciously met before in this lifetime. You know those feelings you sometimes get that you've been somewhere before only you know you haven't?"

"Yes, I know what you mean." It was a great relief to know what he was talking about. I was remembering how I had felt in the Himalayas when I was there—as though I had lived there alone for a long time. As a matter of fact, I remembered feeling *familiar* when I reached the top-of-the-mountain cave of the monk who gave me the saffron scarf. The familiar feeling was the reason I took his warnings seriously and why I have the scarf to this day. I always felt it meant something more than what the lama said, but I wasn't sure why I felt it.

John asked one of his assistants for some tea and then he sat down on the bench with me just below the bookshelf.

"I know I'm talking too much," he said, "but when I get into this stuff, I just can't quit. It's so important . . . see, for people like Pythagoras or Plato or any of those guys, all the misfortunes in life like disease, deformities, injustices, and all that, were explained by the fact that each life embodiment was a reward or punishment of a preceding life embodiment, and as each soul progressed, that person was rewarded with more choices of how to reincarnate, all with the moral purpose, of course, to work out his or her own individual karma. A really superior soul, for example, would choose to work out his karma through choosing a life embodiment of self-sacrifice, but each identity has his own thing. And apparently the older and higher in spiritual accomplishment the soul, the more it can remember of past life embodiments."

"But," I asked, "what if a soul doesn't want to progress? What if a soul wants to forget the whole thing and say screw it?"

"Well, there's a lot written about that too. A soul can choose to advance or regress. If it chooses to continually regress, it will eventually lose its humanity and become animal-like with no choices for advancement or moral atonement left to it. That is what was spoken of as Hell. If you don't choose spiritual evolution, you don't get the chance after a while, and that's Hell."

"So that's what they meant when they said, if you didn't believe in God you'd go to Hell—a kind of never-never land of nonexistence?"

"Sure. And the reverse, of course—God, meaning the everlasting eternalness of the soul and the attainment of moral atonement. Do you know what atonement means?"

"I don't think so."

"Just analyze it. It means at-one-ment. At-one-ment with the original creator or with original creation. We are both creators and, unhappily, destroyers. But when we identify most strongly with creation, we are closest to at-one-ment. You know, when you begin to unravel a little bit of it, the whole tapestry begins to make sense."

"So this business of reincarnating souls makes even the worst kind of evil and suffering have meaning?"

"Of course, everything happens for a reason. All physical suffering, all happiness, all despair, and all joy happens in relation to the Karmic Laws of Justice. That's why life has meaning."

John stopped and began to lift his arm to make another point. Then, perhaps seeing the look on my face, he stopped and said, "Let's go have our tea."

We walked into his office and sat at a window shaded by a tree outside.

"How come you got interested in all this *after* you were in India?" he asked.

I sipped the hot ginger tea. "Maybe I was a Himalayan monk in another life who knew all the mysteries of life and I'm going back to relearn what I already know."

He laughed.

"Do many people around here believe in reincarnation and Karmic Justice and all that?"

"Sure. You know that. There are lots of us weirdos around." He winked and got up. "Okay, so you have your books on psychic readings. See what happens after the next week or so. I'll be here if you want to talk some more."

We finished our tea.

I thanked him, paid for my books, and walked out into the traffic on Melrose Avenue. Whatever John needed to believe was his affair, but at least I had listened, and now I would read.

I went home to Encino. Marie fixed me some tea and hot French bread with Brie cheese. She always kept the Brie in good French fashion, at room temperature until it melted to the edge of the Limoge china plate she always placed it on. I loved her sense of detail. It didn't matter that she didn't like me in her kitchen.

I knew I shouldn't be eating cheese and bread, but I didn't care. I took it upstairs with me, sat down with my new books, and began to read about Edgar Cayce.

🐾 Edgar Cayce was born in 1877 near Hopkinsville, Kentucky. He was a simple and devoutly religious man (a Christian) who was essentially uneducated, having had to cut high school to go to work.

He had suffered from chronic asthma and went to a well-trained and highly respected hypnotist to seek relief when no traditional doctors were able to help him.

While under hypnosis a strange thing happened to Cayce. He began to speak in the third person and with a voice that had no resemblance to his own. He used the word "we" and began to prescribe a treatment for himself in great detail. When the session was over, the hypnotist reported what had happened and suggested that Cayce follow the instructions. Out of desperation Cayce tried it. The asthma soon disappeared. But when the hypnotist described the "voice" that was apparently speaking through him, Cayce was horrified. He considered it blasphemous. The Bible had instructed man never "to suffer any spiritual entity other than God." And Cayce was a man who believed in the Bible.

But Cayce also had great compassion for people. Since the Voice seemed to be one that served to help people, he decided to go along with it for awhile. Cayce soon learned to put himself into trance in order to help others. The Voice (which described itself as "we") always used medical terminology and prescribed from what was obviously a thorough knowledge of medicine, a subject about which Cayce knew nothing. If the prescribed treatments were followed accurately, they always worked. Cayce began to trust the process as much as those who came for help trusted him.

Word of Cayce's strange power spread. People from all over his community and finally the country began to contact him. He didn't need to see or meet the patients who sought help. The "we" seemed to be able to enter their minds and bodies, explore the condition in question, and prescribe treatments which if followed exactly, continued to always work.

The New York Times did an extensive investigative story on Cayce and pronounced that it had no explanation. There was no evidence that Cayce was speaking from his own subconscious (he knew nothing of the medical profession) and as far as "spiritual" entities were concerned, the *Times* couldn't comment.

Cayce became famous all over the world.

Soon people began to question Cayce's "Voice" about more cosmic issues. "What is the purpose of life?" "Is there such a thing as life after death?" "Is reincarnation of the soul accurate?"

The Voice answered in the affirmative and began to

speak of the past lives of the people who inquired. It connected past-life experiences with certain maladies that an individual might be suffering now.

Again Cayce became flabbergasted and confused. Such cosmic connections had never occurred to him. Medical treatment had become acceptable to him but he considered past life information anti-religious. The Bible said nothing about such things. For awhile, he refused to accept the information in the readings. It was too outlandish. But soon, with continuing examples of confirmation of past-life identities, he began to wonder. Too many people returned to him with proof that there had been a Mr. or Mrs. So-and-so living in the identical conditions in the past that he had described. Of course, they had no proof that *they* had been those people, but whenever they investigated in detail, *they* all reported they had indeed felt strangely yet extremely familiar with what he described.

The morality of karma and reincarnation was heavily emphasized in each reading. For example:

A thirty-eight-year-old woman had complained of being unable to commit herself to marriage because of a deep-seated mistrust of men. It turned out that a husband in a previous incarnation had deserted her, immediately after their marriage, to join the Crusades.

A girl of eighteen had a terrible overweight problem which she couldn't control. Other than her obesity, she was extremely attractive. The readings submitted that two lifetimes ago she had been an athlete in Rome with both beauty and athletic prowess, but she frequently ridiculed others who were heavy and couldn't move well.

A young man, twenty-one, complained of being an unhappy homosexual. The readings reported that in the French Royal Court he had taken great delight in baiting and exposing homosexuals. The readings submitted: "Condemn not then. What you condemn in another, you will become in yourself."

The files and records compiled by Cayce were among the most extensive in medical history. The fourteen thousand readings produced examples of health karma, psychological karma, retributive karma, family karma, mental abnormality karma, vocational karma . . . on and on.

But what came through in the readings more strongly than anything else was the need for the assertion of free will. The Voice said that the basic error that man makes is his belief that his life is predetermined and therefore he is powerless to change it. It said that the lives we lead *now* hold the higher priority and the assertion of our free will in relation to our karma is our most important task. It was up to us to get in touch with ourselves spiritually so that we might achieve some insight as to what our purposes in life are. For every act, for every indifference, for every misuse of life, we are finally held accountable. And it is up to us to understand what those accounts might be.

✿ As I read about Cayce and the "readings" of other psychics and trance mediums, I found myself fascinated with the idea that they might be true. Wherever the information came from didn't matter as much to me as the sense it made. Maybe it *was* a psychic's subconscious talking; maybe they *were* just good actors.

But even if that were true, the morality of their message was unmistakable. And a good set of values to live by.

"All the answers are within yourself," they said. "Only look." ✿

Chapter 8

🐾 I read far into the night, and the next morning I
got up early and walked into the Calabasas mountains
to think. The mountains are craggy and steep with an
eye-caressing view of the Pacific. Nestled in the high
hills was "The Ashram," a kind of rough-and-ready,
spiritually involved health camp ("spa" to those who
had a lot of money). I loved the activities at The
Ashram and often went there to get in shape for a
television special, or whenever I knew I would be
doing two shows a night in Vegas or Tahoe. I'd eat pure,
raw food, take the long, ten-mile-straight-up-mountain
walks, exercise in the open air, and got in touch with
what the Swedes who ran the place called the "prana"
in the air. The Swedes were Anne Marie Bennstrom
(who founded The Ashram) and her assistant, Katerina
Hedwig. They seemed to know just about everything
there was to know about health. I trusted them anyway,

because I always felt terrific when they got through with me.

Now, climbing the fire trail, I ran into Katerina, whom I adored. I called her Cat for short. She was leading a group of "inmates" on one of the torturous climbs. I only had to look at Cat in order to feel better. She *was* joy. Bubbly, funny, and light-heartedly intelligent, she and Anne Marie were also deep into spiritual exploration and were devotees of Sai Baba, an avatar in India.

Cat was a big woman and as strong as the mountains she climbed. She was also gentle but forceful, and her infectious personality had led me through a particularly arduous workout period when I first returned from the political campaign trail for George McGovern and finally from China—twenty pounds overweight. She made the pain and the discipline possible to endure. I also teased her that her nickname was Cat because she became a "cat"-alyst for events that followed which were responsible for completely changing my life.

We trudged up the fire trail together. For a while I didn't say anything. Neither did she. I was glad, because when you're climbing straight up you haven't enough breath to talk anyway. At the crest we stretched and looked out over the Pacific. Cat seemed to sense that I wanted to talk but didn't know how.

"Well, fickle lady of fame, how are you?"

'Fickle lady of fame?' It was such an odd way to refer to me.

"Hey," I said, "are you saying that you think I'm fickle?" I laughed, not really sure why I felt the need to do so.

"Yes, about fame you're fickle. You're not really sure you want it, are you?"

Cat had the damndest way of immediately zeroing in on the conflict a person might be feeling.

"Fame?" I said, "I don't think I've ever cared all that much about recognition, only about the quality of the work. And right now I care more about what I'm looking for."

"You mean yourself."

"Myself? I care more about myself?"

"I mean you seem to care more about finding out who you are than you do about fame. Isn't that true, Shirley?"

"Yes. . . . Yes," I said, "and it's a struggle. Because suddenly now I'm into a dimension of myself that I didn't know existed, much less ever explored before."

"You're talking about your spiritual dimension?"

God, it sounded so banal to hear another person put it into words. But then no words were safe havens anymore. I remembered how often I had been judgmental about the words people chose to use when describing a deeply moving experience relating to some abstract occurrence in their lives.

"Yes," I said, "I guess you could say I'm really curious about this spiritual stuff. I don't know what's going on but the more I hear about it the more I want to hear?" I felt myself make the statement as though I were asking a question.

"Oh, Shirley, that's wonderful!" Cat said, her gay laughter enveloping every word. "It's so satisfying to be drawn to the spirit, isn't it?"

I shoved my hands into the pockets of my jogging jacket. "Drawn to the spirit?" I asked. "Is that what I'm experiencing?"

"Why sure, Shirley," Cat smiled. "God and spiritual recognition are everything. That's why we're here. It's the whole explanation of life and purpose. For me it's all I live for. I don't care if I never have another man, and you *know* how lusty I used to be. Well, forget about it. I feel my own spiritual light and I'm in love with that and I don't need anything else."

Jesus, I thought, if I could be in love with my own spiritual light it would save me a lot of plane trips and a lot of grief, too.

"Yeah, well," I said, "I guess I should plunge on ahead but I'm not sure I quite know how."

"Oh, Shirley," Cat went on, "I know a wonderful entity you must meet. Anne Marie is with him now in

Sweden. But she's talking about bringing him over here."

"Wait a minute, Cat," I said, interrupting her all-out enthusiasm, "an entity in Sweden? What kind of entity?"

"A spiritual entity. His name is Ambres and he comes through a man named Sturé Johanssen."

"Comes through? Are you talking about trance channeling?"

"Oh," she said, surprised that I didn't understand, "oh yes. Sturé is a very simple carpenter who lives in Stockholm, and a spiritual entity called Ambres uses him as an instrument to speak through. His readings are incredibly beautiful, Shirley. You should hear him. Of course he only speaks Swedish and an ancient Swedish at that but either Anne Marie or I will translate for you. He is such a strong, powerful, benevolent entity, Shirley. Oh my, you would love him."

"Stockholm?" I asked. "Jesus, that's a long way to go to talk to a spirit."

Cat laughed. "Well, maybe sometime next year Anne Marie will bring Sturé and his wife here to the States. Then you can have a session."

"Does his stuff work the same way that Edgar Cayce's stuff worked?" I asked, remembering what I had just read on Cayce.

"Yes," said Cat. "They both worked as trance channelers for entities on the other side to come through."

We walked on for a moment, Cat excitedly animated at the prospect of my being exposed to a dimension of life that she had long ago accepted. But I wanted to double-check her feelings.

"Cat?" I asked. "Do you honestly believe there is an 'other side' and that disembodied spiritual entities can talk to us and teach us and stuff like that?"

Cat turned and looked at me in astonishment. "Do I *believe* it?" she asked.

I nodded.

"No," she answered, shocking me into stopping dead in my tracks. "No. Not at all," she reiterated. "I don't believe it. I *know* it."

I realized that, because this was Cat, I had just heard a powerful statement of faith. And she said it with such love. Any other suspicious question I might ask her from then on would be a reflection of my own inability to accept Cat's fundamental value system. I would be judging or questioning the very depths of what made up her character and personality. I might fancy myself as a kind of adventurous human reporter, but I certainly wasn't going to ridicule another human being's belief system or "knowingness" as Cat apparently defined it.

"Well," I said, "this Ambres seems like an interesting entity to get to know." I felt like an imposter as I heard the word "entity" come out of my mouth.

"Oh, Shirley, when Anne Marie and Sturé and his wife come to the States we'll give you a call. Too bad you have no reason to go to Stockholm. Don't you need to buy a pair of skis or something?" We laughed as we continued to walk, segueing into a conversation about food-combining and the latest info on what dairy products do to the digestive system. Soon we embraced and said goodbye, promising to follow up on our newly initiated spiritual exploration.

I went immediately home, feeling a strong urge to call Gerry in London. I just needed to speak to him. In fact, I felt I needed to see him. I guess I wanted to hear him and touch him and experience him as my other *real* world. I didn't feel much like seeing any other friends, and I had some time to myself before rehearsals for the new show began.

As I called him I was reminded of how conditioned I had been to checking out my feelings with the man I was involved with. Somehow my own feelings, my own questions, my own searching, my own new interests seemed partially inadequate and only half realized without including *the man*. I couldn't talk to Gerry about what I was into, but it would help me to check out my own perceptions just to be with him. It was hard to admit that I needed to ratify my own identity in relation to the man in my life, but there it was.

I reached him at his office in London.

"Hello," he said, not at all surprised to hear from me so soon after our Honolulu meeting.

"Gerry," I said, sensing that he was rushed, "I know you're busy, but I want to come to London to see you. I have a few weeks and I want to spend them with you."

I could hear him hesitate on the other end of the Atlantic cable.

"Oh," he said finally, "but I'm going to Stockholm."

"In Sweden?" I said idiotically, stunned. I had just agreed with Cat it was too bad I didn't have a reason for going there.

As I think about it today, I would have to say that this was the beginning of a series of events which, as they unfolded, gave me a definite sense of pattern. Of course one could say most anything in life is simply coincidental, but after awhile, when coincidence becomes multiple, a redefinition of "accidental" is necessary.

In any case Gerry went on about his trip to Stockholm.

"Yes," he said, "I have a Socialist economic meeting and I'll be there for a week."

"Oh," I said, "so why don't I come to Stockholm? I love snow."

He didn't say anything. I heard him excuse someone from his office politely and shuffle some papers.

"Gerry?" I said.

"Yes, yes," he said. "Hello."

"Gerry. I need to talk to you. I need to be with you. I miss you. I mean, I really do. And I guess I need to know how you really feel."

I felt I was acting like a school girl pursuing her hero. I waited for him to say something. Every moment seemed to have some horribly anxious meaning. Finally he said, "Yes. Yes, I miss you too."

He was so uncomfortable, but I pressed on.

"So is it all right? Would it be convenient if I met you in Stockholm? I'll make all my own arrangements."

"What did you mean, you want to know how I really feel?"

He sounded frightened.

"What's wrong, Gerry?"

"I'm upset."

"I know. Why? Upset at what?"

"I'm upset at pleasure."

"What pleasure? What do you mean?"

"I'm upset at the pleasure it gives me to know what I mean to you."

"Why? Why would you be upset by that?"

"Because," he said, "I can't understand *why* I'm so important to you. And it makes me feel inadequate."

I didn't know what to say. I didn't know what he was really saying.

"Do you want to see me, Gerry?" I asked.

"I'm longing to see you, but I'm afraid I'll disappoint you. I hate that," he said. "I hate feeling that I'll disappoint you."

"Well," I said, "maybe the important thing is not to disappoint yourself. Can we talk?"

"Come to Stockholm in two days," he said. "I'll be at the Grand. You arrange accommodations somewhere else." He hesitated a few more moments. Then he whispered, "Goodbye," and hung up.

I sat there thinking about what it must feel like to feel inadequate to another person. It was a feeling I had never really experienced as far as I could remember. I had felt *dependent* on others, especially regarding the "man" syndrome, but the *inadequacies* I usually felt were to myself and that could be just as bad. The standards and goals I set for myself were sometimes impossible to live up to and made me too self-demanding. Maybe Dad was right. Maybe I didn't want to disappoint myself. I didn't want to do what he had done.

But Gerry wasn't the only man who had complained of feeling inadequate with me. I remembered several important relationships I had had which ultimately ended because the men simply became afraid they couldn't live up to my expectations of them, and because of it weren't comfortable with themselves. I wondered where the burden of responsibility for such breakdowns lay. Was it with me for demanding too much? Or did it lie with a feeling of low self-esteem the men had in themselves?

I remembered going to several psychologist friends about the question, and they pointed out that behind every woman that a man found himself involved with was the haunting image of his own mother. And their mothers were the figures they couldn't live up to. Very few men saw their own women clearly. Instead they perceived them through the haunting screens of their mothers. And thinking of going to Sweden to meet Gerry, I remembered a very well documented research report I had read studying the problem of Swedish suicide. The high suicide rate was not caused by socialism or the weather or any of the popular cocktail-conversation myths. Instead, they found that most of the Swedish suicides were caused by the high standards and expectations that Swedish mothers placed upon their children who in turn felt they simply couldn't "live up to it." And out of intense depression and frustration, they felt so inadequate they resorted to suicide.

Maybe men everywhere were suffering a less intense but still disturbing sense of double imagery where women were concerned.

And in this age of female liberation, where women complained about feeling addicted to having to have a man, men might be suffering from these childhood pressures that exposed a basic lack of belief in themselves, which was just as devastating for them. In both cases, the problem lay in *self* identity. Gerry said he couldn't understand *why* he was important to me, as though he, with all his intelligence and talents and accomplishments, wasn't worth my attention. He was obviously and publicly a very successful man. So his sense of inadequacy had to come from something deep inside. And just by my acknowledging that he *was* very important to me in a very personal sense, I was bringing his own personal insecurities to the surface.

So female liberation was certainly important, but it seemed to me that male liberation was just as important.

In fact, if men were freer about who they really were, it wouldn't be so necessary for them to colonize the women in their lives to such an extent. Maybe, in my case, because I was so personally *un*colonizable, it made them examine the real meaning of equality. And if there was resistance to true equality in the relationship, it would inevitably dissolve. And how *could* a man feel equal if he didn't believe he was worth loving?

I didn't know anything about Gerry's mother, but in the long run it didn't matter. The real question was what he now thought of himself. It seemed to be *the* question for all of us.

I began to realize, from a new perspective, that *self* realization was the most painful but important search of all. None of us felt whole and self-loving enough to understand that our own self-identity was the answer to a fulfilled happiness. What we really needed most was a complete relationship within ourselves. Maybe that very problem—either in human or cosmic terms—was what Moses and Christ and Buddha and Pythagoras and Plato and all the religious and philosophical sages down through the ages had been trying to tell us . . . know thyself and that truth will set you free.

Suppose one of the paths to understanding who each of us really was lay in having knowledge of who we might have been in lifetimes previous? There were many examples where psychiatry just didn't seem able to go deep enough to get to the root of an individual disturbance. Maybe past-life understanding could. If mothers and fathers and childhood experiences in our present lifetimes molded and conditioned how we related to life and reality today, why couldn't experiences that went even further back affect us in the same way?

I remembered speaking to Paddy Chayevsky, before he died, about the novel he was writing, *Altered States*. He had done extensive scientific research on it and was saying that every human being carries, locked in his or her cellular memory, the entire experience of the human race from the beginning of creation. I guess my mind was following along the same lines. What was the difference between cellular memory recall from the beginning of time and past-life recall? Surely one form of memory was at least as miraculous as the other.

I wondered if I might in fact have known Gerry in another life, and if I had, what our karma was that we were going through such an obstacle course in our relationship now. And I wondered if we were going about working it out in the right way.

I called Cat and said I was going to Stockholm. She wasn't surprised. She gave me the address and telephone number of the trance medium and I said I would look him up.

Chapter 9

"A lifetime may be needed merely to gain the virtues which annul the errors of man's preceding life. . . . The virtues we acquire, which develop slowly within us, are the invisible links that bind each one of our existences to the others—existences which the spirit alone remembers, for Matter has no memory for spiritual things."

—HONORÉ DE BALZAC
Seraphita

I had been to Stockholm several times on tour and it was a place that intrigued me. The city lay under wall-to-wall snow when I arrived, looking like a picture postcard from a Nordic fantasy.

A friend I called met me at the airport.

It was seven o'clock in the evening. A veil of snow filtered down and I wondered how soon it got dark every day during the famous Swedish winters. I had been to Sweden once before during the winter and when my nose ran it froze on my face. During those days in the late fifties Sweden was something of a social and physical mystery to those of us who had heard only a little about the small country that had *voted* for socialism. I remember feeling chilled stirrings when I sat in the hall where the Nobel Peace Prizes were given and heard that there was no preferred seating or class

distinction in Sweden. I had heard it was a country of
free love and if a wife or husband wanted to sleep with
somebody 'else, no one cared. But I had come to learn
that that image was not accurate, and that many Swedes
found such an image difficult to live with; particularly
the Swedish women. They were basically as conserva-
tive as everyone else in the world, even though government policy allowed more legalized personal freedom
than anywhere on earth.

I had been in Sweden during the Festival of Lights
called Santa Lucia which commemorated the end of the
long dark days and the beginning of the slow trek
toward another summer. Swedes lived for the sun and
seemed to hibernate in their minds until it came. A
kind of institutionalized depression came over the Swedish
people during the winter months—which was most of
the year. "Summer came on a Tuesday last year" was a
favorite Swedish joke. The winter in Sweden certainly
wasn't going to lighten my relationship with Gerry.

My friend took me to dinner and after some oysters and herring, I went to the hotel where he had
made a reservation for me in a small suite overlooking
the harbor. The living room had bay windows and the
bedroom a double bed. I knew I would be happy there.
I fell into bed and about four hours later woke up with
the urge to vomit, which I did for the rest of the night.
It was one of the oysters.

The sun came out about nine the next morning to a
day that was overcast from then on and slightly misty. A
sheet of ice in the bay across the street was broken up
every hour by a tugboat that circled around and around
while lines of dump trucks piled all the snow they had
scraped from the streets that morning into the bay.
Sightseeing boats lay clutched in the ice in the surrounding frozen water waiting for spring to come.

I had breakfast and went for a short walk. I wanted
to be in when Gerry called so I hurried back. Slick ice
packed the city streets but the Swedes had no trouble
at all negotiating corners and curbs. I felt as though I'd
fall down at every juncture.

When I returned to the hotel, the woman manager

came to see me asking if I had any requests. After
asking for a hair dryer with Swedish current and an
extra blanket, I was sure I'd be very comfortable.

There was a private entrance to the hotel where
anyone leaving or entering could do so unnoticed and
she promised that the telephone operators would protect my identity from the journalists.

I waited in my room for the rest of the day. Around
six o'clock he called.

"Hi."

"Hi."

"How are you?"

"Fine."

"When did you get in?"

"Yesterday evening."

"Yesterday evening? I thought you'd be coming in
around five o'clock today."

"No," I said, "I told you I was coming on the
16th."

"Oh. Can I come over?"

"Sure. Have you had anything to eat?"

"No, I'll stop along the way."

"Come now. I'll have something here for you. That
way you'll get here sooner."

"All right. Goodbye."

His voice sounded more authoritative, as if he was
in command of himself.

I left the room door open so he wouldn't have to
wait after he knocked. And in about half an hour, there
he was.

He came in wearing big fur gloves, the ones I
imagined his wife disapproved of, looking very white
and drawn.

I crossed the room to embrace him, but he went
straight to the window and looked out, getting his
bearings on where my hotel was in relation to his.

He wore his trench coat with no fur lining, a tweed
suit that I had seen in the fall, and a pair of leather
shoes with big rubber soles.

"My grandmother became very famous," he said,

"for skating on thin ice in a bay like that wearing a skirt that was only a few inches below the knees."

"Well," I said, "maybe you'll become famous for skating on thin ice wearing trousers."

He smiled.

He walked to the other window. "And see the string of lights that look like a penis at the top? Just beyond that is my hotel."

A rising string of lights looked like a penis to him? Interesting . . .

I stood next to him at the window. He turned from the window and cupped one of my breasts in his hand.

I invited him to sit down with me. I had ordered two double decker club sandwiches that had turned out to be lettuce and tomato salad on toast.

He sat on the sofa and began to cut into one of the sandwiches. He talked of upcoming budget cuts, the problems of having to raise taxes in an election year, and an American journalist whom he had been talking to all day. He asked me how my rehearsals were going. I said I would be starting soon. While I talked, his eyes sopped me up—my hair, my movements, my clothes, my body . . . but he didn't touch me. I, in turn, felt too intimidated to touch him. We continued to talk . . . about the boat people from Vietnam and how much happier they would be in France if Europe was where they wanted to go, Sihanouk at the United Nations and the fact that the English Left was split down the middle on the Vietnamese invasion of Cambodia. We avoided the subject of us until we both got our bearings.

He lay back on the sofa. I could feel he was exhausted, and that he had been that way for some time. And I could feel that he knew it was all right for me to know. I sat close to him and touched his hair. He didn't object. He leaned his head against the back of the sofa. His arms rested in his lap. He didn't reach for me at all. I laid my head on his chest and looking up at him I kissed him gently on the lips. They were still slightly cold from the weather outside. Lifting his head, he turned away from me and slowly reached for more of his sandwich. I waited for him to finish.

He lay back again and sighed.

"Listen," I said, "why don't you let me give you a massage? You don't have to do anything but lie there. Okay?"

Immediately he got up and headed for the bedroom. He turned around and waited for me to take off his coat and shirt and tie. I tried but I couldn't get his tie undone. He laughed.

"I thought you said I wouldn't have to do anything."

He untied it himself and stood with his arms beside him. I didn't make any move to take off his trousers. I turned him around, gently pushing him face down on the bed. I reached for some Albolene cream and began to rub his back. He sighed with pleasure and curled his arms under him. I took off my slacks and sweater so I could straddle him around the waist and use the massage technique I had learned in Japan with more strength.

My nails were a problem so I used the base of my hands. His shoulders and arms were so muscular, my hands felt ineffective, but he sighed deeply.

"You know," he said, "this is the first massage I've ever had in my whole life."

I knew he was telling me the truth, regardless of how unbelievable it sounded. But then with Gerry there was so much he didn't know about self-pleasure. His skin was cold. I knew how warm my hands must feel to him. I massaged his neck until I felt him relax. I put more Albolene cream on my hands and moved down to his back and waist. He began to undulate under me and I playfully smacked him.

I continued to knead his back and waist. He reached around and put his arm around my waist. I knew he was too tired. But he wouldn't stop. He wound the other arm around me too.

This whole scene was unreal. We were perfectly free to make love together but somehow he wanted it to be as if it really wasn't happening.

I tried to squirm away from his hands, still massag-

ing his back. He reached around and pushed me toward
him until I fell on him pressing myself against his back
and squeezing him with my legs. He turned over.

Before I knew what was happening, he clasped me
to him and we were making love. His arms held me so
tightly I could hardly breathe. He held me tighter.
Over and over I whispered that I loved him. His only
reply was to breathe as though he were home again.

Afterward he rested. Neither of us said anything.
He stayed still as though he never wanted to move.
Suddenly I felt afraid. I stirred under him.

"Gerry," I said.

"Yes?"

"I'm afraid. I need to talk." I stammered when I
said it and lay beside him.

He stared at the ceiling for awhile and then leaning
on his arm looked deeply into my eyes.

"I have thought very hard every day," he said. "I'm
going to state the problem. I'm not stating any solution
because I haven't reached one."

I could feel my stomach turn over.

"I love you," he said. "I love you deeply, but half
of me resists it. I hold myself back subconsciously
because I know that I'm not strong enough to tolerate
the consequences of our relationship either in a political
or a personal sense. I feel that I have been in a kind of
mental and physical hole with this relationship and
what became so clear to me is that I am not strong
enough. I have been confronting myself up 'til now, but
now I see it clearly and I want to be fair with you."

He patted my hair and smiled shyly almost as a
child would smile, guiltily at the truth of what he was
saying.

"Please don't pat my hair and smile shyly," I said.
"Just treat me seriously and tell me the truth."

His face went solemn. He understood that although he hadn't known me very long, I was more
serious than I had ever been in my life.

He looked deeper into my eyes. "Without you I
can push my feelings under, but when I see you, I love
your face, your hair; I love listening to the things you

tell me. I love touching you. I love you and I love loving you. All those feelings come back and I can't cope with them."

I wanted to cry.

He took a long beat.

"I don't understand why you love me. Subjectively, I suppose I do, but objectively, I don't." He waited for me to say something.

"You don't understand *why* I love you or *that* I do?"

"I don't understand either. So now, I've stated the problem," he went on, "let's not talk about it anymore."

I didn't say anything. He seemed afraid that he might have given me the cue to walk away.

"Let's get under the covers," I said.

We did. I still didn't say anything. He decided to continue.

"The world is a crazy place right now. I want to help my party and my country into a better period, and politically our relationship could lose me the election. I know that is a terrible thing to say, but it's the truth, and I can't do that to my party. They depend on me to win again, nor do I want to lose my seat in Parliament. But personally acknowledging our love would make it three times harder for me. My wife and children have been so patient in putting up with me. There is no stormy loving passion in my relationship with her, but she and they have been a stabilizing force in my life. Morally, I can't do anything to hurt them. I have worked most of my life, usually to the point of exhaustion, and they have tolerated it. You see how this is morally unacceptable to me? And even if I leave out everyone else's feelings, I know I'm not strong enough to tolerate my own feelings if I hurt them or my party. And even as I say this to you I feel that I am speaking from a hole, but from this hole I see things clearly."

I turned over inside the covers and rested on my arm and looked into his face.

"Gerry, tell me something."

"Yes?"

"I feel that along with your own loneliness, that

you feel that your family has held you back. Is that true?"

"Yes," he said, "that's true too, but we have a very intricate relationship with each other and maybe it was good that they held me back. Otherwise I might have grown into a weed."

"A weed?" The self-image was so inappropriate. Did he mean that if he was free of them he would strangle all other growth around him? That was what weeds did. Or did he think he'd just grow wild and unruly without the discipline of a family? I was turning the imagery over and over in my mind. I remembered how it struck me when I had read once that there was no such thing as a weed but only a plant in the wrong place.

"My wife is very harsh and judgmental of others," he said. "That's why I know she would never accept our relationship. I've never been able to understand that streak in her, but it's very strongly there. She's monopolistic. She rules the family with an iron hand."

"An iron hand?"

"Yes. And I think that's been good. But she would be very harsh in understanding my need for you."

The pangs of conscience I had been feeling rapidly vanished.

"But if you are unwilling to be what you'd call immoral to her, why do you accept her being immoral to you?"

"I don't think she's being immoral."

"Well, what's immorality anyway? Isn't it immoral to be harshly judgmental of someone you love?"

"But they have all been so sweet and patient. I can't hurt them now."

I tried to grasp what he was saying, particularly when I wasn't asking for any commitment from him.

"Well, listen darling, no one is suggesting you do anything. I'm certainly not. Please understand that. I'm more concerned with what you think you're doing."

"What do you mean?" he said.

"Well, has it occurred to you that you are afraid of bursting out with a new freedom?"

"How do you mean?"

"Well, bursting out with freedom carries a lot of pain and responsibility with it. Maybe you were ready to do that when you met me, but only up to a point. And maybe you are legitimately retreating back into your hole so you can avoid it for a little while longer. A new freedom for you can mean a better relationship with your family too."

He blanched. "I don't know."

"Well, maybe you're in your hole because your own potential might frighten you too much. I feel as though I fell in love with your potential and you're afraid of it."

He didn't say anything.

Then I said, "I guess I have to ask you, don't I?"

"Ask me what?"

"Could you do without me? Do you want to do without me?"

His face looked pained and drawn. I waited for him to answer, churning inside because he was taking so long and also because he was making a superhuman effort to be fair.

"I don't know," he said. "I suppose I would have to say yes. I could give up my feelings and go back to the loneliness you recognized. Yes, I think I could."

I could feel myself shaking inside. It seemed to be up to me now to make it easier for him and walk away *because* he loved me.

I stifled the tears. "What should I do?" I asked. "I don't know if I could stand how lonely I'd make you by leaving, to say nothing of myself."

"Yes," he said, "it would make me desolate if you left me."

"And if you can't understand that I love you that much, then how can you understand how you love me? If you loved yourself more, you'd be freer to love me and others too."

His face went quizzical. "I can't understand that," he said.

"What I mean is, you have to love yourself before you can really love anyone else."

"I still don't understand," he said.

"It's as though you've dedicated your entire life to helping others unaware completely that you were doing nothing to help yourself."

He got out of bed.

"Does this mean you don't want to discuss it any further?" I asked.

He laughed and fell on top of me sheepishly. "But there is a limit to how much I can take," he said. "You are very strong."

"Relentless is the word. But you are ready for relentlessness or you wouldn't be here."

He sat up beside me and said, "All right, there are three solutions as I see it. One—to continue this deception politically and personally. Two—to effect your solution . . . and . . ."

"Wait a minute. What's my solution?"

"The solution you suggested a moment ago. You know . . ."

He couldn't even say the words, "Leave me and walk away."

"And three—to reflect a while longer."

"We're reflecting right now, aren't we?"

He laughed.

"Well, at least we're *really* talking about it," I said.

He looked out the window.

"You know," he said, "this is the longest personal talk I have ever had."

"I think you're wrong," I said. "I think it's the *only* personal talk you've ever had. Is that true?"

"Yes."

We looked at each other.

"Look," I said, "I don't want to mess up your marriage and I don't want to mess up your political career. But I also don't like participating in deception of any kind whether it's personal or political on any level."

"I know," he said.

"As far as a solution is concerned, I would be happy if you would be more free when you're with me, that's all. And in that respect, we can buy some more time."

"Okay," he said, "I understand. I'll try to be more

free if you'll continue the deception awhile longer."

"Okay, it's a deal," I said, "but one more thing.
You're right that there is a limit to how relentless I
should be, but there is also a limit to how 'fair' you
should be. Please stop being so fair and just enjoy
yourself with me and I'll stop being so relentless."

"All right," he laughed.

He rolled his eyes and shook his head in mock
despair. He was wonderful to talk to: no hostility, no
giving up, no arguing; just a deep and desperate desire
to understand what was going on between us.

He dressed and so did I. He said he had a youth
meeting in some other city and wouldn't be back in
Stockholm until the day after tomorrow. But we would
see each other as soon as he returned.

I had agreed to more deception, but I didn't want
to mention the true and real immorality he was commit-
ting by keeping this from his wife for what would be a
whole year. And I didn't mention that I suspected what
worried him the most was that if she knew about us,
she would be harshly judgmental of him *in public*,
which would not only lose him the election, but also
shatter all the illusions he had as to how *moral* she
really was . . . or wasn't.

I walked him to the private entrance, showed him
how the key worked, and watched him walk away in the
snow muttering about the night watchman who might
recognize him.

Then I remembered something he had said that
was too complicated for me to understand.

"I like to be admired," he had said, "but not by
those people who really mean something to me."

I thought about that all night while I tried to sleep.

To be admired by people you care about carried
with it a responsibility to live up to that admiration. It
was more than public relations; it required substantial
qualities which could stand the test of scrutiny and
continued observation over a period of time.

Most people didn't seem to allow themselves close
personal contact. It aroused too much anxiety, was too
difficult to sustain . . . for a few days maybe, but on a

long-term basis it became too threatening. The irony was that all of us looked for love. We spend our lives searching for another to share it with. And when we find someone with the potential for fulfilling that need, we back away.

Chapter 10

"I think immortality is the passing of a soul through many lives or experiences, and such as are truly lived, used, and learned, help on to the next, each growing richer, happier and higher, carrying with it only the real memories of what has gone before . . ."

—LOUISA MAY ALCOTT
Letters

❧ I didn't see Gerry again for three days. During that time I sat in my hotel room and thought. I slept about four hours a night. I left to take frozen walks in the snow, but I was unaware of the cold. I turned over my whole life in my mind. I read some of the books I had bought at the Bodhi Tree, especially on Edgar Cayce. And then I pulled out the address and telephone number for the Swedish trance medium who channeled Ambres.

I called my friend who had met me at the airport. Lars and his wife were in advertising; they were upper-middle class, although the Swedes didn't like to think they still had a class society. I had met them when I was on tour in Stockholm a few years before.

They had been very discreet in meeting me at the airport and refrained from asking me why I was in Stockholm now. We chatted for awhile on the telephone and in that context I mentioned that I had been reading some metaphysical books, particularly on the psychic readings of Edgar Cayce.

"Oh yes," said Lars. "Edgar Cayce. I know quite a bit about his work. He was very astute."

I was slightly taken aback that in Sweden Edgar Cayce was known when I in America had only recently heard of him.

"It's strange and coincidental you should mention him," Lars went on, "because just tonight we are going to a psychic session with a Swedish trance medium. Would you like to come along and meet the spiritual entity?"

"A trance medium?" I said. "Lars, *you* are seeing a spiritual entity?"

"Yes," he said simply.

"What's his name?" I asked.

"Ambres," he said.

Well, to put it mildly, the "coincidence" was not lost on me. I had been flipping through the Cayce book as we talked. Now I closed it firmly and said yes, I'd love to come. I was definitely in Sweden for reasons other than Gerry. Things were really getting interesting.

I was ready when Lars and Birgitta picked me up a few hours later. They didn't ask what I had been doing since I arrived, so I volunteered that I had an idea for a new book and was spending time away from my hectic life in America and needed peace and quiet in the Swedish winter. They seemed to accept my explanation, but then Swedes rarely expose their feelings.

They drove me toward the outskirts of Stockholm where the trance medium and his wife lived. They told me the trance medium's name was Sturé Johanssen and his wife's was Turid. The spiritual entity that Sturé channeled was becoming famous all over Sweden.

"Many people are coming to the teaching sessions of Ambres," said Lars, "because he helps so many with medical diagnoses."

"How do you mean?" I asked, remembering that Cayce had channeled what sounded like much the same thing.

"Oh," said Lars, "people come from all over Sweden

with needs of every description. Some are suffering from chronic problems of health, some with terminal diseases, some with psychological confusion, some just with questions about where mankind came from and where we are going."

"And this Ambres can provide answers for all of that stuff?"

"Well," said Lars, "if people follow his holistic directions perfectly, they usually find some relief, and most of his instructions have to do with understanding the power each of us has within ourselves to know everything if we'd only recognize it and believe in it."

"What if someone is suffering with terminal cancer? Ambres can put it in remission?"

"No," he said, "Ambres doesn't put it in remission. He helps put each person on the right course mentally and spiritually so that they can attempt to do it themselves, or at least to deal with the emotional problems involved. It's basically a holistic and spiritual approach."

"Does it work?" I asked.

"Well," Lars replied, "the basis of Ambres' teachings is educating us that we have the power and the knowledge to become anything we want to become. That *we* have dimensions and understanding that we are not aware of. He teaches that our positive energy is awesome, just as his is, only *he*, as a spiritual being without a body at the present, knows it, and we don't."

"Well, what is a spiritual being really? I don't quite understand."

"We are all spiritual beings," said Lars. "We just don't acknowledge it. We are spiritual beings of energy who happen to be in the physical body at the present time and Ambres is a spiritual being of energy who does not happen to be in the body right now. Of course, he is highly evolved, but then so are we. The difference is that we don't believe it."

Shades of what David had said to me ran in and out of my mind. Snippets and phrases from articles and books I had read played around in my head. Sai Baba in India had said what sounded like the same thing.

Likewise, the spiritual master Krishnamurti. "We are capable of everything there is," they had said, "and the acknowledgement of our seemingly invisible spiritual power would hasten our improvement."

"So," I said to Lars, "you and Birgitta really believe an actual spiritual entity is speaking through Sturé Johanssen?"

"Oh certainly," said Birgitta. "First of all, if he isn't an actual spiritual entity of a highly evolved nature, then Sturé Johanssen is not only a magnificent actor, but he has within himself information and remedies that have saved lots of lives, both physically and mentally. He has also told people things that were so deeply personal that it would be hard to comprehend how Sturé would know. Nor does anybody know where he would, from himself, get the medical information he uses in diagnosis. But each person must have the faith in themselves. Ambres also provides past life information that checks out to be so familiar to people that it has a great bearing on the lives they lead today."

I opened the car window and breathed deeply.

"You mean, past-life information relating to present-day relationships is possible to ascertain?"

"Yes," said Lars, "but Ambres emphasizes heavily that *this* lifetime is the most important because otherwise we'll get obsessed with the past rather than concentrating on the present."

"Does he always answer past-life inquiries then?"

"No," Birgitta answered, "not always. Many times he assesses the questioner and concludes that present-day evaluation is much more necessary. With others he will give quite extensive past-life readings. It depends on the individual."

I sat awhile in silence as I listened to Birgitta and Lars itemize how helpful Ambres had been in solving questions and issues that had plagued some of the people who had come to him for help. And others who had been simply curious to see how the phenomenon of spiritual channeling worked.

"Listen," I said finally, "would you say there is much of this sort of thing going on?"

"You mean elsewhere in the world?" asked Lars. "Or just here in Sweden?"

"I don't know," I said. "Anywhere, I guess."

"Well, we have lots of friends in America and Europe who are interested in spiritual metaphysics. And yes, trance channeling of spiritual entities is becoming more and more common. It's almost as though the closer we come to the end of the millennium, the more spiritual help we are getting if we'd just take advantage of it."

"Well, are some of these trance mediums phony or frauds? I mean, how can you tell the difference between one who is only acting and one who is really in trance?" I asked.

Lars thought about what I asked as though he had never considered the possibility. He looked at Birgitta. They both shrugged.

"We don't know," he answered. "I suppose you'd sort of know it when it was happening if it was phony. The material coming through is usually too complicated, or too personal, for the medium to be putting on an act. In any case you would certainly be able to distinguish the difference by the results you yourself got. We've never experienced a fake, so we don't really know."

"Are many of your co-workers in your advertising firm into this stuff?" I asked.

"Only a few," answered Lars simply, "those who are interested in spiritual growth. We tend to shy away from people who aren't willing to be open-minded at least, but there are many, like us, with whom we have become close friends. People who are searching for their own spiritual understanding become those whom we can really communicate with. The others are only acquaintances. They seem to be living on the surface of life rather than in it."

I took another breath of the pristine Swedish winter air. "What about Sturé Johanssen? What is he like as a person when he's not channeling?" I asked.

"Sturé is a carpenter," Lars explained, "and not at all interested in the spiritual world."

"So does he mind being an instrument when he

could be spending his time building bookshelves or something?" I asked.

Lars laughed as the car plodded through the icy streets of Stockholm. "No," he answered. "He says if it helps people, then he's all for it. He's a good man at heart. Simple, but really a good man."

"And what does Ambres sound like compared to how Sturé sounds?"

"Sometimes it's quite difficult to understand Ambres' language," said Lars, "because it's such ancient Swedish, something like what it would be for you to listen to biblical English. His phrasing is entirely different from Sturé's, and even different from the Swedish of today. Ambres says there is *no* language to express some of the knowledge he would like to give us."

"What do you mean?"

"Well," he said, "when he's trying to teach us about dimensions or concepts we've never even thought about, he says any language itself is a limitation."

"I'm sorry," I said genuinely, but I must have sounded doubtful, "can you be more specific?"

Lars nodded. "Our spoken and written languages," he said, "only really describe those dimensions which relate to our five senses. Our physical world. We are only just beginning, through the advancement of astrophysics and psychodynamics, to know that we need to develop language which relates to the worlds that are invisible to us. Little by little, we are beginning to perceive the exciting dimensions of what we simply and sometimes sarcastically refer to as the metaphysical world. That is why Ambres sometimes has a difficult time helping us to understand life from a non-physical plane point of view."

I shut my eyes as we drove, wondering what it would be like not to be "physical." I found that the minute I got into discussions of the metaphysical and heard people using words like "occult," "astral plane," "cosmic vibrations," "etheric memory," "soul," "God" —the standard vocabulary of a study as old as time—I reacted with nervous derision, sarcastic laughter, suspicion, or outright contempt. This time was no exception. Yet I wanted to know more. I wanted to "experience" a medium myself.

Lars continued as I held my eyes shut. "All sciences have their own vocabularies," he said, "usually incomprehensible to laymen, to say nothing of their mysteries and marvels and miracles that we take on faith. And the same for all religions. We accept scientific marvels without really understanding them, and we accept religious miracles on faith. I wonder why we, in the Western world, have so much difficulty with the whole concept of experience and thinking that is popularly known as the 'occult.'"

I opened my eyes. "Because," I said, "when you think of 'occult' you think of dark forces and *Rosemary's Baby* and stuff. It's scary. Spirits from the dead and all that aren't very mirth-making, are they?"

Lars chuckled. "Well," he said, "many people have exploited the occult to focus on the dark side of the metaphysical world. But the light side is inevitably beautiful. You can take anything in nature and focus on the negative, but the positive beauty of it can change your life."

I rolled up my eyes into my head. Sure, I was sitting in a car in Stockholm with a man and his wife who sounded just like David in Manhattan and Cat in Calabasas, California. Was this stuff going on all over the world?

As though Lars heard my thoughts, he said, "Millions of people all over the world are so interested in this stuff that they support an entire industry of books, teachings, schools, individuals, and literature of all kinds devoted to the metaphysical dimensions of life. I wouldn't call it the occult anyway. I would call it an interest in the spiritual dimension of life."

Lars and Birgitta began to speak at the same time. Again they emphasized how "gloriously involving" their spiritual interests had become. They said it had made them happier and more loving people. Through their many sessions with Ambres, they had made lots of new friends who also found themselves believing in the same things. And there seemed to be no question in

anyone's mind that Ambres was a genuine spiritual
entity speaking from the astral plane.

I didn't want to be disrespectful, but I asked one
more time, "And you *honestly* believe that Ambres is a
real spiritual entity?"

Birgitta turned to me as Lars smiled patiently. "It's
almost impossible to explain to anyone who hasn't the
open-mindedness to at least consider it possible," she
said.

I peered out at the Stockholm countryside, ponder-
ing. I wondered how many other Swedes in their
postcard-perfect houses were into spiritual exploration.
Every corner, every house, every tree was a snow-
covered postcard. The leather interior upholstery of
Lars's Volvo gave off a faint fresh smell. It was comfortable,
modern, austerely luxurious. The Swedish houses were
modern and clean, nothing opulent, but individualistic
in their personalities, I thought. Sweden had its problems,
but somehow seemed to be moving into the twenty-first
century with a studied balance of socialism and democracy.
I wondered if they would make it as time went on. I
wondered how prevalent or deep their spiritual interests went. It was remarkable to me that a successful,
high-powered advertising man would be driving me to a
spiritual reading with a trance medium.

About ten miles outside of Stockholm we pulled
into what looked like a quiet residential community.
There were quaint street lamps at every corner. Sandboxes
and swings decorated each line of condominiums which
were built exactly alike, but were somehow individualized with flower boxes, snow men, and decorations
fashioned by each family.

Lars stopped the car and I got out. I looked around
at the look-alike community. "You know," I said, "I'd
probably walk into the wrong condominium at least
once a week. It sort of forces you to look more carefully
at the individuality of each house so you don't make a
mistake."

Lars smiled. He and Birgitta led me to one of the
condominiums and rang the bell. A cheerful female
voice came from inside and soon a plump, rosy-cheeked

woman opened the door and greeted us with a stream of Swedish.

"This is Turid," said Lars. "She says she's sorry she doesn't speak English. She knows your movies and she is very happy you want to meet Ambres."

Turid ushered us into her living room which looked like a Swedish version of a small place in the San Fernando Valley: a low, modern couch, bookshelves, a Tiffany-style lamp hanging over a smooth wooden modern coffee table. There were people sitting around the table. Spreading green ivy spilled from vases on the tables.

"Sturé made all his own furniture," said Lars.

With Lars translating, Turid introduced me to her other friends as Shirley. She never mentioned my last name. After the initial pleasantries at her front door, it didn't seem to matter to her.

"Sturé is resting," she said. "He'll be out from the bedroom in a moment." She invited us to sit down and have some beer and cheese which was spread out on the handmade coffee table.

The three of us wolfed down some cheese and Swedish crackers. "Sture and Turid are devoting their lives now to bringing about spiritual communication," said Lars. "But Turid is concerned that Sturé might be draining his energies with trance channeling, but they want to be helpful to as many people as possible."

"Why?" I asked. "I mean, does that mean that Sturé has completely given up his regular work as a carpenter?"

"Close to it."

"Well, where do they make enough money to live on?"

"People contribute what they feel is commensurate with what they learn from the channelings."

So here was this Swedish carpenter who suddenly found a spiritual voice speaking through him giving up his regular life and work to help people by providing himself as an instrument for communication from a spiritual entity, very much like Edgar Cayce. Was this similar to what had happened with Moses and Abraham and some of the ancient prophets spoken of in the Bible? Were the same patterns occurring today that had happened then—only in modern-day terms?

"Why do they do it, Lars?" I asked.

"Well, they don't know. They just feel they have to. They are aware that the world is deteriorating and they feel this is a way to provide spiritual knowledge to prevent that human course of action. I feel the same way, as a matter of fact. We listen to what Ambres says and it has changed the way we relate to our lives. I can make more positive and compassionate decisions when I know more about my purpose as a human being."

The other people talked quietly among themselves, eating cheese and drinking beer. Some discussed occurrences in their lives. Others discussed spiritual truths that they said they didn't quite understand.

I looked up. Sturé came quietly into the room. He was about five-foot-nine, solidly built with a stocky, sturdy walk and an even modulated voice. He seemed very shy, but his handshake was strong when Lars introduced us. He greeted me in Swedish. His face was extremely kind. He was about thirty-five. He stood around for a moment shyly greeting his other friends until Turid motioned that the two of them should sit. They sat side by side in hard-backed chairs with a glass of water on a table beside Turid.

"We must begin immediately," she apologized, "because we have others to see later."

She gently turned off the lights and lit a candle on the coffee table in the center of the room. Sturé sat quietly, seemingly preparing himself to relax.

"May we observe a few moments of silent meditation," asked Turid.

We all bowed our heads and waited until Sturé was in the proper trance state for Ambres to come through.

As I sat in the candlelit darkness, I wondered what Gerry would think if he saw me. He was intrusive, and I deliberately concentrated on the candle. I had never been much for doing anything communally, usually preferring to do my own thing in private and in my own way, at my own pace. But in so many of the books I had

been reading, it seemed that communal energy benefit-
ed everyone more than one's individual energy. Certainly
any performer or speaker knows about audience energy.
And anyone who has been in a live audience has felt
and shared in that community or feeling. As a matter of
fact, the books said a positive collective energy apparently was much stronger, more intense, and more beneficial and healing in *any* human endeavor, according to
the spiritual point of view. Presently I became aware of
a sense of unity with the others in the room.

About ten silent minutes passed. My tape recorder
purred quietly beside me. Lars sat directly over the
recorder. He reminded me again that the ancient Swedish
would be difficult to translate quickly. He said he would
try to keep up.

I looked over at Sturé. He sat quietly, breathing
deeply but calmly. His eyes were shut. His hands
rested unmoving on his stocky thighs. His brown curly
hair was cut just above the ears. I was conscious of
focusing on small detail. After about fifteen minutes, he
began to quiver slightly . . . quiver as though an electrical charge was surging through him. Turid took his
hand, almost as though she was grounding him with a
physical touch. She smiled. Lars whispered into my
ear.

"Because of the electromagnetic energy of Ambres'
spiritual entity, Sturé needs Turid's earthbound energy
to neutralize his body. That's why they need to work
together."

Sturé's body suddenly became rigid and sat totally
upright. His eyes opened. Then his head strained forward and cocked itself to one side. His whole body
shook and when it stopped, he opened his mouth and
said something in a guttural voice in Swedish. The
voice didn't sound anything like the man I had just
been introduced to. Lars leaned over to me and
whispered, "Ambres is saying, 'Greetings' and he is
happy we have gathered together. He is identifying
himself and he is giving us a reading on the level of
spiritual energy in the room."

I don't know what I thought. I wanted to stop Lars

and ask how such energy levels could be obtained by this Ambres, but before I could raise any questions, the session had already progressed into a dialogue between Ambres and the people who had come to learn from him.

Lars translated as quickly as he could. Then I realized that most of the people present were not interested in *how* it worked. They had already accepted the process. They were interested only in the "teachings" that Ambres was imparting. And from their questions it didn't seem they were interested in past-life information or energy levels either. They were asking Ambres questions about the beginning of Creation!

Lars tried to keep up with the translation. I tried to keep up with what was happening. In a swift but careful rhythm, Ambres talked. I say Ambres because it "felt" like Ambres. I felt certain that Sturé had nothing to do with it. He was only a kind of telephone through which some spiritual entity spoke. In fact, I could "feel" the personality, the humor, the ancient rhythm of the thoughts of this entity called Ambres. He gestured and laughed and made succinct and overt points with his own energy, not the energy of Sturé. At least, that's what it "felt" like to me. His back was rigid and formal, not at all like the casual body movement of the man I had observed a half hour before.

Lars translated in capsulized statements as Ambres described God as Intelligence. He described the first stirrings of God's thought and the creation of matter. He described the birth of worlds, and worlds within worlds; and universes, and universes within universes. He described God's love for his creations and his need to receive love reflected in "feeling." And he described God's need to create Life.

I could see what Lars meant about the limitations of language, found myself identifying with how Ambres must have felt, saddled with the limitation of earth language!

About two hours passed. Lars continued to translate in generalized fashion. Ambres passed from the rise and fall of civilizations to the creation of the Great

Pyramid, which appeared to have considerable significance and which he described as a "library in stone." I
somehow felt I could visualize what he was saying. The
others in the room asked questions in Swedish and
Ambres acknowledged that he realized there were other "entities" present who spoke only "another tongue,"
but he said he was an ancient Swede and even if he
could speak "other tongues," the "instrument" could
not do so comfortably. It would drain too much energy
from him because of the strain to form words in a
language he knew nothing about.

Even with his monumental account of the beginning of Creation, this entity Ambres seemed to have an
understanding of humor on a human level. I wondered
how long ago *he* had been human, or if he *ever* had
been, but the session raced on beyond my mundane
questions. I could only feel that everyone present was
more advanced than I. I sat back and tried to absorb
what was happening.

Ambres-Sturé would get up and walk around the
room with a hunched-over stride. He appeared to be
nothing like the Sturé I had met. Sometimes he laughed
deeply and made jokes to emphasize a point. He went
to a drawing pad tacked up on the wall and drew
diagrams and cosmic geometric designs and spirals to
make his descriptions more graphic. He asked the
group questions as though he was a master teacher
conducting a class. The group was involved and excited,
confused sometimes over a crucial point which he patiently
explained again. A few times he scolded someone who
obviously hadn't done his homework. Then he sat down
next to Turid again.

"The instrument is losing his energy," said Ambres.
"He must now revitalize."

He said he hoped he would have an encounter
with us again. He said we should take care of each
other. Then, he said a prayer in his ancient tongue
giving thanks to God for the opportunity to serve.

Sturé trembled. The electrical charge known as
Ambres seemed to leave his body. Turid quickly thrust

water into her husband's hands. Sturé drank all of it. He slowly came around to his own consciousness and stood up.

I looked around not knowing what to think. The guests talked quietly among themselves, asked me if I understood enough of the Swedish to comprehend what was going on, and I said yes, not wanting to admit that the process itself would take me awhile to understand, much less the information. But they seemed to understand anyway and said once I found it acceptable, it would be beneficial for me.

Beneficial? It was enough to scramble my brains. I was just glad I had read the Cayce stuff before coming.

I walked over to Sturé.

"Thank you," I said. "I hope you're all right. I've never seen anything like this."

Sturé shook my hand as Lars translated. He seemed tired but calm. His eyes looked liquid and kind. He said he hoped I had learned something from Ambres, said he would like to talk to him someday himself, and gave a little shrug as though he didn't understand what was really going on either. I was struck by his direct simplicity. Turid put her arm around me.

"Ambres is a great teacher," she said. "I'm so glad you could hear him. Sturé needs to rest now."

She guided Lars and Birgitta and me to the door and said we could talk tomorrow if I wanted.

We said goodnight to everyone and left. Snow was falling outside. The snow man in the sandbox was a square bulk now, newly fashioned by fresh snow as the children of the neighborhood slept.

The three of us walked under the white sky to the car.

"What did you think?" asked Lars.

I wanted to say something profound.

"I guess I need time to think," I stalled.

"You know," I said, "I'm beginning to feel that I was somehow guided to come here. There's too much happening to me lately to believe in accidents anymore. I think I was *supposed* to come to Stockholm."

Lars and Birgitta smiled and led me through the falling snow to the car. We didn't say anything to each other.

Then, as we drove back to Stockholm, each lost in our own thoughts, I began to wonder about the string of "coincidences" in my life. I was aware that I was beginning to feel some preordained plan, unfolding according to my own awareness and willingness to accept what I was ready for. As though the events and incidents were bound to happen if I let them. The timing was up to me, but the inevitability felt fixed and predestined. I was surprised at what I was thinking. I had never believed in such things. Yet the serried coincidences of my relationship with Gerry: its very nature, based on earthbound frustrations, political realities, and negative obstacles coincidental (that word again!) with my slow friendship and understanding of David with his spiritual point of view—all this was greatly forcing on me an awareness of other dimensions.

I seemed to be a middle-ground observer of dual realities. And I felt I was gradually developing an understanding of both points of view which, as I thought about it, seemed to represent the dualities in life (something like what my father pointed out)—the grounded Earth reality and the Cosmic Spiritual reality. Maybe they were both supposed to be necessary for human happiness. It was becoming more and more clear to me that to call one point of view the only true reality was limited, prejudiced, and probably incorrect. Maybe all human beings were Mind, Body, and Spirit as the great ancients had tried to tell us. That was their legacy. Maybe I had to *re*learn it.

I said goodbye to Lars and Birgitta and said I'd be in touch. ᘝ

Chapter 11

"There is a principle which is proof against all information, which is proof against all arguments, which cannot fail to keep a man in everlasting ignorance; that principle is contempt, prior to investigation."

—HERBERT SPENCER

When I walked into my hotel room, the telephone was ringing. I picked it up.

"Hi," said Gerry. "How are you?"

"Fine," I said.

"I'm sorry I'm a few days late."

"That's okay. I know you were busy."

"Yes."

"How are you feeling?"

"The snow on the trees is paradise."

"Yes," I said, "the countryside must be beautiful."

"My wife came from London."

I felt the breath go out of me. I didn't know what to say. I felt paralyzed. Had he known she was going to come? Had he *asked* her to come?

"Hello?" he said.

"Yes. I'm here."

"Well . . ." he said, "I'll be over later."

"Yes, sure. I'll be here."

I went into a tailspin. I felt sick and angry. My

stomach felt as if it had a hole in it. I wondered what
Edgar Cayce or Ambres would prescribe for this and
tried to force my mind into a peaceful and spiritual
space. I couldn't. I decided they were full of crap when
it came to living a reality on Earth. I managed to laugh
at the vulgarity of my thought.

When Gerry came to me I was withdrawn. I
couldn't communicate. We made love, but I was afraid.
He said nothing—either about his wife's presence or
my reaction. Neither did I.

He asked me if I thought his hair smelled of
perfume. I said he knew I wasn't wearing any and
hadn't for months.

When I opened the bathroom door to see if he
needed anything, I saw his huge body crouched in the
tub in an embryonic position, washing and looking as
though he hadn't been born yet.

He was gone for the next two days and nights.

I wrote. I wrote everything I was feeling.

I wrote until my head spun. I relived everything
that was happening. I wrote to understand it. I wrote to
decide what to do. I tried to hang on to who I was,
what I wanted, what I wanted to do with or without
Gerry. I wrote to try to understand myself. I wrote
about my life and my thoughts and my questions. I
wrote for days.

Whenever Gerry called I told him I was writing.
He said he was glad I was doing something. It made
him feel less guilty about not being able to see me. I
told him he needn't worry. I was one person who would
always find something to do. Then I felt guilty that I
was writing partly about him and not saying so.

On the sixth night he finished working at about
nine-thirty, called, and said he wanted to come to me
but felt he should go home to his wife. I said fine.

I wrote well into that night, and got up at six and
began again. I never left my hotel room. I wrote what I
was living and feeling, like an extended diary, a way of
talking to myself.

He came the next night. We ate and talked. He ate
kiwi fruit and melon. He wore a thin turquoise tie

which was a gift from the small town he had visited the day before. His hair fell across his forehead as he gestured with his hands cupped and scooping into the air. I made no move toward him at all.

I crossed the room to get him more tea. He reached out, stopped me, and pulled me to him. I stood still. Slowly and with delicate sweetness he kissed my eyes, my chin, my hair, and finally my lips. He encircled me with his arms. I left mine beside my body. He pressed himself against me. I stood still.

With a kind of sly certainty he led me into the bedroom. I didn't want to go. He was taking the initiative and I wasn't sure I wanted it. He lowered me onto the bed and kissed me long and deeply as though he was experimenting with his own right to take what he wanted. I responded but with no aggressiveness. He pulled my thick wool sweater off and felt my body underneath. His hands moved all over me.

He undid my slacks and pulled them off. His hands wound in and around and underneath me. He reached up and held my head and squeezed my hair.

"I love you," he said.

I said nothing.

"I said I love you."

I said nothing.

Then like a dam bursting, he cried, "I love you, I love you, I love you . . ."

We lay together until some kind of reality swam back into focus.

He sat up and looked over me and out of the window. His face looked a hundred years old, as though his mind had seeped through it and dripped down his cheeks. He looked down at me.

"What are you thinking about?" he asked. It was the first time he had inquired about what *I* was thinking.

"I'm thinking about how unreal all of this is," I said. "I've been in this room watching a tugboat going in circles breaking ice. I've watched six layers of snow fall over the curb downstairs. I've eaten Swedish crackers and butter and nothing else. I've written and written and written until my hand aches. I've become the

furniture and the rug and the cold air. And now you're
here. You're here and it's so unreal to me."

"Maybe what we're doing is what's more real," he
said.

"Yes," I said. "Maybe." I shook my head to shock
myself back to normal. "So now," I said, "you have to
return to your unreality."

He got up and headed for the shower. I remained
lying on the bed. He turned around and ran back into
the bedroom.

"I love you," he said.

I held him in my arms.

"Thank you," I said. "Thank you."

He beamed. His dark eyes glistened. He walked
toward the shower again. Again he returned.

"I love you," he said.

"Yes," I said. "I love you too."

"But I still can't understand why. I still can't understand why you want me."

"Neither can I," I answered. "In fact, most of this I
don't understand."

He shook his head.

"And more than anything else," he said, "I want to
spend a whole night with you again."

"I think," I said, "it's because you can't have that
right now."

"No, I know myself better than that."

He nodded seriously. He got up again. This time
he made it to the shower. He returned wet and cold. I
dried him off. He pulled me towards him and hugged
me close.

I dried his hair with the hair dryer while he put on
his shoes and socks.

When he was dressed we discussed his schedule
for the next two days. He had meetings and press
conferences.

I told him I had to get back to America soon. He
said he couldn't see me the next day; it was crammed
too full. I said fine, it didn't matter.

He put on his coat and fur gloves and walked to
the door. Instead of proceeding through it as he usually

did, he turned around and said, "And how's your writing coming?"

"Fine," I said. "Fine. I'm just not sure where I'm going with it."

He looked at me. "Maybe it should just fade away," he said. His words smacked the air. I didn't know what he meant, or maybe I did.

He winked at me and said, *"Ciao,"* and closed the door behind him.

Deep confusion swept over me. Then it was followed by guilt . . . then a kind of double vision. I didn't know what was real again. I hated the feeling. To be unclear about the emotional horizon was the worst thing that could happen to me.

I started writing again—I had no one to talk to but myself. My self.

❧ Everything seemed to be feeling like an illusion. *Was* it an illusion? Was physical reality only what I *thought* it was anyway? A simple day in the life of anyone was just a series of acting scenes; acting what we *thought* we felt. Shakespeare had said it. Maybe all of life was a stage and we were merely actors on that stage playing out our roles. Was he talking about reincarnation when he wrote that? So, if today was acting, was yesterday an illusion? And tomorrow?

Maybe Gerry and our meetings and my work and our world wouldn't even be there tomorrow. Or, maybe what was driving me crazy was the pressure to define reality in physical terms. Perhaps the truth was that everything was real on every level because everything was relative and needed to be taken into account. Maybe we loved and laughed and worked and played in an unconscious effort to remind ourselves that we *must* have a *purpose* beyond this reality. If *that* purpose was real, was each of us using someone else to bounce off so as to define our own purpose more clearly? Did we simply use others we loved to try out our own hidden potentials, our unseen capacities to get some definition of our selves? Were we looking for the source of our own meaning from another time? Or had we actually known each other before? Were Gerry and I really working out some relationship that had been unresolved in another life? If that was so, and if somehow we came to understand that, perhaps then we would no longer need one another. Was that the final joke? Maybe that was the profound reason for humor. Maybe all of life was a colossal cosmic joke because it would continue on its own course regardless of what we did or didn't do. Maybe we should just smile our way to the end, because maybe the end was only the beginning anyway. It might be true that the cycle would start all over again until we got it right. That really wasn't so bad. We'd certainly not need to fear death. If death never even happened, then life was a joke on us. So, we might as well smile through it while we worked our way through our purpose.

Gerry became more clear in my mind. As I wrote about him I understood things more objectively. I began to see his role in my life with more clarity. I wasn't so compulsively intense about either his or my confusion and I began to feel that whatever we meant in each other's lives had a reason, a purpose behind it. In the scheme of his life and in the scheme of mine, the purpose might not be so clear now, but it probably would be soon.

I wrote as though I were talking to myself. The hours melted into one another. I never left the hotel room. I began to wear the walls. I knew every circle of the tugboat doing its icy duty each day in the bay below my window by heart. I watched the days become longer with each successive snowstorm. And now, at the end of another week, the city below me lay carpeted in white, while a veil of new snow made it even whiter.

I walked through the snow. I must have walked five miles . . . through the city and into the animal park, rolling knolls of white snow cream spreading all around me. The sun was sharp and crisp. I felt I could hear myself breathe in the silence miles ahead of myself. Three deer watched me as I walked by them ankle deep in snow, crunching softly. I held my head to the sun. Five white swans flew across it. A man walked by in the distance smoking a pipe.

Gerry hung silently in the air with me as I walked. He was like this air, this country, this environment. It was a pastel environment, not overtly splashed with color or accents. It was an environment that seemed to cover its intentions, as though its real meaning was hidden. It didn't reach out—it lay back almost waiting to be discovered, to be touched, to be walked through and understood. It wasn't exactly afraid of itself as one might think at first. No, it waited on itself instead; with its long, silent patience, those who were new to it might feel rejected and excluded from integrating into it. But that wouldn't be a legitimate response. That wouldn't be giving the detached stillness a chance to come out of itself.

And so maybe it was with people.

To feel emotionally starved because of the lack of overt clarity and discernible communication was to deny the inner richness of communicating with silence. Indeed, the silence could probably be even more full, and if I felt a victim of no communication, that was my problem because it probably wasn't true. I had been used to explosive communication in my life. What I was experiencing now was implosive communication. I had to find what was inside of me and so did Gerry.

I walked all day and came home just in time to see Gerry on Swedish television discussing Third World economic problems.

I had heard it all before but watched carefully anyway. He was assured and strong in the way he presented his proposed solutions. I was reading the *Herald Tribune*, waiting for his call, when I heard the hotel door open.

He looked as though he had run all the way. He was totally out of breath, his face frozen, his eyebrows and eyelashes sparkling with melting snow. I kissed him quickly. He was still on a "high," vivacious and anxious to know what I thought of his appearance on television. We talked about how he was learning to orchestrate his personality for TV. He ate two chocolate-filled biscuits and drank lukewarm tea. We talked about Jimmy Carter and China and the variety show I hoped to do from Peking. We talked about everything under the sun but what was concerning me most. I decided it was time to introduce Gerry to the things that had been happening to me—to us—the things I had been writing about (he had *not* asked).

"Gerry?" I said bravely.

"Hmm . . ."

"Are you curious about what I've been writing about?"

He looked surprised. "Yes," he said, "of course."

"It's about us," I went on, and seeing the look of carefully checked alarm on his face, "in a way, that is."

"In what way?"

"Look, a whole lot of strange things have been happening to me lately, at least since we met. There's been one coincidence after another throwing us together. There's the strength of the pull between us which is illogical in the circumstances. You and I know it is much more than just a physical thing, but *why*? All this time with you I've been having these pre-cognitive feelings and recognition feelings. Gerry, tell me honestly—do you feel that you have known me some place before?"

"Good God! I don't understand you. In any case, what difference would it make?"

"Well, maybe if we could figure out what we were before, we could sort out what we should be now."

He took a long breath. "Darling, you've been alone too long in this room . . ."

"No, dammit!" I was suddenly out of patience. "Don't patronize me! I just want to *talk* about this. I'm not overwrought, I'm not nuts, and I'm not stupid. And there seems to be a whole lot more to this world than you're willing to acknowledge."

He gave a wry grin. "Well, that's probably true at any rate," he said. "What, specifically, are you thinking about?"

"Reincarnation, for one."

"I've no objection to reincarnation—it's fine for those who need it."

"Gerry, I'm not talking about starving peasants. There are a lot of people, all up and down the social and intellectual scale, and all through time, who believe in reincarnation. But specifically, I'm talking about *us.*"

"Oh, for God's sake! If you're suggesting that we have actually lived some previous life together, Shirley, so *what*? What the hell difference would it make since we can't remember anyhow?"

"Well, it might make a difference if we could find out through channeling." I knew I was doing this all wrong.

"What the hell is channeling?"

"I mean," I swallowed, "talking with disembodied spirits through a channel—people do it all the time to find out all kinds of things."

Gerry looked aghast and then very concerned. "Shirley, have you been going to mediums?"

"You don't have to make it sound like a dirty word," I told him.

"No, no! Of course not, I didn't mean it that way." He took a deep breath. "You're right, we do have to talk about this. What, exactly, is it that you have been doing?"

Feeling guilty and defensive, and resenting it, I told him about Cat and Ambres, about Edgar Cayce, about the reading I had been doing. He listened in silence as I slowly wound down. Then he looked at me in what, I realized with surprise, was embarrassment.

"Gerry, what are you thinking?" I asked.

He shook his head. "I don't know what to say," he muttered. "I mean, you just can't be serious about this."

"Why not?"

"Well, my God, isn't it obvious? These mediums are psychos, or weird, dragging stuff up out of their own unconscious. Or else they're taking you. You surely don't believe they're actually communicating with *spirits*?"

"*They* aren't communicating. They're just channeling—they don't even remember what's been said."

"Whatever they're doing, it's utter rubbish. They

do it for money, exploiting gullible people who want to be told some sugary nonsense about dead relatives or some other damned thing."

"Edgar Cayce took no money, the advice he gave was sound, and it didn't come from his unconscious because he had no medical training."

Gerry looked at me helplessly. "Why in the name of God do you have to get involved with this sort of thing?" he asked desperately.

"I'm just trying to find an explanation for us," I said, "or maybe just for me. I'm beginning to think I can't do it for us . . ."

"I should hope not! Look, darling [he so rarely used endearments, and that made twice in the same conversation—he must be really upset], you really mustn't go on with this business. I mean, it can't possibly gain you anything. Ninety percent of these people are charlatans and everyone knows it—all your friends are going to think you've gone soft in the head. And God knows what the public would think if it ever got out."

It was interesting that he was concerned with my public image. I suppose it was logical that he should be, being himself at all times very aware of the importance of his own. But he still had not considered in any way the possibilities of the world I was exploring: it was something completely outside his ken, he couldn't see it, he could not begin to acknowledge the possible validity of its existence.

"What d'you mean 'if it ever got out,' Gerry? This is what I've been writing about."

"You can't," he said flatly. "Not for publication."

"Why *not*?" His rigidity was pushing me into a false position, because in fact, at this point, I had no intention of publishing.

"Because every intellectual you've ever known, anybody with half a brain to use will tear you to pieces—" he stopped, floundering and unhappy.

I was amused at his bland assumption that *all* intelligent people would share his views and touched by his obvious distress for me. But his blanket rejection of all I was talking about seemed to preclude further discussion—if indeed, there had been any! Leaning forward, I murmured, "Oh, the hell with it," and kissed his nose. "It's warm," I said.

"What's warm?"

"Your nose. It was cold when you came in."

He fingered my earrings and swept back my hair. I knelt beside him. He lifted my face and, in the middle of a word, kissed me and stroked my eyes.

He lifted me onto him and when I raised the soft material of my negligee into the air and let it fall around our bodies, he watched the movement and made a soft noise. We never undressed. We made love just as we were leading our lives, the pleasure of it hidden from view.

I fell against him. He kissed my eyes and neck.

"You're leaving tomorrow?" he asked.

"Yes," I said, "I have to go."

"I love you more than I can say," he said.

I felt myself go into a sad limbo.

"When do you think we'll be able to spend a whole evening together again?" he asked.

"Well, it's January now," I said. "Do you figure by September when your election is over?"

He swept his arm up and, hiding his face behind it, stifled a cry under his breath.

"Well," I said, "let's wait and see."

"I have to get up now," he said. "Otherwise I'll be too melancholy to bear it. Where will you be?"

I told him I didn't know. I would be traveling.

He tried to get up, but stopped himself. He looked at our bodies and said, "This next move of yours may be impossible. We are one person, you know."

I smiled. He lifted me up and over him and stood up.

"That was an extremely complicated maneuver, wasn't it?"

"Not as complicated as we are."

When he toddled off to the bathroom with his trousers piled around his ankles, I couldn't believe he wanted to be Prime Minister of England.

When he returned I was still on the sofa. He

looked down at me and said, "You're lovely. You're really lovely."

"When is your birthday?" I asked.

He said, "Tuesday, how did you know?"

I said I just had a feeling.

He said his deputy leader's birthday was on the same day and he would be extremely disappointed if Gerry didn't get back to England and help him celebrate it.

I said, "What about celebrating *your* birthday?"

He said, "That doesn't matter."

I grabbed his arms and shook them. "Doesn't matter? Gerry, *what about* your *birthday*!!" Then I stopped. I stopped in the middle of a thought.

He said, "Yes?"

I said, "Nothing."

I took some pictures of him with my Polaroid camera and flash. He submitted to it and then was curious to see how he looked. Slowly the image bled through in color.

"Oh," he said, "I look dreadful." Gently I shook his arm again.

He raced to the hallway for his coat and fur gloves. He put my hotel room keys on the coffee table, picked up his briefcase, and with more aggressive speed than ever, he headed for the door. I stood still without following him. He opened the door and turned around to look at me as though he was burning whatever I looked like into his memory.

"You are really beautiful," he said, and then he was gone.

I ran to the door and locked it. When I walked back to the living room I saw he had forgotten his glasses.

I raced into the hallway and whistled. I heard him retrace his steps. As he retrieved his glasses from me he said, "When is your birthday?"

"April twenty-fourth," I said.

He nodded as if to say it was another date in the future he could look forward to. Then he said, "What do you think we have together?"

I sighed and ran my fingers over the hair in his eyes.

"I know," he said, "to get to the fruit on a tree, you have to go out on a limb."

He looked into my eyes and walked away. He didn't look back. I walked inside and closed the door.

I lit a cigarette and went to the bay window. Opening it, I blew smoke into the air watching it mingle with the steam of my breath in the winter air. Snow was falling thickly now.

I looked down into the street. He walked into the courtyard below. I whistled softly. He looked up and waved. His fur gloves and black coat were outlined sharply against the solid white background. Snow tumbled around him as he walked into the street looking for a cab. The street was empty. I felt him decide to walk. He looked up and waved again. I waved back and threw him a kiss, but he had already disappeared determinedly into the thick cold silent white Swedish night. ❧

Chapter 12

"The 'soul' is indeed a vague conception and the reality of the thing to which it refers cannot be demonstrated. But consciousness is the most evident of all (invisible) facts . . . The physiologists are very fond of comparing the network of our cerebral nerves with a telephone system but they overlook the significant fact that a telephone system does not function until someone talks over it. *The brain does not create thought (Sir Julian Huxley has recently pointed ed out this fact); it is an instrument which thought finds useful."*

—JOSEPH WOOD KRUTCH
More Lives Than One

The flight back to America was a strange one. I didn't really know who or what I had just left or who or what I was returning to. Something remarkable was underway in my life. But it had no name and eluded description. It spoke to something very ancient and yet I had the feeling it was the forerunner to what could be a new age of thought for me. The experience with Ambres had been fascinating but the questions I had asked Lars and Birgitta still bugged me. Pragmatic child of my time, I decided, for one thing at least, to check out the process of channeling.

In the weeks and months that followed, I read and

investigated and checked. I asked questions and, wherever possible, I listened to tapes. I found there were a remarkable number of mediums, or trance channelers, functioning. With the exception of Edgar Cayce, almost no one spoke of these people by the name of the medium. The personality channeled was dominant, and among these there were a few whose reputations stood out above the rest, largely in terms of the clarity and cohesiveness of the messages channeled. Like experts, or talents, in any field, some mediums were better than others. (I established also that, like any professionals, there were days when absolutely nothing would go right: in that case, some relied on past experience, some faked, and some said flat out that nothing was working and everybody would do better to go home).

But I was struck also by the variety and strength of personality demonstrated by the different entities who were channeled through. The rather hazy odor of solemnity that surrounds the phenomenon of channeling in the minds of most people (perhaps because their own mood in approaching the prospect of a discussion with a disembodied spirit would be somewhat somber?) seemed to be at odds with the reality. There was rich humor and occasional downright flippancy in some of the channeled personalities, for instance. Whoever, or whatever, these entities were, they conveyed enormous individuality of character and an aura, not so much of solemnity, as of experience.

Moreover, channeling was something that had been going on for some time and several famous people not only "believed" in it but had practiced it, including Abraham Lincoln, who used Carpenter (the medium actually lived in the White House with the President) for regular consultations, J. P. Morgan (who used Evangeline Adams), William Randolph Hearst—and many, many more from widely varying fields. The work of Sir Oliver Lodge and Mrs. Piper was of course well known. There seemed to have been almost a fashion for this kind of thing around the turn of the century, and not only channeling, but table-tapping, the use of the planchette, and the ouija board. No doubt it was entertaining, but equally clear was the fact that many worthy and serious people took channeling—and all that it implied—very seriously.

It was also clear that some could not handle the sheer volume of information being channeled through, much less the quality of its nature. The cosmos is a staggering concept: to relate each individual human to such vastness was often more than the listeners could bear. And when it came to the particularities of extraterrestrial life, the structure of the atom, the cohesion of all matter, all thought—these were matters to which most people had not given very much attention. The entities communicating this information frequently appeared to have no idea of how much the party on the other end of the telephone, so to speak, could absorb.

In sum, it seemed as though there was an individual pace, or rhythm, which each person gradually developed in assimilating the mind-boggling floods of information that came through. When dealing with the mind and the emotions, concentrated force-feeding simply did not work. It even appeared to alienate a good many people.

I turned my attention to the more modern channelers and the entities who communicated through them.

Best known of the current channeled spiritual entities appeared to be a spiritual master known as D.K., channeled by Alice Bailey, and later by Benjamin Creme. Seth, channeled by Jane Roberts, was a particularly interesting case and one which presented more than one facet of the phenomenon of channeling.

Since 1963, when Mrs. Roberts was first approached by Seth, she and her husband (who, from the beginning, had taken notes on what Seth said) had accumulated a library of notes on the sessions. Some of this material has appeared in several published works, one actually dictated by Seth himself. What I found most interesting was the strong doubt evidenced by Mrs. Roberts in the early contacts with Seth (*The Seth Material*).

Having no previous contact with, nor interest or belief in, psychic phenomena, Mrs. Roberts was assailed one night while writing her own poetry by a torrent of words which demanded to be put down on paper. Scribbling furiously for hours, she eventually discovered herself writing the title of what she describes as "that odd batch of notes, *The Physical Universe as Idea Construction.*" (These subsequently proved to be a synthesis of material that Seth would later develop). But at the time, knowing nothing of Seth, Mrs. Roberts was made uneasy, astonished, and upset by both the event and the content of "her" writing.

In the weeks and months that followed, after Seth had virtually insisted on "coming through," she and her husband conducted many tests to prove, or disprove, the existence of Seth as a separate personality, or the disembodied entity he claimed to be. In fact, it took Seth a considerable time and some quite spectacular displays of special abilities to prove to Mrs. Roberts that he was not a part of her own subconscious!

Nevertheless, actual "proof" of channeling, that is, a physical presence on Earth acting as a channel of communication for another kind of presence on a different plane, was hard to establish in scientific terms. In the end, proof of the process came down to content: if a channel spoke in a foreign language, or displayed a talent (such as playing the piano) or practiced a professional skill (such as medicine) or conveyed information, let's say, from a distant place or about a particular event or person which the channel had no way of knowing, then it would appear that the foreign language, or the talent, or the skill, or the knowledge, had to be coming from another source.

(Over a period of time to follow I was to come across many instances of such "proof," but by then the process had become commonplace to me—not unimportant, but rather like the preparation of a good meal: one was grateful for a good cook but the meal was what counted.) In fact, even at the end of two or three months of intense reading and questioning I had decided that the process was of lesser relevance. At least one aspect of the channeled information I was reading about cropped up again and again and that related to past-life recall. I was probably more curious about this as it seemed I might learn something helpful about my relationship with Gerry, but what had taken my real attention in the vast volume of material available for study was the fact that so much of the message seemed to be universal—that is, entities channeling through a variety of people in many countries in different languages were saying basically the same thing. Look into yourselves, explore yourselves, *you* are the Universe...

More and more, as I read and thought, the *message* forced me to reexamine motives, to rethink, or perhaps to think for the first time, about values and aspects of living I had heretofore simply accepted.

I had been used to living in a world where, by the very nature of the life we led, it was nearly impossible to get the time to look into yourself. Where just to stay alive, to say nothing of staying on top, seemed to require attitudes that were just the opposite... if you weren't carefully checking out the progress of your neighbor, you had the impression that it wouldn't be long before you'd be left behind yourself. If you were a successful person, you had to keep going in the rat race to stay there. If you were poor, you had to keep going to survive. There was never any time for just yourself, to do nothing, to enjoy a sunset, to listen to a bird sing, to watch a bee bumble, to hear what you were thinking, much less what anybody else was thinking.

Human contact seemed superficial, striving for meaningful goals, wanting deeper meaning but only talking around it. Competitive living left no time for what we were, who we could be, and what we could mean to each other. I had seen very few relationships with real and lasting meaning—my own included. They hadn't seemed able to survive our own scrutiny of them.

And instead of going deeper, we chose to respond to urges to be comfortable, to just accept the limits and restrictions imposed by safe superficiality, to be successful and well-attended creatures of comfort with protection and warmth and no challenges from what could be frighteningly new and unknown... no challenges from what more we could be or were, no challenge from what more we could understand, no challenge from how that might threaten us, and no recognition of what it could mean to end up alone.

Alone . . . that was the cold word. Everyone was afraid of being alone. Yet it didn't really matter who we lived with or slept with or loved or married. In the final analysis, we were all alone—alone with ourselves—and that's where the rub came. So many relationships were failing because the people involved didn't know who *they* were, much less the person or people they were involved with.

But could that now be changing? Were people now beginning to search into their own depths as a kind of instinctive survival mechanism to offset the polarity of violence and disturbance that was clearly stalking the world? Were they finding the potential for unbridled joy in themselves—as Lars and Birgitta had described? It could be that thousands of people all over the world were involved with this mystery of whether or not there was a life beyond the physical, or in addition to it, rather, and hence necessarily, something we called a "soul." I found myself giving more and more credence to spiritual teaching, the helpfulness of meditation, the essential decency and rightness of the emotional message, and the boundless possibilities of metaphysical reality. If all energy was eternal and infinite, then our own unseen energy—thought, soul, mind, personality, whatever you wanted to call it—had to go somewhere. I was finding it increasingly difficult to believe this energy merely dissipated when the physical envelope decayed. And apparently a great many other people felt the same way. Was I rapidly being drawn into a groundswell of human realization? If Gerry represented the old, intellectual, rather cynically pragmatic approach to the meaning of life, it could be that that was why both of us found the relationship ultimately unsatisfying. I wanted to "be." He wanted to "do." I was beginning to think that each of us had only half the equation.

I wondered what other friends of mine would think of what I'd been reading and thinking. Anything of a spiritual nature would undoubtedly embarrass them, or make them laugh, given the kind of world we live in.

But the psychics I was reading about were all saying the same thing. Rudolf Steiner, Leadbetter, Cayce, and so many countless others—all claiming the fundamental existence of a Divine Will—an energy force from which everything else sprang. The same Divine Will was in all living things. We were part of it and it was part of us. The task was to find that divinity in ourselves and live by it.

And I wondered, if we indeed found life on other planets, would it too know what we knew, or would "they" have a clearer understanding? Science seemed virtually certain that there had to be life on other planets. The chances against its having developed were remote. And if there were, would that life have a different Divine Will or would it be the same? Was the energy force at the center of all the cosmos attending to life on other planets as well as life on our own?

The ancients said, "Study yourself, for in the self one may find the answers to all problems that may confront you. For the spirit of man, with all its attributes, physical and mental, is a portion of the whole great spirit. Hence the answers are all within the self. Your destiny and your karma depend on what your soul has done about what it has become aware of. And know that every soul will eventually meet itself. No problem can be run away from. Meet yourself now."

I thought that what the ancient seers said was no different from what modern psychologists said, or religions, or science, or Shakespeare for that matter. It was all the same: "Know yourself, have the courage to look, and it will set you free."

To know oneself perhaps it was necessary to simply be aware, to acknowledge one's own soul. To know the sum of the lifetimes that soul had experienced seemed outrageously impossible and maybe even irrelevant. But many people I knew did want this knowledge and moreover accepted the theory of re-embodiment as readily as they accepted the sun coming up each morning.

Eventually I was to learn that a very accomplished actor, and one with whom I had had wonderful professional experience and a warm personal relationship, was certainly one of these people—Peter Sellers. And an experience he lived through, which he confided to me, helped to confirm his belief to himself that his soul was in fact separate from his body.

I had made two pictures with Peter. One was called *Woman Times Seven,* in which he played a supporting role as one of my seven husbands, and the other was *Being There,* in which I played a supporting role to the most brilliant acting job of his entire career. Peter always *became* the characters he played, offscreen as well as on. In my opinion he was a genius, but he suffered personally from what he called a lack of knowledge of his own identity. He said he knew the characters he played better than he knew himself, that he felt he had *been* those characters at one time in a way that could only be described as "having lived them in the past."

One day toward the end of filming *Being There,* we talked about it. We had returned from location in Asheville, North Carolina, and were shooting some interiors on the Goldwyn lot in Hollywood. When I arrived on the lot that morning, I was struck with the feeling that something was wrong. I didn't know if it was because memories of the films I had made there flooded back to me—*Irma La Douce, Two for the Seesaw, Children's Hour,* and *The Apartment*—or whether something was actually going on that I'd learn about later.

Peter wasn't in great form that morning. Probably because he was tired, I thought. He was working ten hours a day with a pacemaker in his heart and he had never been a candidate for the marathon. We sat together in the back of a mock-up limousine waiting for the lighting to be set up.

Suddenly Peter clutched his chest and grabbed my arm. It wasn't a huge overt lunge or anything. Actually, it was very insignificant as far as anyone else could tell, but I knew something was really wrong. I casually called over the production manager and whispered to him to have a doctor stand by. He nodded and went away. Peter went on talking about acting and parts and how he felt he *knew* all the characters he had played. In fact, he was quite specific about feeling that he "*was* each of those characters at one time or another."

At first I didn't realize what I was hearing, but as he continued, I understood he was talking about having lived those characters in some of his own past-life incarnations.

"Oh," I said casually, "you mean you feel you are drawing on those experiences and feelings that you actually remember living in other lifetimes?" I was very matter-of-fact. "That's probably why you are so good at acting. You just have better past-life recall on a creative level than most people have."

His eyes lit up as though he had finally found somebody he could talk to, to share this belief of his.

"I don't go into this with many people, you know," he said, "or they'll think I'm bonkers."

"Yes," I said, "I know. Neither do I. But there are probably more cosmic closet believers than we are aware of."

He seemed to relax a bit.

"So what was that pain you just had?" I asked.

"Oh, just a touch of indigestion, I guess."

"Well maybe," I said, "but maybe it would be good to talk about it."

He didn't seem to want to go into it immediately. He fumbled and talked about food and what was right and wrong for him to eat and what it was like living with "this goddamn toy contraption I have in my heart."

I listened. I knew he still hadn't gotten to what he wanted to say.

"This sound stage gives me the creeps," he said.

"Why?"

"Because."

"Because why?"

He wiped perspiration from his forehead and took a deep breath.

"Because," he said, "this is the sound stage where I died."

I tried not to overreact. I remembered reading in the papers what an awful brush with death he had had.

"Rex Kennamer saved my life," he said, "and I saw him do it."

"No kidding," I said. "How?"

Like a person recounting a scene that had happened to somebody else, he said:

"Well, I felt myself leave my body. I just floated out of my physical form and I saw them cart my body away to the hospital. I went with it. I was curious. I wondered what was wrong with me. I wasn't frightened or anything like that because *I* was fine; and it was my body that was in trouble. Then I saw Dr. Kennamer come. And he felt my pulse and saw that I was dead. He and some other people pushed down and up on my chest. In fact, they pummeled the shit out of me . . . literally, I believe. They did everything but jump up and down on me to get my heart beating again. Then I saw Rex shout at somebody and say there was no time to prepare me for heart surgery. He commanded somebody to carve me open right there on the spot. Rex took my heart out of my body and massaged the hell out of it. Did everything but toss it up in the air. I was so curious watching him. He just refused to accept that I was dead. Then I looked around myself and I saw an incredibly beautiful bright loving white light above me. I wanted to go to that white light more than anything. I've never wanted anything more. I knew there was love, real love, on the other side of the light which was attracting me so much. It was kind and loving and I remember thinking, 'That's God.' I tried to elevate myself toward it as Rex was working on my heart. But somehow I couldn't quite make it. Then I saw a hand reach through the light. I tried to touch it, to grab onto it, to clasp it so it could sweep me up and pull me through it. Then I heard Rex say below me, 'It's beating again. I'm getting a heartbeat.' At the same moment a voice attached to the hand I wanted to touch so much said, 'It's not time. Go back and finish. It's not time.' The hand disappeared on the other side and I felt myself floating back into my body. I was bitterly disappointed. After that I don't remember anything until I regained consciousness back inside my body."

When Peter finished, I tried to continue to sound matter-of-fact. "Yes," I said, "I've read a lot of Elizabeth Kubler-Ross's stuff and she has so many documented accounts of so many people describing the same phenomenon when they were pronounced clinically dead. But apparently it wasn't time for them either, and they came back to tell about it."

Peter looked at me closely in that way he used to have of openly questioning whether he should go further. I tried not to press him but I didn't want him to stop talking about it either.

"You don't think I'm crazy?" he asked.

"No," I said, "of course not. I've heard about too many people describing the same phenomenon. They can't all be nuts. I think the important thing is to figure out what one comes back *for*." I said *"one"* instead of "you" because with Peter, if you pressed too hard on the personal stuff, you could lose him. As I have said, the identity of "Peter Sellers" completely eluded him. He had often said to reporters that he understood his characters to the core and many other mysteries of life besides, but Sellers? Nothing . . . he didn't have a clue.

Peter squirmed around in the mock-up.

"Are you all right?" I asked.

"Yes," he said, "but all of this . . . this set . . . that camera . . . these lights . . . this car . . . reminds me that I haven't yet understood just what you said. I don't know why I'm here! I don't know what I came back for this time! That's why I act like I do. I don't know. I can't figure out my purpose. What am I supposed to be doing?"

His eyes filled with tears. He began to whisper under his breath, "I know. I'm a pain in the ass to so many people. And I know they think I'm crazy. But I'm crazy about the right things. I'm not sure they are."

He wiped his eyes with the sleeve of his immaculate costume in the character of Chauncey Gardiner. He blinked and sniffed as Chauncey would have.

"I know I have lived many times before," he said, "and that experience confirmed it to me, because in *this* lifetime I felt what it was for my soul to actually be *out* of my body. But ever since I came back, I don't know why, I don't know what it is I'm supposed to do, or what I came back for."

He took another deep breath, a long agonized sigh—still maintaining the persona of Chauncey Gardiner.

A few minutes later the camera crew was ready. Hal Ashby, the director, walked onto the set and we went into the scene as though nothing had happened. We were shooting our first scene in the picture on the last day of filming. Life was an illusion . . . just like the movies.

    ✿ About a year and a half later, I was sitting with some friends in my apartment in Malibu. I had been traveling and didn't know that Peter had had another heart attack.

We were chatting amiably when suddenly I jumped up from my chair.

"Peter," I said. "Something has happened to Peter Sellers."

When I said it, I could feel his presence. It was as though he was right there in my living room watching me say it.

I felt ridiculous. Of course, all conversation stopped.

Then the telephone rang.

I disguised my voice and said hello. It was a newspaper reporter. "I'd like to speak to Miss MacLaine," he said. "Well, actually I wanted to get her reaction."

"To what?" I said.

"Oh," he said. "If you haven't heard, I'm sorry, but her friend Peter Sellers just died."

I turned in toward the room. I could feel Peter watching me. I wanted to tell the reporter he was mistaken. I wanted to say, "Yes, you probably *think* he's dead, but he's really only left his latest body." I wanted to say, "Listen, he did the best work of his life in our movie, and he did it portraying one of the gentlest, sweetest souls that ever walked this earth. There was nothing else left to accomplish, he probably couldn't figure out what else he was hanging around for, so he must have gone for the white light *.* . . and besides, he really missed his mother."

But of course, I didn't. Though Peter would have loved it . . .

Instead I said, "Shirley isn't in. But I'll give her the message."

I turned away from the phone.

"What happened?" asked my friends.

I could feel Peter smile.

"Nothing," I said. "Some reporter was trying to tell me that Peter Sellers just died."

Chapter 13

"Why should it be thought incredible that the same soul should inhabit in succession an indefinite number of mortal bodies ...? Even during this one life our bodies are perpetually changing, though by a process of decay and restoration which is so gradual that it escapes our notice. Every human being thus dwells successively in many bodies, even during one short life."

—FRANCIS BOWEN
"Christian Metempsychosis"

When I first got back to California from Sweden I had called Cat at The Ashram. I told her I had seen Ambres in Stockholm and that I wanted to talk with her. At the time I asked her to meet me for a mountain walk. In the undulating hills of Calabasas perhaps I could clear up my intentions. During our walk I told her about my experience with Ambres and that the whole thing was so puzzling that I had been writing about it to try to clear it up. Her blue eyes lit up like neon saucers and she clapped her hands.

"Great, Shirley!" she said. "Oh! That's great! You're going to write about being drawn into the spiritual dimension? You know, there are so many people who would love to read about what you're doing, and you know they're ready out there to read about this stuff. Really they are!"

This was going further than I had intended, but nevertheless I asked why she thought anyone would be interested.

"Because nothing else these days is working for them," she said. "So many sense that there is another way to lead their lives . . . and the spiritual path is about the only one they haven't tried."

We walked for a little while longer and then she said, "Would you like to have a great spiritual channeling in English? I know a very well-respected trance medium here in California. He's busy channeling all the time but he's coming down from Santa Barbara to channel for some of the guests here at The Ashram. Maybe he could work in a session with you."

"Oh, really?" I said, marveling once again at how Cat was a catalyst in my life. "Have you had a session with him?"

"Oh, Shirley," she said, seeming to spread her arms and her radiant energy all over the mountain tops. "Yes! And you will love his light, and you will love the spiritual entities that speak through him!"

Cat always talked in exclamation points and had such a sunny nature I couldn't imagine her *not* loving anyone, disembodied or otherwise.

"Sure," I said, getting into the spirit of the thing as it were, "that would be fun. What do you think would happen?"

"Oh," she said, "several entities come through as a rule, and it's just as though they're right in the room with you."

"And what do I do?"

"Just ask anything you want. They can tell you about your past lives, or help with physical diagnosis and pain, or with diets that are good for your vibrations— anything you want . . ."

"Well," I said, "after hearing about the creation of the world from Ambres I'd like to hear something a little more personal."

"Besides," Cat was striding merrily along, "you need a good spiritual rest."

I wondered how on earth Cat could translate channeling into being spiritually restful. Well, maybe for her it was . . .

❦ Three months and a mini-library of books later I felt the time had come for me to do some personal channeling investigation. Through Cat I made an appointment with Kevin Ryerson, resolving at the same time that I would try to be noncommittal, bland and several other things I am not . . .

My doorbell in Malibu rang at six-forty-five the following evening. I opened it not knowing what to expect. Looking at me under a slouched beige hat was a young man, about twenty-nine years old, with direct, kind, deep blue eyes. He was wearing a beige suit to match the hat, a beige vest, and beige shoes and beige socks. He wore an overcoat (also beige) slung over one shoulder and smiled directly into my face. His smile was innocent and gentle. Ironically, he didn't seem to be aware of his amusingly theatrical garb. Looking at him made me want a huge slice of beige coconut cream pie.

"Hello?" he said. "I'm Kevin?" His tone went up at the end of the sentence as though he had just asked me a question. "I'm Kevin Ryerson." He gave the impression of being a little uncertain, yet relaxed somewhere way underneath.

"Yes, Kevin." I opened the door and ushered him in. "Please come in and sit down."

I watched him closely as he walked through the door, unaware that his beige coat was dangling nearly off his shoulder. He moved smoothly, though with a slouch, planting his heels down first as he walked.

"May I leave my vehicle where it is outside?" he asked.

"Your vehicle?" I said. "Oh, you mean your car. Yes, sure. It doesn't matter."

"Thank you," he said. "My lady may drop in to meet me. I'd like her to be able to directly recognize it."

"Your lady?"

"Yes," he said, "we were just recently wed and we had planned a celebration dinner later tonight depending on the time periods we would be occupying?"

I hesitated a moment not knowing how to react to his use of the English language. It sounded so affected. Combined with the way he walked and the way he dressed, it made me wonder whether he could be taken seriously.

"Oh, sure," I said perfectly casually. "I don't know how long a session like this will take. You would very likely know better than I."

Kevin walked into my living room and sat down rather formally in one of my chairs.

"Yes," he said, "you direct your questions to the spiritual guides and they will determine the length of time required."

Kevin seemed strangely out of time, anachronistic. Or maybe I was just reading such an impression into his odd formality. Maybe that was what happened when you were with a trance medium.

I asked him if he would like a drink or a cup of coffee or something.

"No," he said, "alcohol inhibits my accuracy. But tea would be fine."

I fixed the tea, telling myself firmly not to confuse the message with the messenger.

"So, you've just recently gotten married?" I asked, making small talk and wanting to know what it was like to be living with a trance medium.

"Yes," he said, "I pretty well did in the bubble gum brigade before deciding to settle down."

I laughed out loud. He seemed to swing back and forth between the Knights of the Round Table and the rock generation.

"Hmm. And will you be having children do you think?" I asked.

"No," he said, "my lady and I would like to go out

and change the world, but we can't afford a babysitter."

I served Kevin the tea.

"Are you familiar with trance channeling?" he asked.

"Well, slightly," I answered. I told him about Ambres in Sweden and about other people who had described their experiences to me. I said I was familiar with the Edgar Cayce material. Kevin said modestly that he was an expert on Cayce and admired him very much. "A great soul," he said. "I have several Cayce books that are impossible to find. You're welcome to them."

We chatted on about Cayce and spiritual guidance and medical diagnosis through the phenomenon of trance channeling. We discussed Sir Oliver Lodge's research with the British Society for Psychical Research in England, and his experiments in contacting the soul of his dead son. We discussed the case of Mrs. Piper in Boston and how her information always checked out to be infallible.

Kevin talked in a relaxed way, appeared to be well read in metaphysical matters, articulate, and surprisingly humorous with his intelligent assessments of some of the circumstances he found himself in as a result of his psychic and metaphysical talents.

"I didn't know what was happening to me either when this all first started," he volunteered. "Spirit came through during one of my meditations. I didn't even know it. But someone ran and got a tape recorder and got the whole thing. When they played it back to me I freaked. I knew nothing about the medical information I had channeled through. I didn't know the voices that came through me either, and I certainly didn't make up the past-life information while fabricating a phony voice."

It was difficult for me to accept what he was saying at face value. Why should I believe that he couldn't or wouldn't fabricate strange voices and intricate stories about past lives? I thought of Ambres in Sweden. If I had understood or spoken Swedish I would have asked *him* more questions too. Well, I'll just keep listening, I thought. I folded my arms.

"I couldn't explain it in any rational way," Kevin

continued. "I just knew that I must be channeling spiritual guides. My sister can do the same thing. And it always freaked out our parents who just plain didn't understand any of it. Then I began to read about other people who found themselves capable of the same thing—even kids eight and nine years old, channeling through languages they didn't speak, and stuff like that. So I relaxed and just let it happen, and it's helped a lot of people."

I looked at Kevin, quietly sifting what he'd said through my mind, remembering all the other case histories I had read. He sipped his tea. He seemed so modest, so unpretentious, even though he was dressed as though he had come straight from Western Costume. I had always trusted what a friend of mine described as my built-in "bullshit detector"—that inbred sense of skepticism. But I decided against questioning him about his garb for fear of intimidating him.

I wondered what my ideal impression of a credible trance medium would be. Each individual was just that—an individual. What would a "typical" trance medium sound or look like? What would a "typical" psychiatrist or doctor or lawyer be like? Were there trance mediums who faked ninety percent of what they did, just as there were practitioners of other professions who made mistakes or were careless on "off" days or who really didn't give a damn *any* day of the week? Didn't one, in any case, have to judge pretty much by *results*? Was invisible reality something that could ever be proved?

And, for that matter, what *was* invisible reality? It was, quite simply, something one *believed* to be true. Praying to a deity called God was investing faith in an invisible reality: when a baseball player made the sign of the cross before stepping up to the plate, he was invoking a higher invisible reality; when a basketball player crossed himself before attempting a tie-breaking foul shot, no one in the bleachers laughed at him; there were supposed to be no atheists in foxholes, and the moving spectacle of loved ones praying to an invisible God in a hospital emergency room was all too familiar.

Millions of people spent every Sunday participating in the invisible reality of worshipping something they could not prove. None of this seemed to require skepticism in order to be credible. The invisible reality was accepted and had been for centuries. No one questioned it. In fact, faith in an invisible reality was what reverence was all about.

"Well," said Kevin finally, "whatever one thinks of channeling invisible spiritual guides, it is an individual decision. People usually just 'know' whether it feels reasonable or not. I don't try to convince anyone. I just try to understand it and learn as I go along. I feel quite guided by my spiritual friends and continue to develop my metaphysical talents. You'll have to make up your own mind."

I thought about what he said, wondering if my having a session with him actually constituted believing in what he was saying. Was it a way of asking to be convinced? I found myself analyzing my own "open-mindedness" in a new light. Was open-mindedness an act of gullibility? I sipped my tea.

"So, are you religious, Kevin?" I asked.

He choked involuntarily on his tea. "Are you kidding? What church would have me? I'm treading on their territory. I say folks have God inside them. The Church says it has God inside of *it*. There's a phrase in the Bible which states that one should never countenance spiritual entities other than God. Most Christians go by that. But then the Bible says nothing about reincarnation either and it's quite well known that the Council of Nicea voted to strike the teaching of reincarnation from the Bible."

"How do you know that?" I asked.

"Well, most serious metaphysical students of the Bible know that. The Council of Nicea altered many of the interpretations of the Bible. The man Jesus studied for eighteen years in India before he returned to Jerusalem. He was studying the teaching of Buddha and became an adept yogi himself. He obviously had complete control over his body and understood that the body was only the house for a soul. Each soul has many mansions. Christ taught that a person's behavior would determine future events—as karma, as the Hindus say. What one sows, so shall he reap."

I didn't question these rather sweeping assumptions. I offered Kevin a cookie. He seemed to like sugar. He ate it in two bites.

I thought about the similarity between the Cayce readings and Ambres and Buddha and the countless numbers of people who had been professing the same kind of belief.

"So," I said, "what's going to happen here?"

Kevin swallowed another cookie. "All right," he said, "right. Now . . . two, three, or maybe four spiritual entities use me to channel information. The first who usually comes through to greet people calls himself John. There are some of us who feel that he is the most highly evolved of all the disincarnate entities. He speaks in a biblical lingo that is sometimes hard to follow. If you prefer, or if John senses a difficulty in communication, another entity comes through. He calls himself Tom McPherson because his favorite incarnation was that of an Irish pickpocket a few hundred years ago. He can be very amusing. Lots of folks like working with him. Others find him too humorous to take seriously. Some folks prefer their spiritual guides to be solemn. Then there's Dr. Shangru, a Pakistani of a few hundred years ago, well-versed in medical matters, and Obidaya, whose favorite incarnation was that of a Jamaican who understands modern-day racial problems."

I felt my mind trying to turn off again. It sounded like a comic strip with a collection of unlikely characters. But wait a minute, I thought. This only bore out everything I had been reading. If these entities *are* entities from the "astral plane," then they would have individual personalities just as we in the body had.

"Wait a minute," I said. "Let me adjust. You say this Tom McPherson was an Irish pickpocket? Does that mean that was all he ever was?"

"No," said Kevin, "as I said before, it's just that his pickpocket personality was his favorite incarnation. He teaches from the vantage point of that lifetime."

"Oh," I said, "okay, why did he like being a pickpocket?"

"Ask him," Kevin replied. "But I think it's because of his sense of humor."

"Okay, so do you hear these entities when they speak through you?"

"No," he answered. "I am not aware of my conscious mind. But I can speak to them on the astral plane when I am sleeping if I want to. And I can feel them guiding me when I'm in a consciously aware state."

"Do you believe everyone has spiritual guides?" I asked.

Kevin looked surprised. "Why sure," he said, "that's what the soul does after it passes out of the body. Souls that have died, so to speak, help those who are still in the body. Why, that's what spiritual understanding is all about."

"What *is* what spiritual understanding is all about?"

Kevin sat up in his chair and leaned toward me. "Haven't you ever had the feeling that you were being guided to do something by a force you didn't understand?"

I thought of all the times in my life when I thought I was listening to my intuition which seemed to almost compel me to make a certain decision or meet a person or go to a place. I thought of my experiences in Africa with a force that seemed to protect me when I traveled alone, or the time in Bhutan in the Himalayas when I felt impelled to inquire and investigate what the lamas were doing as they sat meditating in their monasteries 18,000 feet high above the clouds. I had seemed to recognize some similar force way back then, nearly twenty-five years ago. That force had motivated my curiosity and my drive to question what I couldn't see.

"Yes," I said now to Kevin. "I must admit I've felt guided by some kind of force throughout my life. What does that mean?"

"It means," said Kevin, "that, along with your own intuitive certainty, you were being guided by your spiritual friends and guides and teachers. You might have defined it simply as a force but now I'm suggesting that you become more aware in your understanding of what was really going on."

I stood up. "What does it feel like to know that spiritual entities speak through you?"

"Sometimes," he said hesitatingly, "sometimes I'd like to be a gardener instead of the custodian of the garden. But maybe that's my karma. We all have our roles in life, don't we? Maybe mine is to be a human telephone."

Kevin suddenly looked so vulnerable sitting in his upright position with his tea cup balanced on his beige knee. I wondered what his life was like, what he did on Saturday nights, how he felt about politics. Had others who had gone through their spiritual questioning also gone through the same *personalization* of what they learned?

I didn't realize it then but Kevin Ryerson would come to be one of the telephones in my life. And, on this Friday night in Malibu, I was about to talk to some new friends... *Real or not, I once again was reminded that each person experiences his own reality,* and no one else can be the judge of what that reality really is. But it wasn't simply a matter of believing what one wanted to believe. It was more a question of taking care to refrain from being so skeptical that one automatically shut out challenging ideas and new perceptions.

Chapter 14

*"Every new-born being indeed comes fresh and blithe
into the new existence, and enjoys it as a free gift:
but ... its fresh existence is paid for by ... a worn-
out existence which had perished, but which con-
tained the indestructible seed out of which this new
existence has arisen: they are one being. To show the
bridge between the two would certainly be the solution of a great riddle."*

—ARTHUR SCHOPENHAUER
The World as Will and Idea

I lowered the lights in my living room. The ocean
tumbled gently outside. I put the tape recorder on, and
asked Kevin if he needed anything.

"No," he answered, "I think I'll be going out now."

"Okay," I said, "I'll be here."

"Right," said Kevin. "See you in a while then."

He leaned back, placed his hands over his chest
and crossed them. He closed his eyes. I moved the tape
recorder closer to him. Slowly he began to breathe
deeply. I waited. He sat still for about three minutes
and breathed even more deeply. Then very gently his
head toppled forward onto his chest and a catch spluttered
slightly in his throat. His head straightened up and
cocked to one side. About thirty more seconds elapsed.
Then he opened his mouth and his body shuddered.

His breathing changed rhythm. Slowly his mouth transposed into a smooth smile. His eyebrows lifted, giving his facial expression one of momentary surprise. His hands moved to the arm rests. In a raspy whisper which didn't sound in Kevin's vocal range, I heard,

"Hail. I'm John. Greetings. Please identify yourself and state purpose of gathering."

I cleared my throat and shifted onto the floor next to Kevin's chair.

"Yes," I began, "my name is Shirley MacLaine. I am from Richmond, Virginia, in the United States, but I am speaking to you from Malibu, California. I am a performer who also writes, and I can't really say why I'm here."

"As such," said the Voice.

As such . . . I guessed that meant okay. I remembered Kevin had said one of the spiritual entities spoke in a biblical lingo.

"We are taken to find ye have investigations. We sense your vibrational condition as such and have familiarity with it."

There was a pause as though he was waiting for me to ask a question or say something. I didn't know where to begin.

"Yes," I said, "well, could you tell me please who 'we' might be?"

"As such," he said, "we are those who have known ye in lives past."

He startled me.

"You people have known me in past lives?"

"As such."

"Are you my spiritual guides then? Is that why I am here?"

"As such."

"Oh, I see," I said inaccurately. He went on.

"To understand yourself now you must understand that you are more than what you seem now. The sum of your talents, the sum of your feelings, are those which ye have experienced before . . . and all that ye are is part of the oneness of all. Is that to your understanding?"

I squirmed around on my carpet. Didn't everyone

have certain talents, feelings, and thoughts which did not correspond to present life experience? "Excuse me," I said, "on what do you base your information either about me or anything cosmic?"

With barely a pause he said, "On that which ye would term the Akashic Records." He stopped as though I should be thoroughly acquainted with his references. He seemed so distant, so pseudo-Biblical. I felt detached.

"Ye are taken to find that Akasha is that which ye might term the collective unconscious of mankind, stored in ethereal energy. This energy could be termed as the mind of God. Ye are taken to find that communication of said ideas is difficult given the limited dimension of language."

"Yes," I said, "I can see what you mean. And while we're at it, why do you speak the way you do?"

There was a pause. Then he said, "I will endeavor to bring my language more up to date, as you would term it." He went on immediately, "This stored energy called the Akashic Records is as vast scrolls housed in vast libraries. You, as an individual, would be thought of as a single scroll within the libraries, or as a single soul within the mind of God."

"Excuse me," I said. "Isn't what you are saying just a little too simple?"

"All truth is not so much simple as it is designed to be easily revealed."

"Well, if it's so easily revealed, why don't we know it?" I asked.

"Man refuses to accept that he is in possession of all truth and has been from the beginning of time and space. Man refuses to accept responsibility for himself. Man is the co-creator with God of the cosmos."

No, I thought, in the church we are taught that *God* created everything.

But "John" was plowing on.

"Only when man accepts that he is part of the truth he is seeking, are the truths themselves apparent."

"So you're saying that if I understand myself and where I come from, I will understand everything?"

"Correct," he said.

"Well," I said, "I've never really been sure there is such a thing as God until maybe lately. With what's going on in the world, why should anyone believe in God?"

"You are saying," he asked, "that you need proof of your own existence?"

"Well, I don't know what you mean. No, I'm sure I exist. Yes."

"You have a mind?"

"Of course."

"The mind is a reflection of the soul. The soul is a reflection of God. The soul and God are eternal and unto each other."

"So you mean if I'm to understand what this God thing is, I must know myself?"

"Correct," he said, "your soul is a metaphor for God."

"Huh? Wait a minute," I said. "I can't prove either one—soul or God. I don't mean to be disrespectful, but that's a tricky way of confirming that there's a soul."

"Tricks," he said, "are a game of mankind, not of God."

I felt strangely embarrassed.

"Well, I could become very arrogant if I really believed *I* was a metaphor for God."

"Never," he said, "never confuse the path you take with the truth itself."

I felt slightly shamed. I waited for him to say something else.

"Pause," he said, "another entity is desiring to speak."

"What?"

Kevin shifted his position in his chair. His arms rearranged themselves. His head swiveled to the other side. He covered his face for a moment and then crossed one leg over the other.

I got up on my knees trying to understand what was going on.

"Tip o' the hat to ya," said a completely new voice. "McPherson here. Tom McPherson. How are you doing out there?"

The accent was funny. I laughed out loud. Kevin cocked his head as though *he* wasn't really doing it. The expression on his face made me feel he wondered why I found him so funny.

"My, my," said the McPherson voice. "I didn't expect a reaction like that quite so soon. It usually takes me a while to work up to that."

Kevin had said this McPherson character was amusing. I felt as though I could *feel* his personality coming through. It wasn't just the sound of the voice, it was almost the presence of a distinct new energy in the room. It was remarkable how he seemed so separate from Kevin. Being an actress, I had to hand it to Kevin. If he was acting, it was a superb transition.

"Is your whirring box going?" said McPherson.

"My what?"

"Your whirring box."

I looked down at my tape recorder.

"Oh that," I said. "Yes. Is it all right?"

"Oh, yes," he said, "of course. I just wanted to make certain you captured the details."

"The details?"

"Quite right," he said.

Kevin coughed. He cleared his throat and coughed again.

"Excuse me," I said, "but what's wrong with Kevin's throat?"

"Oh, nothing," said McPherson. "I'm just having a little difficulty adjusting to the vibrations of the instrument."

"Oh. You mean you try to adjust your energy vibrations with Kevin's energy vibrations?"

"Yes. Quite right. Over here we work with vibrational frequencies. Do you have any of your brew about?"

"My brew?"

"Yes, I believe there is an herbal brew about?"

"Oh, you mean tea?"

"Quite right."

"Why yes," I said. "Would you like some?"

"Very good."

"The cup is very small. Shall I put it in Kevin's hand? Will he be able to handle it?"

"Oh, yes," said McPherson.

I filled the cup and held it in front of Kevin. He made no move to lift his hand. His eyes remained closed.

"Just place it in the young man's hand. Thank you."

I lifted Kevin's right hand and slipped the cup into his palm.

"The cup is not so much small as it is tiny," said McPherson.

I laughed. I didn't like these little cups myself.

"Have you a mug about?" asked McPherson. "I believe you have glass mugs in your cupboard?"

I looked over to my kitchen. He was right. I did have glass mugs. Only I never served tea in them.

"I'm partial to mugs," said McPherson. "A bit of the old pub feeling. Helps me to think clearly."

I climbed from my knees, walked into the kitchen, and fetched the mug. I continued talking to McPherson as I went.

"So you really are an Irishman? Do all Irishmen think better with mugs?"

"Quite right," said McPherson to my back.

I returned and poured more tea into the mug and exchanged the cup.

"Well, it's not like the pub, but anyway," said McPherson.

Kevin raised the mug to his mouth and took a sip. His eyes were still closed. He swallowed the tea.

"Can you actually taste the tea?" I asked.

"Well, I sense it more than I taste it. I use the instrument's oral faculties to gain a sense of it."

He took another sip.

"If it was too hot, would you feel it or would Kevin feel it?" I asked.

"I would react to protect the instrument," said McPherson. "I wouldn't feel the pain, but there would be empathy on my part, yes."

"And if it was really hot, what would you do?" I asked.

"Probably use a better command of the instrument's system to deaden the pain."

There was a silence. I could feel McPherson waiting for me.

"May I call you Tom?" I asked.

"Very good."

"I hear you were a pickpocket," I said.

"Quite right. Although pickpocketing was more what you would term my 'cover trade.'"

"Your cover trade?"

"Quite right. Actually I was what you would term a diplomatic spy."

"A diplomatic spy? For whom?"

"For the English Crown, I'm sorry to say."

"You were a spy for England and you're Irish?"

"Quite right. I was Irish even though the name McPherson is Scottish. I took the name of McPherson to disguise my Irish identity as there was deeper prejudice against the Irish than the Scots in those days. Hasn't changed much either."

"Well, why were you spying for the English if they were so prejudiced against your people?"

"I like to think of myself as a freelance spy. The Crown simply hired me to lift important papers from Spanish diplomats. I was very good at that sort of thing. Therefore I call myself a pickpocket. It is more humorous for me."

I sipped some tea, trying to make heads out of tails and not getting very far.

"So, now you ply your trade more positively to help others down here, do you?"

"Quite right. Balance and karma and all that."

"Didn't you get points against you for being a pickpocket—diplomatic or otherwise?"

"Quite right. I am working off some of my karma now by being of service to you."

"I see." I was alternately amused and skeptical

"Have you any more of your brew about?" asked Tom.

"Yes, certainly." I poured another mug of hot tea.

"Did you wish to make any other inquiries?" Tom asked.

Now I poured some tea for myself, considering what would be a productive line of approach.

"I was discussing the existence of the soul with someone the other night," I said, "using déjà vu as an example of previous existence. You know, when you feel you're in a place where you've been before but know you can't have been? Or you have that back-of-the-head feeling about an experience that it has all happened before?"

"Quite right."

"Well, some people were saying that cellular memory or ancestral memory (like some of the scientists are also saying) was really the explanation. They believed that we just inherit genetically the memory of things our ancestors might have experienced. Now, how would *you* debate the issue of the existence of the soul?"

There was a moment of silence.

"How would *you* do it?" he said, "now that you have had time to reflect?"

"Well, I guess I should have said that there are cases of people—say, in tribal societies in Africa—whose ancestors have never moved out of their environment. Yet they have memories of North America, India, etc."

"My goodness," said Tom, "that *is* a good argument. Then of course you also have heard of your telepathy and mind-out-of-body experiences. Many people in your time have spoken publicly of out-of-body experiences. They were actually experiencing their souls as separate from the physical envelope."

I remembered how many people indeed had described this experience when going through a close brush with death. Most described the same white light as Peter Sellers had, drawing them with a compelling sense of love and peace, while looking down at their own dying body. Some did not want to return to the body. Many such experiences have been recorded in

Life After Life by Dr. Raymond Moody. In my own acquaintance were a surprising number who had reported having the experience.

"And," Tom was continuing, "as for déjà vu being simply a form of cellular memory, there are many individuals who have had memory patterns of places their ancestors had never been."

"Yeah," I said, "that's what I said. But maybe some of *his* ancestors had been to Africa—like the Romans, for instance—and their cellular memory recorded their reactions and the offspring inherited those cellular memories."

"Possibly," said Tom, "except for one thing. Déjà vu also occurs in the modern context. For example, you may have déjà vu when you walk into a house that's only a few years old. That's hardly inherited cellular memory."

"What is it, then?"

"That is the result of the soul astrally projecting to the new house. Something like your experience in what you call the floating dream that you loved so much. You remember that experience?"

He stopped me in my tracks. I had never mentioned that to anyone.

"My goodness," I said, "how did you know that?"

"Oh, a bit of the old spiritual voo-doo, so to speak."

I needed a moment to adjust to what had just happened. Could this have been a predictable guess? Did he tell this to everyone he channeled for? I choked back a cough.

"Just give me a moment," I said.

"Quite right," he said, "one thing we have plenty of is time."

I felt confounded. Could it be that certain dreams were astral projections of the soul?

"Have you any more inquiries?" McPherson asked.

I collected myself.

"Well," I said, "why is there such resistance to the study of the soul as a realistic fact? Why isn't as much time and money spent on researching the existence of the soul as there is on splitting the atom or nuclear energy?"

"Well, for one thing," he answered, "the material isn't available. The soul is not a material thing. Also the field of soul study has a tendency to have scorn and ridicule heaped upon it and professional reputations go down the tubes, so to speak, very easily."

"But *why* is it so scorned?"

"Because it is considered to be a ludicrous waste of time. Superstition and the like. Serious people who admit to such investigations are sometimes made to feel ridiculous. But as a friend of yours said recently, 'To get to the fruit on the tree one must go out on a limb.'"

I was silent—floored. He had used the same analogy as Gerry. I had been most careful never to even mention Gerry to anyone, much less what he said.

McPherson went on. "You must be patient with your Gerry. We are being patient with you."

I was struck dumb. How the hell could this guy know about us? He not only knew about Gerry, he knew what Gerry had said.

"Do we have a revelation here?" asked Tom.

"Oh God," I said.

"Quite right," he responded cheerfully.

I sipped more tea and tried to sort myself out. A few moments passed.

"Would you like to continue?" said Tom.

Jesus, I thought, this stuff could be real. There were so many questions I had to ask. "Okay," I said under my breath. Then, "Okay. Tell me, why is there such a gap between science and the Church?"

"Well," said Tom, "because science just lately (in cosmic terms, of course) feels it has rid itself of the shackles of religious superstition and is now enjoying its freedom and golden age. The attitude is understandable. To research those domains of the Church which was its former jailer would only rebuild the power base of that old traditional persecutor."

"Is the soul under the dominion only of the Church?"

"Quite right. That is, it is considered so in the

orthodox sense, yes. Actually, one's soul is, um, a highly personal matter, in a manner of speaking."

"But would proof of the soul's existence radically alter the attitude of science?"

"Yes, of course. But quite honestly, science feels there is no basis on which to inquire about the existence of the soul. Also, there isn't much money in that kind of research."

"You mean, if you research electricity you can turn it into an electric light? Or, if you research the atom you can turn it into a bomb?"

"Quite right."

"But if you research the soul there is no material profit in it?"

"Quite right. Could I have a bit more of your brew?"

I poured more tea. It was almost gone.

"So," I asked, "are there research groups who solely devote themselves to the soul?"

"You turned a nice one there," he said.

"I turned a nice one where?"

"*Solely* for the soul? Very good."

"Are you aware," I asked seriously, "that you are performing for me right now?"

"Quite frankly," he said, "I believe I am sensationally entertaining at all times. This is my natural nature. There's another: 'natural nature.'"

"You're quite a punster, aren't you?"

"No," he said. "I don't feel I'm being, so to speak, overly campy. No, it's all a natural extension of my personality."

I sat quietly for a while considering this outrageous tea party we were having. I wondered if I was so gullible I was swallowing a whale. The tape recorder whirred in the silence.

"Well," I said.

"Quite right," said Tom.

"Well, I'd really like to know something more about my past lives. Would that be all right?"

"Very good," said Tom. "Has the instrument any alcohol in his system?"

"No," I said. "He said it inhibited trance channeling, so I don't think so."

"Very good then. One moment please. Would you remove the mug please?"

I got up, took the mug from Kevin's grasp, checked my tape recorder, and settled down again. ↯

Chapter 15

"In view of the endless duration of the immortal soul throughout the infinity of time . . . shall the soul remain forever attached to this point of world-space, our earth? Will it never participate in a closer contemplation of the remaining wonders of creation? Who knows but that the intention is for it to become acquainted at close range, some day, with those far distant globes of the cosmic system . . . which from this distance already provoke our curiosity?"

—IMMANUEL KANT
General History of Nature

A shudder went through Kevin. His head moved around until once again he had assumed the character of John.

"Hail," said the John voice. "You have inquiries as to your past lives?"

"Yes," I answered.

The telephone rang.

John reacted and cocked his head.

I waited.

I could feel John "adjust his vibrations," as McPherson had said. The telephone rang again. Again, I didn't answer.

"You will find," said John, "that to understand the soul within yourself today, you must also understand something of the previous civilizations you have known."

"Really?" I said inanely, feeling sort of ridiculous and nonplussed.

"Indeed," said John, "you were incarnate several times during the five-hundred-thousand-year period of the most highly evolved civilization ever known to man. It was what the Bible symbolized as the Garden of Eden. I would like you now to understand one very important concept. The level of achievement in any civilization is judged by its spiritual evolvement. Technological advancement is important and attractive, but if it detains, detracts, or deters spiritual understanding, it bears the seeds of its own destruction. You are bearing witness to such a simple truth in your present civilization on Earth today. Your spiritual understanding is lagging at great lengths behind your technological knowledge and as a result, you are witnessing progressive insanity, depression, confusion of purpose, and total human inequality and despair."

"So where is the hope for us then? I mean, if we're going backward instead of forward, why are we living?"

"A good and important question," said John, "which brings us to the subject of karma yet again, and makes it necessary for you to grasp your basic identity and the understanding of the power of your free will to understand your divinity and partnership with God."

"Excuse me," I said, "but can I ask where religion fits into all this, please?"

"There is much that I am saying that your worldly religions would take exception to. Your religions teach religion—not spirituality. Religion has exploited man for the most part. Your world religions are on the right track basically, but they do *not* teach that every individual is fundamentally the creator and controller of his own destiny. They teach that *God* assumes such a role. What I am endeavoring to explain is that each individual is a co-creator with God. This does not sit well with your churches and religions because they prefer to have control over mankind, rather than help teach that mankind can only control itself through self-knowledge and through knowledge of its *past* and of its purpose in the present and future."

I was aware of how explosive such a concept would be. But didn't many people within the Church pursue self-knowledge? Weren't there many people who, while following the precepts of the Church, still searched restlessly for truth beyond precepts?

I looked out the window across the dark ocean. A fishing boat blinked its light in the darkness. I wondered how many of the great truths in life one might never be able to see or prove or confirm. It was unsettling and anxiety-arousing. Was the truth only truth when we could "prove" it? I couldn't cope with what I was thinking. I looked away from the window and back to Kevin and the "disembodied spiritual entity" he was channeling.

"So," I said anxiously, and finding myself slightly breathless, "so I lived way back in some ancient civilization?"

"Yes, several times," said John. "Twice as a male and once as a female."

I was quiet as one of the finer points of reincarnation hit home again. "Have we all experienced living as different sexes in order to be able to empathize with the opposite sex?"

"That is correct," said John. "Certainly. How else could mankind reach an understanding of itself and its identities without such diversified physical experiences?"

I leaned forward again. "Could that be a metaphysical explanation for homosexuality?" I asked. "I mean, maybe a soul makes a rocky transition from a female to a male body, for instance, and there is left over emotional residue and attraction from the previous incarnation?"

"As such," said John. "The sexual preference of such individuals plays an important part in the requirement for understanding that we are all basically the same because we have all experienced being both sexes; our souls, if you will, are basically androgynous."

"Androgynous?" I asked.

"Yes, high spiritual understanding knows no sexuali-

ty differences because the elements of both sexes are
simultaneously present. The polarities are evenly opposed.
Your ancient prophets and Christ figures such as Jesus
and Buddha, et cetera, were not so much celibate as
they were vibrating at an even and perfectly balanced
frequency. Their yin and yang were so evenly distribut-
ed that sexuality was of no interest to them because
there was no conflict and therefore no tension. It was
not a subject they needed to sublimate or repress. It
simply didn't interest them because of their peaceful
spiritual level of achievement."

"I'm not sure I'd be ready to trade."

John paused a moment. "We don't recommend the
abstaining of sex," he said. "Definitely not. Sex in
human terms is also a pathway to God if it is enjoyed
spiritually as well as physically."

I looked at the tape recorder. "Excuse me," I said,
"are we getting off the subject?"

"Yes," said John. "But sex is a fascinating subject,
even for me."

I laughed. "And who are you?" I asked. "I mean,
were you once in a physical body?"

"Oh yes," said John. "I have embodied many times
as both male and female but recently have remained in
astral form."

"I see," I said. I was curious but I really wanted to
know about myself.

"So, who was I in my previous lives?"

"According to the Akashic Records, you were incarnate with a twin soul."

"Oh? What exactly is a twin soul?"

"That question takes a great deal of explanation
which I will endeavor to accomplish later. For now, let
me begin by explaining *soul mates*."

"Soul mates?" I asked. I had heard the term from
time to time, usually in reference to people who said
they had found their other half.

"Soul mates," John continued, "were actually created for one another at the beginning of time, or what
you call at the moment of the Big Bang. They vibrate at
exactly the same electromagnetic frequency because

they are identical counterparts of one another. Twin
souls are more common to find because they have
experienced many lifetimes together in one form or
another. But *soul mates* were actually created at the
beginning of time as pairs who belonged together . . . So
you see, there is more to your Big Bang theory than you
imagine . . . and quite romantic at that, wouldn't you say?"

I made some noncommittal noise.

"So let me begin there," said John, "where, as I
said, we knew each other."

"Oh?"

"Yes, we were teacher and pupil. You were one of
my brightest, and what you would term today, 'pet
students.' "

I looked around my living room wishing I had
someone to share this with. "So we knew each other?"

"Correct. It is no accident that you are here today.
We believe you have matured to the understanding that
there is no such thing as an accident?"

"Who's 'we' again?" I asked.

"Your spiritual guides, of whom I am one," said
John.

"You mean, I was drawn here somehow by you and
these guides?"

"That is correct," said John.

"How?"

"By your own need to explain your behavior and
your questions and your search for the truth and by
psychic guidance from those of us who feel you are
ready for more of your own truth."

"Is that what is meant by Spiritual Guidance?"

"That is correct."

There was a pause as John the Voice seemed to be
gathering his thoughts, or some kind of information, or
both. Quite casually the Voice resumed and said:

"We have isolated your vibration during one of the
lifetimes that you spent with an entity with whom you
are also now involved. We believe this entity is living in
your British Isles. Would that be correct?"

"Gerry?" I said with a rather high-pitched squeak.
"Are you talking about Gerry?"

"As such. We have also isolated his vibration and find that the two of you were man and wife during one of your previous lifetimes."

"Oh, my God," I said, amused and flabbergasted. "Did we get along then? I mean, was communication better between us then than it is now?"

There was another pause.

"Your Gerry was equally devoted to his work then. And we must admit it was to the detriment of your union. However, he was doing important work involving cultural exchanges with the extraterrestrials who were endeavoring to be of help technologically and spiritually."

"*Extraterrestrials?*" John seemed to sense my astonishment. He replied more firmly than usual.

"As such. There were extraterrestrials visiting this planet then, as now."

"Oh, Jesus." I took a breath. "Well, could you tell me more about that? I mean, what are you really saying? Are you saying that we have had outer space visitations since the beginning of time?"

"That is correct. There are planets more advanced in knowledge than your Earth, just as your Earth is more advanced than some other planets."

I deliberately relaxed myself and breathed deeply. I supposed the logic of what he was saying held together in its own terms. But I wished I knew what questions to ask.

"Well," I said, floundering around in my own head. Maybe this was all an act, but what if it wasn't? I didn't want to waste an opportunity to learn something. "Well," I said again, "what kind of knowledge were these extraterrestrials bringing?"

John answered immediately. "The only important knowledge is the spiritual knowledge of God within man. Every other knowledge flows from that."

"*Every* other knowledge?"

"That is correct. Your scientific knowledge, for example, depends on your understanding of vibrational frequencies and how they pertain to the universe. God is love—which is the highest vibrational frequency of all. In your physical world light is the highest and fastest speed frequency. But to beings who have more knowledge, more control, *thought* has a much higher frequency than light. Thought is part of God, just as thought is part of man. Therefore, when *thought is love* your frequencies are vibrating at the highest level of energy. That is what the extraterrestrials were teaching just as you of the Earth plane will someday teach it to others. Is this to your understanding?"

I didn't know how to answer.

I cleared my throat and tried to stretch my mind to understand. I couldn't personally relate to what John was saying in any specific or detailed and understandable way. The implications of what he was saying were so stunning that I couldn't really think of a good question. I wanted to get back to myself. *That* I could cope with.

"Excuse me, please," I said. "Could I just ask you about me? I'm having enough trouble just relating to that."

"Of course," said John. "You must proceed at your own pace."

"Okay," I said, relieved. "Thank you. So Gerry and I were man and wife. Does that mean we were twin souls?"

"No. But you were and are a twin soul of the entity you call David."

I stopped him. "You know about David, too?"

"That is correct. You had several lifetimes with the David entity during that early period, as well as many others down through the march of time."

Maybe that was why I felt so comfortable with David now.

But John was continuing. "Your David is a good teacher and you can trust him. But we feel that you already feel that. You must learn to trust your feelings more and refrain from approaching so many issues in life from strictly an intellectual perspective. Intellect as a marvel is limited. Feelings are limitless. Trust your heart . . . or your intuition, as you term it."

Trust my intuition? Yes, I could see that as I thought back on my life I could fairly say that whenever

I went against my intuition I got in trouble. "You're saying that if we all follow what is in our hearts we'll be fine?"

"No. Not necessarily. There are wrong, or hurtful, feelings to be overcome. But mankind, and all life, is basically good. You must learn to give it a chance. Life represents the thought of God and God is love."

Frankly, all this talk of "God" was embarrassing me. "Okay," I said, "but what do you call God?"

"God, or the God Force, of which all things are a part," said John, "is the Divine Energy that created the Universe and holds it together harmoniously."

"You would describe what's going on here as harmonious?"

"In the ultimate scheme of life, yes, it is harmonious in the sense that matters are balancing out. But you must understand the process of each soul's progress and reembodiment and purification to understand the harmony."

"Wait a minute," I said. "Isn't the Bible supposed to be the Word of God?"

"Yes, in the main it is. Although much of what exists in your Bible today has been reinterpreted."

"Reinterpreted by whom?"

"By various persons through time and through various languages. Ultimately, by the Church. It was to the advantage of the Church to 'protect the people' from the real truth."

"The real truth being what?"

"The real truth being the process of each soul's progression through the ages. The real truth being each soul's responsibility for its own behavior in the realization of its own divinity."

"You mean reincarnation?"

"That is correct. That is the word you use to term it. That is the carrying out of Cosmic Justice toward an ultimate harmony."

"Well, would the Church deny us that truth?"

"Yes, because such a truth would make the power and the authority of the Church unnecessary. Each person, that is, each entity, becomes responsible to itself for its conduct. It does not need a church. It does not need rituals, and stratifications, and cubbyholes to crawl into to get absolution issued by the Church. Let us say simply that the authorities in the Church desired to 'shelter' mankind from a truth they felt you were not prepared for."

"You mean in somewhat the same spirit that governments act today?"

"As such."

I stretched out on my carpet. I didn't know what to think, nor could I think of any more questions. Kevin sat impassively in the chair. The tea on the table was cold.

"Will there be any more inquiries then?" asked John.

I looked out at the blinking lights of the fishing boat.

I thought of some of the people I had talked to who found me naive and gullible for even considering the believability of disembodied spiritual masters speaking through a medium. How could I fall for such stuff, they said. I had always replied that I felt I was simply learning. I wasn't sure what it meant really but it somehow confirmed to me that there were more dimensions to the reality of life than one understood—in somewhat the same way that the dimensions of our own personalities and characters were a mystery to us until we began to explore those aspects which we were not familiar with and certainly were not aware of because we couldn't "see" them.

But why did *I* feel more comfortable than some others in allowing myself to explore dimensions of unprovable possibilities? I really didn't know. It just felt all right. That's all I could say. It didn't threaten me. It didn't upset my emotional investment in what I was already sure was real: it did not seem to destroy my image of myself. This whole exploration simply seemed to be expanding what my perceptions of reality already were. So I wondered, then, why some of my friends, and Gerry in particular, found this pursuit of a new knowledge along spiritual paths, through mediums and

reincarnation, so threatening in terms of my credibility.
Why were they so worried for me? Out of love and
protectiveness certainly. They didn't want to see me
ridiculed—any more than I did. But it was more than
that. They were also threatened themselves. Why?
Why *not* ask questions seriously and delve into areas
and possibilities that were not necessarily "provable"?
What "real" harm could it do? Would it shatter the
conditioned images they had of themselves? Would it
confuse their own views of "reality"?

I turned over onto my knees.

"John," I said, "why do so many people find this
phenomenon of trance channeling a disembodied master such as yourself through a human instrument so
unacceptable?"

There was a slight pause.

"Because," he said, "they do not remember the
experience of having been disembodied themselves.
People think that life is the totality of everything they
see. They believe that man himself is simply a body and
a brain. But personality is more."

"How do you mean?"

"Personality is the intangible aspect of consciousness which is only lodged in the body for a brief period
of cosmic time."

"But they don't believe that concept is real."

"Real?" asked John. "Is a thought not real? Yet how
does one scientifically prove that? Thought is energy.
Those who question the physical existence of a thought,
or of thought energy, question with deep skepticism
their own identities."

"Yes, but aren't questions good? I mean, absolute
certainty in something creates egomania and corruptive
power."

"That is correct. But it is worrisome when skepticism becomes so profound and demoralizing that it
restricts the potential of learning glorious truths which
would be in their favor."

"But how can I convey to them that being open-
minded is actually wise?"

"You do not have to do that. You who *are* open-minded simply say what *is* from your point of view. Give the skeptics the freedom to be skeptical. If you did not I would accuse you of being an enslaver. Give them the privilege of continuing their doubt. There will come a time when they too will want to know and they will be drawn to dimensions which are more true. They will seek a greater counsel when they are ready. If people insist upon remaining within their "logical" belief systems they are safe within their own perceived reality, and thus are safe within the position of power they hold, whatever that power might be. They will not change their perceptions and thus be required to change themselves or grow into an expanded awareness of themselves."

"But what about the security of one's ego?" I asked.

"Most people are suffering from *altered* egos. Altered by society, by the Church, and by education. Their true egos know the truth. I am as believable as anyone else. You cannot see me but there are many aspects of yourself that you cannot see either. People are searching for these aspects in themselves every day. But while they search they require that their worlds remain secure. To believe I am as real as they would be to deter them from their comfort zones—the zones they understand and can control. When you begin to understand more you are essentially understanding that there is so much more to understand that is beyond your grasp."

"No, but that isn't what people say to me. What they tell me is that the whole theory of reincarnation is too *tidy*. They say it is too simple-minded to be real."

"As I have said before to you: the truth *is* simple. It is man who insists on making it complicated. And man cannot just *learn* the truth as one would learn a lesson. He must *experience* aspects of it in himself in order to go further. Learning and experiencing the truth of itself is a struggle. A struggle toward simple awareness. You must remember that the natural habitat of the human is not Earth; the natural habitat of human beings is the ether. Each individual already knows the Divine truth. They have simply complicated it and forgotten that they know it."

"But my intellectual friends say that believing one knows *the* truth is the ultimate act of arrogance."

"Each person knows his own truth. That is correct. But the only truth that matters is the truth of the relationship that one has with the source, or the God force. And *that* truth is limited when intellectual skepticism is applied to it. Because one does not need intellect to know God. In that respect, all individuals are equal. Your intellectuals seek to separate themselves from the masses in order to feel elite. They rely more on their intellect than they do on the God force within themselves. Many people, and not only intellectuals, are embarrassed to acknowledge the spark of Divinity within themselves. But the intellectual skeptics are more likely to be conflicted, confused and unhappy within themselves. All people seek peace. The path to inner peace is not through the intellect but through the inner heart. Within the inner heart one finds God, peace, and oneself. Intellectual skeptics avoid themselves. The *self*, however, knows the Divine truth because the self is itself Divine. Is this to your understanding?"

I sat up feeling that, yes, I did understand. None of this felt religious either. It just made sense. And I could not understand why some others I knew had to make such a big deal of it—either couldn't understand or didn't want to.

"Why are there wars, John? What causes people to want to conquer others?"

"Because those who feel the need to conquer do not understand the truth of themselves. However, if a closed-minded tyrant is exposed to inner knowingness, inner awareness, he soon loses the intent of his conquest. He sees how vast *he* really is and does not need to secure his own immortality by conquering others. When the human mind experiences an expansion of dimensions on many levels it becomes more peaceful, more satisfied. The skeptic's view of higher knowledge of self is most limiting. Your dogmatic religions, for example, are most limiting for mankind because they demand unquestioned reverence for authority—an exterior authority. *You* are God. *You* know you are Divine. But you must continually remember your Divinity and, most important, *act* accordingly."

"John, you mentioned extraterrestrials before. I don't quite know what to think about that, but are they involved with the same struggle of inner knowingness?"

"That is correct," said John, "perhaps they are operating, at least some of them, on a higher level of awareness and a higher level of technology also. But they are not to be revered as Godlike. They are merely teachers. They have visited your Earth over the eons to bring knowledge and spiritual truth because they have found through the evolution of time that the spiritual understanding of the individual is the *only* understanding required for peace. All other knowledge stems from that."

"And the possible extraterrestrial references in the Bible were real? I mean in Ezekiel and all that?"

"That is correct. They appeared at that time on your Earth to bring higher knowledge of God and spiritual love. They always appear when they are most needed. They serve as a symbol of hope and higher understanding."

"Will I ever meet one?"

There was a pause. "We will speak of these matters again at another time. Think about what I have said and what you are willing to learn. Will that be all for now?"

My mind felt so stuffed I had to say yes. "Thank you, John," I said, "whoever you are. I just can't think of anything else right now. I have to absorb what you've said."

"Very well," said John. "Seek to be at peace with yourself and with God and his work, for you are part of that work. God bless you."

> "*Something unknown to our understanding is visiting the earth.*"
>
> —DR. MITROVAN ZVEREV,
> Soviet scientist

🐾 Kevin shuddered as though the vibration of John's spirit passed through his body and was gone. His hands lifted to his eyes and covered them. Then he rubbed them as though waking from a deep sleep.

"Hello?" he asked drowsily, trying to focus on the room around him. "Hello?"

I stood up and stretched and walked in a circle in front of him.

"Hello," I said, "I'm here."

"How did it go?" asked Kevin.

"My God," I said. "It was incredible. I just don't know what to think."

Kevin straightened up in the chair and then stood up. "Just do what feels right," he said. "Did what came through *feel* right? They've told me to just trust my feelings. There's nothing else you can do once you begin to ask these questions."

"But they were saying incredible stuff."

"Like what?"

"Oh, about previous lifetimes. A whole lot of stuff about people I know now that I'm supposed to have known in other lives. And John and McPherson as well."

"So?"

"Well, do you believe all that?"

"I believe what feels right."

"And does reincarnation feel right to you?" I asked.

"Well, it would have to, wouldn't it? I mean I am an instrument through which many spiritual entities speak, aren't I? So the existence of the soul in many dimensions makes sense to me. Otherwise that makes me either an actor or crazy. And as far as I know I'm neither."

I looked at Kevin closely.

"Yeah," I said hesitantly, "but John also said a lot of stuff about extraterrestrials having provided all kinds of spiritually advanced input for the human race. Do you believe that?"

He sat down. "Sure," he said, "why not? Not only are they mentioned all through the Bible, but they figure in one form or another in nearly every culture on Earth. So why wouldn't they exist? Besides, I know lots of people today who say they've seen them."

"Have you ever seen a UFO?" I asked.

"No," said Kevin, "I have not yet had that pleasure."

"But you believe it anyway?"

"Of course. It feels comfortable to me. And besides, who am I to argue with all the authorities who say there is a good chance they exist? I know there are a lot of people who say they don't, but there's no proof of that either."

Absently Kevin sipped what was left of some cold tea. Then he looked at the mug.

"Where did this come from?" he asked.

"McPherson. He said he needed an Irish-type mug to think more clearly."

"I was holding this mug?"

"Yeah."

"Interesting."

"Yeah."

"What time frame would it be right about now?" he asked.

"Good question," I said. I got it sorted out. "A little before ten."

"I'll be picking up my lady then." He walked toward my door.

"Well, could we get together again soon? I know how busy you are. But would it be possible to work me in?"

"Let me check with my lady and I'll be getting back to you."

I opened the door and thanked him.

With his low-slung slouch, he slid his beige western costume overcoat over his shoulders. He moved out

and descended the stairs like a character in *The Lodger*
(an old movie I had seen in my childhood).

I watched him walk to his "vehicle" on the street.
As I looked after him, I wondered if trance mediums
needed to be involuntarily theatrical in order to sustain
an identity of their own.

I fell into bed. I couldn't sleep. My legs were
vibrating with a strange almost magnetic energy from
inside. I shifted my position. It didn't help. The energy
continued to vibrate . . . I was almost afraid of it because
it was so unfamiliar. I felt the same vibration in my
fingertips and around my lips. It felt physical but at the
same time I could feel the energy emanating from my
mind somehow.

I tried to focus on small, familiar things—the softness
of the breeze coming through my window off the Pacific,
the slap of the waves, the walk I would take in the
morning through the mountain of wildflowers. I went
through some familiar choreography which I often did
in order to fall asleep. I counted each step and movement to the music. I felt the meaning of the music in
my mind. I stretched the muscles in my legs attempting
to neutralize the magnetic stream of energy flaming
inside. It was such a foreign energy, yet somehow
positive. I pictured the pleasure of a hot fudge sundae
dripping with thick, sweet chocolate over cold vanilla-
bean ice cream.

I felt I needed somehow to ground myself in the
here and now on Earth. I laughed to myself. What the
hell was going on? What was real? Had I in fact lived
someplace with Gerry and with David five hundred
thousand years ago? If I really believed this stuff there
was no way I could continue walking around in this
world the way I'd always done. It was bound to change
my perceptions. Was that what happened to Walt
Whitman and Pythagoras and Aristotle and Thoreau
when they came to the conclusion that reincarnation
was not only possible but probable? No wonder the
people in Asia had a different concept of time than we
in the West did. They grew up in the belief of the
reembodiment of the soul from lifetime to lifetime.

Jesus, I thought, maybe time and space are so relative they are not measurable. Maybe they both exist at the same time. Maybe the soul inside my body was telling me that *everything is real*. And if that was true, then reality had more dimensions than I had ever considered. Perhaps, as philosophers and even some scientists claimed, reality was only what one perceived it to be.

If that were the case, I could understand on a colossal scale what an added spiritual dimension could mean to the planet and all the human beings living on it. What a wonder, what a marvel that would be!

Everyone's perception of reality would be valid. If the soul's experience was all that mattered and one's physical existence was literally irrelevant because, from a cosmic perspective, there was no such thing as death, then every living second on Earth was precious precisely because it *did* relate to a grand overall design *which we had helped to create*, and precisely because every *atom* had a purpose, maybe the purpose of this particular collection of atoms writhing around here on the bed was to convey the message that we are part of the God-force that created all things—it is as much a part of us as we are of it.

In a ball of vibrating confusion, I rolled over and finally fell asleep. ❧

Chapter 16

"And whether I come to my own today or in ten
        thousand or ten million years,
I can cheerfully take it now, or with equal cheerfulness
        I can wait . . .
And as to you, Life, I reckon you are the leavings
        of many deaths,
(No doubt I have died myself ten thousand times
        before.)"

—WALT WHITMAN
Song of Myself

I slept until late the next day. I just could not get up. When I finally did I went to the Colony Market and got a double-dip peach frozen yogurt. Anything with peaches always helped.

On the way home I began to consider how my friends would react to what had happened. My thoughts flashed to my friend Bella Abzug. I had known and worked with her on the McGovern presidential campaign and we had become very close. She was tough, brilliant, compassionate, and pragmatic. I wondered what she'd think. I wondered if there would ever come a time when politicians could engage in their own spiritual search without seeming off the wall to voters.

As I opened the door the phone was ringing. It was Bella.

I told her all about what had happened in my session with Kevin. It took a long time and she didn't interrupt once. Finally I stopped.

"Let's get this straight," Bella said. "This Kevin told you you'd lived a previous life in an ancient civilization with someone you're in love with now?"

"No, not Kevin. Kevin was the channel. I talked with two entities, one called McPherson, the other called John."

"Yes, well," she said, "whoever. Listen, this Kevin character could be just making it up and acting."

"Oh, Bella. That's the first thing that occurred to me. And of course it *could* be true—but if he was he should be getting an Academy Award they haven't invented yet. I've been doing a helluva lot of reading on this business of channeling and I really don't believe I'm being taken in any way. I mean, this is something a lot of people are experiencing every day."

"Well," Bella considered, "not meaning to be funny—would you say you were having a religious experience?"

"God, *no!*"

"Then, what? Are you saying you believe in reincarnation?"

"Bella, I don't know. I really just don't know. The thing is it all seems to be about 'feeling,' not thinking. I *feel* that what those spiritual entities said could have really happened to me. In a way, it's *me* I'm listening to, not anyone else." As I spoke I had realized something. "And I can't stop now and just forget the whole thing. I've got to know more."

There was a long silence.

"My darling," she said finally. "I don't want you to be hurt. Just don't do anything dramatic or public about it, okay?" I said okay. "And call me." I said okay.

❧ An interesting and multi-dimensional period of my life now began for me. I can only describe it as a time of living on several levels. I went into rehearsals for a world tour with my live stage show. I danced, sang, acted, and made jokes with my company during the day

while at night I pored over every book I could find to
help me sort out my feelings and thoughts arising from
the questions I found myself asking about life and
purpose.

My bookshelves began to bulge with esoteric metaphysical material. I was glad that I had an office in my
house in Malibu private enough to shut the door and
lock. I wasn't prepared to answer questions about the
books I was reading.

There were reams of material on reincarnation
alone. I read heavily in this area since it was a subject
that interested me particularly. I was astonished to find,
not only that reincarnation was an integrated part of
most Eastern beliefs (which I already knew) but that
hosts of notable thinkers from the West shared this
view of the cosmic purpose of the soul, even though the
Eastern beliefs were rooted in religion and the Western
concepts seemed to grow more from philosophical roots.
From Pythagoras to Plato to Socrates to Aristotle (even
though he later denied reincarnation, splitting off from
his Platonic master) on to Plutarch and down to the
seventeenth century when a whole school of thinkers
rose known as the Cambridge Platonists; from this
followed many—John Milton, the poet Dryden, the
statesman-intellectual Joseph Addison.

I hit the eighteenth century—the Age of Reason as
it is called, thinking that here I would find rebuttal and
skepticism. Skepticism indeed there was—but not of
belief in the soul and a deity, rather there was a
rejection of formalized religion and of authoritarian
thought. There was in fact an explosion of new thinking
and a ratification of the right to think. This was a time
that saw Isaac Newton, Benjamin Franklin, Voltaire,
the great German philosopher Immanuel Kant, Sir
William Jones the brilliant Orientalist, and the Scottish
historian and economist David Hume (the latter dedicated to reason, but acknowledging that if there was such a
thing as an immortal soul then certainly, in logic, it had
to exist both before and after death!) This was a time of
the flowering of intellect—yet most of these extraordinary minds believed in the rebirth of the soul.

If I was overwhelmed I was rapidly discovering I had good company...

Many writers and poets, such as William Blake and Goethe, gave expression to their beliefs in their work. Goethe wrote of his beliefs in letters. Heinrich Heine, the German lyric poet and critic, was, in fact, remarkably "image" conscious: *Who can tell what tailor now inherits the soul of a Plato, what dominie is heir to Caesar's spirit? ...Perchance the soul of Genghis Khan now animates a reviewer who, without knowing it, daily slashes the soul of his faithful Bashirs and Kalmucks in the pages of a critical journal ...(The North Sea)*

Closer to home, I read my way through reports on the American Transcendentalists—spearheaded by Emerson and Thoreau. These were men in revolt against conventional, authoritarian Western religion, as their forerunners—among them Kant, Schopenhauer, Carlyle, and Wordsworth—had been. Walt Whitman's *Leaves of Grass* is of course a paean to reincarnation. Malcolm Cowley said of Whitman, "The universe was an eternal becoming for Whitman, a process not a structure, and it had to be judged from the standpoint of eternity."

So all through the eighteenth and nineteenth centuries there were great men of letters, philosophers, and scientists; and musicians, artists, poets, historians, essayists—and politicians—all giving voice to a belief in reincarnation arrived at through a pragmatic examination of the wonder of life on this earth, often combined with study of the Orientalists. This included men like Thomas Edison, Camille Flammarion (the French astronomer), Gustaf Stomberg (Swedish American astronomer and physicist), to name just a few.

What, I wondered, did the twentieth century have to say? I found immediately, and again, that there was an enormous body of writing on the subject. I could only begin to scratch the surface. Among the many writers were Henry Miller, Pearl Buck, Thomas Wolfe, Jack London, Mark Twain, Louisa May Alcott—the litany of names was endless. I was delighted to find such diverse characters as Lord Hugh Dowding (British Air Chief Marshal during World War II), Sir Arthur

Conan Doyle, Ernest Seton Thompson (founder of the Boy Scouts of America!), Lloyd George (British politician) and—my God—Henry Ford, all in the same reincarnational boat, as it were; also innumerable scientists, a whole school of modern art headed by Mondrian, Kandinsky, Klee. Malevich (Theosophists, one and all); and Herman Hesse, Rainer Maria Rilke, Robert Frost, John Masefield—to name, again, just a very few of the rich and distinguished roster of believers in the theory of reincarnation.

If the work of one man stood out from the rest, it was that of John Ellis McTaggart. At the age of twenty-five McTaggart had been acknowledged as the most distinguished dialectician and metaphysician since Hegel. C. D. Broad, who succeeded McTaggart as lecturer in the Moral Sciences at Trinity College, Cambridge, said that McTaggart was "in the front rank of the great historical philosophers [who might] quite fairly be compared with the *Enneads* of Plotinus, the *Ethics* of Spinoza, and the *Encyclopaedia* of Hegel."

Needless to say I was not familiar with any of these heady works. But I found what Mr. McTaggart himself had to say in his *Human Immortality and Pre-Existence* made a great deal of sense:

> Even the best men are not, when they die, in such a state of intellectual and moral perfection as would fit them to enter heaven immediately. . . .This is generally recognized, and one of two alternatives is commonly adopted to meet it. The first is that some tremendous improvement—an improvement out of all proportion to any which can ever be observed in life—takes place at the moment of death. . . . The other and more probable alternative is that the process of gradual improvement can go on in each of us after the death of our present bodies. . . . The absence of memory need not destroy the chance of an improvement spreading over many lives . . . a man who dies after acquiring knowledge—and all men acquire some—might enter his new life, deprived indeed of his knowledge, but not deprived of

the increased strength and delicacy of mind which he had gained in acquiring knowledge. And, if so, he will be wiser in the second life because of what has happened in the first . . . we cannot doubt that character may remain determined by an event which has been forgotten. I have forgotten the greater number of the good and evil acts which I have done in my present life. And yet each must have left a trace on my character. And so a man may carry over into his next life the dispositions and tendencies which he had gained by the moral contests of this life. . . .

There remains love. The problem here is more important, if, as I believe, it is in love, and in nothing else, that we find not only the supreme value of life, but also the supreme reality of life, and, indeed, of the universe. . . . Much has been forgotten in any friendship which has lasted for several years within the limits of a single life—many confidences, many services, many hours of happiness and sorrow. But they have not passed away without leaving their mark on the present. They contribute, though they are forgotten, to the present love which is not forgotten. In the same way, if the whole memory of the love of a life is swept away at death, its value is not lost if the same love is stronger in a new life because of what passed before.

If McTaggart's philosophy made sense to me, I found there were those who were concerned—as I was discovering of myself—with a *use* for past life recall: not just simply believing in it, but finding a purpose for it. In particular, psychologists had been using regressive hypnosis to uncover *past-life* traumas which were showing up in this life. A certain Dr. Helen Wambach had conducted a series of experiments, not in fact originally designed to assist patients, (although, in several instances, this was one of the results) but rather to establish the validity of past lives. In her book, *Reliving Past Lives*, she fully describes the genesis of her experiments, how each of them was conducted, and the extraordinary results of her investigations into past-life recall of over one thousand subjects, each of whom made at least three "trips," each of whom was asked the same questions on each trip. The results, written down before they had discussed each trip with anyone else, were then correlated by time period, social strata, race, type of food eaten, clothing, architecture, and other cross-reference points.

This book, perhaps more than any other, left no doubt in my mind that we have indeed lived past lives. For me it became a matter of exploring further for myself—when I could take the time to do so. For I was still in the midst of my tour, accompanied by bags full of books . . .

I played Europe, Australia, Canada, Scandinavia, and America. I played in the theaters at night, and read and scanned, and skimmed and read during the day. I found I was meeting people who, over drinks and dinner after the show, professed hidden interests of their own in reincarnation and memory feelings that they couldn't define or explain. Some had had out-of-body experiences, some had done trance channeling themselves, some had had past-life recall that they were sure was real but were reluctant to discuss for fear of appearing weird.

I talked with Gerry from exotic parts of the world but it was difficult to discuss my growing interest in spiritual metaphysics on long distance lines, or indeed in any way at all. I wished that we could meet, but my schedule never fitted into his availability, and vice versa. With each stilted conversation I was aware of how deeply grounded in his politics he was, and also that my attitude toward his reluctance to express any interest in my concern for expanded consciousness was one of growing impatience. I found myself remembering that "John" had said I should allow people in my life to conduct their awareness capacity at their own pace: allow the skeptics their skepticism. In fact, *I* didn't necessarily believe *all* I was reading and learning—but I longed for someone I was really involved with to be interested in the possibilities of other dimensions. Reality was a subjective truth and I knew my reality was expanding. I felt more aware and more able to cope with ideas of my own inner reality: and I sure as hell wanted to talk to someone about them.

The tour was a joy. The work was hard but rewarding, and some of the people I met along the way seemed quietly involved with their own search for deeper identity. Many told me that psychiatric help did not go deep enough: that there were events and traumas even earlier than the lifetime they found themselves in today. Many said they felt their childhood conditioning and experience did not explain some of their deep-seated fears and anxieties. I listened with guarded astonishment that there could be so *many* people thinking that way.

One episode in particular struck me as it was both coherent and touched off very unexpectedly. An old friend of mine from Ireland whom I hadn't seen for years described a recent trip he had taken to Japan; he said he was calmly strolling along a street in Kyoto when he spotted a Samurai outfit in the window of a Japanese antique shop. He stopped as though riveted and stared at the outfit that he "knew" had belonged to him. He said he remembered the sword, how the material had felt next to his skin and the way in which he swaggered as he wore it. As he stood staring at the ancient garments, scenes of battle flooded through his memory until he remembered having died wearing that uniform. He said he walked in to inquire about buying it but it was not for sale. As he related the story to me he said he was surprised that he felt free enough to actually express what he believed about having lived a lifetime in Japan. I nodded and listened, wondering when I myself would possibly begin to remember lifetimes that I may have had before.

And so for about three months I toured, talked to people, and read. I tried on new thoughts and new assumptions with each country I visited. I began to be more free in applying my new ideas to the life and work around me. I was selective with whom I discussed what I was feeling, but more often than not I found this wasn't necessary.

I returned to Malibu for a rest and to reexamine

my notes and try to sort out my thinking. I wasn't sure how to approach what was on my mind. When one first discovers new awarenesses it can be confusing. So I did a lot of walking on the beach, and sometimes, with one of my books, I would sit under a tree in the small park near the health food restaurant in Malibu.

One afternoon after carrot juice and a tofu burger, a friend of mine with whom I had had a deeply personal love affair happened by and found me under my tree. He was a writer and TV director from New York and he could be extremely caustic and cynically witty. I knew him well—in fact his quirky brilliance had been a major factor in keeping me interested in him for quite a number of years.

At first I felt a tap on the head which had usually been the way he said hello. I knew it was Mike right away. He was puffing on his pipe, casually clad in jeans, T-shirt and leather jacket. You could tell he was intelligent from this costume—the I'm-just-a-bum-who-doesn't-care look.

Without any preamble he said, "What's happening? Where have you been for the past year?"

"Oh, around," I said. "I've been on tour all over the world. Got back a few days ago."

"Ahh," said Mike, "still have that mystical wanderlust, eh?" He surprised me a bit with this insight. But he was continuing, "You've really combined your work with your wanderlust pretty well, haven't you? That's good. I could always tell when you wanted to get out and look around."

I sat up on my knees as he plopped down beside me. "Did you really always know that about me?" I asked, seeing an aspect to him that had not been evident to me when we were together.

"Sure," he said. "But I didn't want you to go, so I never mentioned it. Honest, eh?"

We sat for a moment and smiled at each other. "It's good to see you," he said, really meaning it, and immediately went on. "Something's on your mind. I hear you've been keeping to yourself a lot, except for some secret guy you keep making trips to Europe to see."

Oh, brother, I thought. Sometimes the world was too much of a golf ball.

But I laughed. So did Mike . . . not really expecting me to go into my love life.

"Tell me something, old friend," I said, "do you think I'm naive? I mean do you think I'm the kind of person who believes everything I'm told?"

Mike puffed on his pipe, suddenly serious, as though understanding (as he always had) that I was concerned about character traits in myself that I was unaware of.

"No," he answered, "I wouldn't say you were naive. You've got a really tough inquiring mind. But I do think you sometimes read good into things that isn't really there."

"What do you mean?"

"Well, for example, when you went to China you *wanted* the revolution there to be successful so I think you tended to overlook areas which were a problem. Of course I know you only saw what they wanted you to see so I can understand your positive assessment of what was happening there. But that's what I mean."

"Well, what did you mean a moment ago when you called me mystical?"

"Shirley, you always had an understanding some-how that sounded like Eastern philosophy to me. I don't know. I called it abstract for a while there but you seemed attracted to ideas that weren't exactly meat and potatoes. You know I always wanted to know who collected the garbage, and you wanted to know what was underneath the garbage collector's mind."

"Yeah," I said, going over other relationships I had had where I had heard the same complaint. "Is that a complaint, Mike?"

"No," he answered, "not at all. It's just the way you are. You always wanted to get underneath everything, looking for a deeper meaning. I admire that. It can drive a guy nuts but it made me look deeper too."

I smiled. He smiled. A pair of ex-lovers smiling about appreciating each other. Mike leaned over me and picked up my book.

"What's this?" he asked.

"Oh, just a book."

"On reincarnation?"

"Yeah."

"Oh."

"Yeah."

"Why?"

"I don't know." I swallowed, deciding whether or not to get into the discussion. "I think it might be true. And I'm just reading a lot about it."

Mike looked into my eyes. "So you've gone California, eh?"

"California?"

"Yeah. Everybody out here is into that stuff. Only California could elect a Governor Moonbeam, right?"

"I guess so," I answered tentatively. "But I've found it lots of other places too."

"Yeah? Where?"

"Oh, Mike. All over the world."

"For example?"

When Mike decided to interrogate, you felt like you were on trial.

"Well, on tour I talked with lots of people in Europe, Australia, Canada. Wherever."

"Yeah? What did they say?"

"They told stories. Sometimes they remembered real past-life experiences. Sometimes it was just a feeling they had—or sometimes the déjà vu thing."

"Yeah," he said, "I have proof that there is life *after* death."

"What do you mean?" I asked, pleasantly surprised that maybe we could have a dialogue here. "What proof?"

"The Congress of the United States," said Mike.

I laughed but my tummy turned over. Oh God, I thought, I might as well get the full treatment. "That's funny," I said.

"I'll tell you," he said, "I think we've got enough

trouble in the world here and now. I'm not too interested in whether I was an Egyptian slave five thousand
years ago."

Of course I found myself wondering why he came
up with that particular image but I let it go. "Have you
ever heard of trance channeling?" I asked.

"You mean that stuff Oliver Lodge wrote about at
the turn of the century in England? He got in touch
with his dead son or something?"

Mike floored me. I knew he read nearly everything
there was to read but I couldn't imagine him haunting
the occult bookstores.

"Yeah," I answered, "Lodge did a lot of psychical
research which was never explained—other than the
fact that it must have happened."

"So what have you got to do with that? Are you
getting in touch with Chou En Lai through a medium?"
Mike knew that I thought Chou En Lai was attractive
and that I would probably have gone to any lengths to
meet him!

"No," I answered, "not Chou. But maybe it's
possible to get in touch with disembodied spiritual
guides who were once in the body and are not any
longer."

Mike leaned back on his elbow and chewed on his
pipe. "You want to tell me about it?" he asked.

I took out a cigarette and lit it. Very carefully I
outlined what had been happening. I told him about
Ambres in Sweden, about John and McPherson and
Kevin in California. I told him that many people were
learning through trance channeling all over the world.
And that I realized some mediums might be phony but
that did not rule out all of them. I told him about the
past-life information I had heard about myself, along
with the teachings of spiritual love and God and extraterrestrials having supposedly brought the same message.
I told him how I had read and read about other people
in the world, past and present, who also felt an affinity
toward having lived before. I mentioned all the famous,
intelligent, artistic, philosophic, scientific, and even
religious leaders I could think of to whom reincarnation

was an accepted part of their lives—and I was defensive enough to conclude my presentation by reminding Mike that I was in pretty good company.

He took his pipe from his teeth and sat up, hunched over.

"Shirl," he said, "I'm Mike, remember? I'm on *your* side, right?"

I said nothing. Just looked at him.

"I mean," he went on, "a person goes into a trance and another voice comes out of their mouth and you sit there and believe what you're hearing?"

I kept quiet.

"Look," he went on, "people would have to say what's happened to our Shirley? They tell you about past lives, they tell you about extraterrestrials, for God's sake! It's preposterous! You sound gullible and ridiculous. I don't like to see you put yourself in that position."

I sucked on my straw, making a grating sound on the bottom of the empty cup. "Who is 'people'?" I said. "That's why I asked *you* if you thought I was naive. You see, Mike, I don't feel naive, or gullible. I feel inquiring. I want to know. I feel that anything is possible—and why the hell not?"

"But do you *believe* it?"

"I don't know. I'm just about convinced on the matter of past lives, and hence reincarnation—just on empirical evidence. I'm in the middle of finding out a bunch of other new stuff. It's a process of considering new dimensions. It's a whole damn fascinating world that I'm not willing to throw out the window and I don't see anything naive about that. I've always been open-minded, right?"

"Right."

"Well, I guess that's what I'm continuing to be. The only thing is right now I'm a bit confused about whether there is such a thing as actual 'reality.' I mean reality seems to be so relative."

"Wait a minute," Mike protested, "just hang in there a minute. When a Hollywood producer screws a writer out of his salary—that's *real*."

"Sure. It's real to *him*. Maybe it becomes real to his kids because for the first time in their lives they become conscious of want, or deprivation. But being screwed out of a house, car, TV set, clothing, warmth, food—all that is absolutely meaningless, not *real*, don't you see, to millions of people who have never, ever had those things. And it is just as *unreal* to a handful at the other extreme who have always had everything. So maybe it isn't the money part that's important. Maybe there's a lesson in that. Maybe life is about *lessons* and *that's* reality."

"Well, what's the lesson in a man not being able to feed his kids?"

"I don't really know, Mike," I answered. "It didn't happen to me. But if it had I would try to figure it out rather than let it rest at being pissed off. I would try to find out *why* and not lay the whole thing on someone who had screwed me."

"Oh shit," he said. "Are you saying that you'll just sit back with all this God and love crap and allow yourself to be fucked over?"

Mike's eloquence was uplifting at times.

"No, I'm not saying that. I'm saying that perhaps I wouldn't actually be fucked over. Perhaps, what looks like fucked-overness is really something I needed to experience in order to understand myself better. Besides, that stuff goes on all the time anyway whether you allow it to happen or not. So I guess I'm saying if I decide not to allow it I'll have to go to war, right?"

"War?" asked Mike.

"Sure. You can extend this example to a worldwide scene of haves and have-nots. It's the same dilemma. But if we never really actually die anyway, then life becomes a question of how we handle a situation of injustice rather than not allowing it to happen by violent means."

Mike leaned back against the tree. A cloud passed in front of the sun and a scream of seagulls took off as though they had made a collective decision to leave. "Do you realize," said Mike, "that every despot in the world has taken advantage of that kind of thinking and gone on to cause incomprehensible suffering? To support that philosophy is despicably self-righteous. I mean, to teach that everyone should turn the other cheek is an open invitation to tyranny. I believe in self-determination and revolution if some bastard is doing me wrong."

"So then you're agreeing with killing if *you* are the one who feels it is necessary?"

"If some guy is trying to kill me first, yeah."

"Okay," I said, "I understand that. That is certainly the usual way out. But I'm wondering if we ever really kill our enemies anyway. Regardless of what one's reason is for killing another person, I mean whether it's personal or because some government or maybe religious authority tells one to, if the law of cause and effect is in operation—and that *is* at the root of reincarnation—then what have you accomplished except to accumulate a lot of bad karma? If death, meaning oblivion, a final end, is not a reality, what's the point of killing? If we could 'prove,' as they say, that killing is *not* an answer, is ultimately self-defeating in a literal sense, maybe more than a few good minds would look for other solutions."

"It's a bit esoteric," Mike said. "I can see why you have to worry at it because that's the kind of mind you have. And I guess you're bound and determined to unravel the knot to your own satisfaction. But Shirl, what's it going to do to you?"

"How d'you mean?"

"Well, shit," he said, "people will wonder what's happened to you. I mean they don't know you like I do, they'll think you've gone off the deep end with no paddles in the water."

Mike was genuinely concerned for me just as Bella was—even as Gerry had been. But why such concepts should be so personally threatening to Mike was another issue. Why he couldn't relate with open-mindedness instead of anxiety was of course what I was concerned about, and not just in Mike.

"But Mike," I said, "don't you find nearly everyone has wondered about this stuff in one way or another?

Don't you think everyone has had something happen to them that they can't explain?"

"Sure they have. But they just leave it unexplained. Why do you feel you have to develop this elaborate set of beliefs in order to explain things that are probably better off left alone?"

I was defensive enough to feel somewhat exasperated. "Who *says* they are better off left alone? What's so good about the status quo that the world wants to preserve it as is? I'm looking for *better* answers, Mike. Part of it is just plain cussed curiosity I guess—I've always wanted to know why a rose was red, or a thought was strong. Surface explanations have never been enough for me so I suppose it is inevitable that I would carry my questioning all the way through—wherever it brings me out."

Mike took my hand and patted it. "Well, a lot of other folks couldn't leave well enough alone, like Louis Pasteur or Madame Curie. And look what they came up with. So who knows? But what bothers me is that what they did was *all* they did. They didn't have to depend on audiences not being alienated to make a living. I don't want that to happen to you."

"I don't think that'll happen, Mike. Anyway, it's the most meaningful thing in my life right now—to put it mildly. I just can't leave it alone. And when I go the limit with my identity or anyone else's identity I ultimately get to the fuller identity of what might have gone before this life. I mean I can see where you and I might have had a karmic relationship in a life before this one. I can see that we were together this time around because there was stuff still left to work out from before."

"You mean maybe this conversation is part of working that out?"

"Could be."

"Well. But I can only handle this life. That gives me enough to think about. And I don't see how understanding any of what you're talking about will help me raise the bail for a friend of mine who got busted for coke."

Mike got up and stretched. "Be careful, Shirl. That's all, okay?"

"Okay."

"Wanna walk?"

"Sure."

We put our arms around each other and walked out from under the tree toward the mountains. Mike leaned over and whispered in my ear, "So tell me. In our last lifetime together did you make secret trips to Europe to see me?"

❧ That evening I felt really tired. I decided to take it real easy, maybe not do any writing that night. At the end of the day I sat out on my balcony and watched the wind play on gusts of sand as the sun set. The low glasslike tide reflected a glow of pink-orange. I wondered when the grunion were supposed to run and how they knew they were supposed to. I wondered if fish had souls.

A lone figure walked along the shallow rippling waves about a mile down the coast. I watched him. I always wondered what other people thought about when they walked at sunset. Some walked with purpose, some ambled and others walked as though they weren't walking at all—perhaps they were somewhere else. This lone figure walked as though he were looking for someone. He didn't look much out to sea but more at the direction of the buildings on their pilings. He was eating something, an apple. He carried a pair of sandals in his other hand and walked with a slumped left shoulder. I looked closer as he came nearer. He saw me looking at him from above and waved. It was David.

Oh my God, I thought. Now what? When he reached the front of my building he stopped, smiled, waved again and yelled up at me. ❧

Chapter 17

"I maintain that cosmic religious feeling is the strongest and noblest incitement to scientific research."

—ALBERT EINSTEIN
The World As I See It

"Hi," he said. "It's beautiful down here."

I got up and leaned on the railing. David was wearing a sweater over a shirt and a pair of white gym socks hung from the back pocket of his slacks.

"How are you?" I called.

He threw his cigarette into the waves. "Come on down and walk," he yelled. "Let's walk up to the big rock. Then if you feel like it, we can have some dinner at Holiday House."

I straightened up from the railing.

"But bring a sweater," he yelled. "It'll be cold later."

I got the woolen sweater that had been around the world with me, the green one Gerry loved, and climbed down the wooden stairs leading to the sand, feeling that I was seeing David for the first time—and in some respects wishing I had never met him at all. I was feeling bruised from the encounter with Mike which I was far from having sorted through.

David looked at me hard when I joined him. "Are you okay?" he said.

"Okay, fine, just fine."

"I see," he said, as we began to walk into the sun. "So you've been thinking a lot, eh?"

"Haven't had time, really," I said noncommittally.

He lit a cigarette.

"You sure do smoke a lot," I commented. "Why d'you smoke so much if you're into this spiritual stuff and all squared away with yourself?"

"I don't know," he said. "I guess it helps to ground me. Otherwise I'd be out on Cloud Thirty-nine all the time. Wouldn't you smoke if you really got into it?"

"Smoke?" My voice was a little shrill. "I'd be inhaling giant redwoods if I really believed all I'm learning about."

"Yeah," he said, "it's scary at first, like everything new is, but after a while you learn to desensitize yourself. Smoking is one way to do it. Also, I'm addicted."

We walked a way in the cold sand. The sandpipers did their sundown minuet. I felt I was doing my own minuet with David. For a time I said nothing. Then I thought I might as well.

"I guess you know," I said, "that we're old friends and have been married before?"

"Yeah," he laughed, "I know."

"Who from?"

"Oh, around. We're lifetime partners or something, right?"

"Hmm."

He puffed on his cigarette and looked up into the sunset. He had a way of sounding so sure of things he was almost pompous.

"You know," I said, "I've been thinking. When the astronauts travel out there in space, are there spirits all around the space capsules?"

David laughed and coughed. "Well yeah," he said. "You could say that because the spirit world is everywhere, even around us right now. I mean the spiritual plane is invisible to us most of the time because our consciousness is too dense to see them, but we aren't invisible to them. And you can feel it sometimes, can't you? I mean, don't you really wonder sometimes where certain ideas and inspirations come from? Don't you sometimes feel you are actually being guided by some invisible force? You know how so many of the great minds have talked about really feeling an invisible kind of inspirational force? Well, I think it's probably their spiritual guides as well as a kind of recall from a talent they experienced in a past lifetime. You can see it in child prodigies. I mean, Mozart was probably playing the piano at four because he was *remembering* how."

"David," I said, interrupting his dissertation, "what proof is there that all this stuff is true? I mean really. You can sound like an asshole spouting off these theories like it's fact and Santa Claus is real."

"Well, there's no question about it to me. I just feel it. I believe it. I know it. That's all. Of course there's no proof. So what? But the connection between the spiritual and physical planes is what's missing in the world today. To me, the soul is the missing link to life. I mean if everyone understood that their souls never really die, they wouldn't be so frightened, and they would understand *why* they're alive as well."

Every time David opened his mouth he delivered a spiritual sermon.

"So," I said, "what you're saying is that reincarnation is like show business. You just keep doing it until you get it right."

"Yeah." He had the good humor to laugh. "Something like that. You know," he continued, "I'm convinced that Christ was teaching the theory of reincarnation."

I wrapped my turtleneck sweater closer around my neck. Everything gave me chills these days. When David made one of his statements, he never gave it a buildup.

"Why do you think that?" I said, remembering what John had told me about the Bible.

David swished his feet in the water, breaking the mirrored reflection below us in the sand. "I've read a lot about the interpretations of Christ's teaching other than what appears in the Bible." He looked into my face and hesitated. "You know that nothing is recorded in the Bible about Christ from the time he was about twelve until he began to really teach at about thirty years old. Right?"

"Yes," I said. "I had heard about that and I just figured he didn't have much to say until he got older."

"Well, no," said David, "a lot of people think that those eighteen missing years were spent traveling in and around India and Tibet and Persia and the Near East. There are all kinds of legends and stories about a man who sounds just like Christ. His description is matched everywhere and he said he was the Son of God and he corroborated the beliefs of the Hindus that reincarnation was in fact true. They say he became an adept yogi and mastered complete control over his body and the physical world around him. He evidently went around doing all those miracles that were recorded later in the Bible and tried to teach people that they could do the same things too if they got more in touch with their spiritual selves and their own potential power."

David did not know about my session with Kevin and John, nor that I had met a woman at The Ashram, a kind of protege of Sai Baba's (an avatar in India). She and her husband had written a book and done a documentary film on the missing years of Christ. Their names were Janet and Richard Bock and they had done extensive research on that period in Christ's life on Earth. They had compiled stacks of evidence researched by respected archeologists, theologians, students of Sanskrit and Hebrew writings, et cetera. All seemed to agree that Christ had indeed traveled extensively in India.

As we walked I told David about Janet and Richard and he said he had never met them but would love to compare the notes he had made when he spent two years in India researching the same thing. He said when Christ returned to Israel he taught what he had learned from the Indian masters, that is, the theory of reincarnation.

"But David," I said, "why aren't these teachings recorded in the Bible?"

"They are," he said. "The theory of reincarnation *is* recorded in the Bible. But the proper interpretations were struck from it during an Ecumenical Council meeting of the Catholic Church in Constantinople sometime around 553 A.D., called the Council of Nicea. The Council members voted to strike those teachings from the Bible in order to solidify Church control.

"The Church needed to be the sole authority where the destiny of man was concerned, but Christ taught that every human being was responsible for his or her own destiny—now and future. Christ said there was only one judge—God—and he was very opposed to the formation of a church of any kind, or any other kind of ceremonial religion that might enslave man's free will or his struggle for truth."

This confirmed what Kevin had said, but it seemed logical that anyone heavily into reincarnation would have read about that famous Council.

The sun began to set behind the waves now, sweeping a pink-purple slash across the clouds above the Pacific.

"Anyway," said David, "that's what I believe Christ was really doing and when the Church destroyed those teachings, it screwed up mankind from then on."

I didn't answer him. I thought that if the Church *had* been teaching that our souls were involved in a continual physical embodiment in order to work out Karmic Justice, I would have been interested in it from the time I was little. *That* would have made sense to me. It would have given me a *reason* to believe in the spiritual dimension of man, because *I* would have been responsible for my own destiny (and so would everyone else). It would be up to our own consciences, not up to the Church to judge our behavior. And it also would have explained all the suffering and horror in the world which all my life had rendered me helplessly incapable of understanding or altering. "Whatsoever a man soweth, that shall he also reap," would have taken on a different meaning. And it would have given me a deep-rooted comfort that we did indeed live forever and eternally according to our actions and reactions as we went along. "Turn the other cheek" would have had new meaning also. In fact, it would have been more possible because we would have held our eternal priorities higher than our earthly problems.

The law of cause and effect was accepted in science as fundamental. Why wasn't that same law operable where human life was concerned? Laws were not always based on what we could see, and therefore prove. Morality, ethics, love—these were not visible, tangible things. But that didn't mean they were not there.

I was not an expert in science or any of the given fields of provable facts. But, I was slowly beginning to wonder why these fields mattered so much. I didn't see much value in physical proofs when it came to the struggle of understanding why we were alive. Such a struggle belonged to each individual personally and in the deepest sense. It didn't necessarily belong in the domain of "experts" of any variety. Maybe that's what was meant by "the meek shall inherit the earth." Perhaps the meek who didn't see any need to act "strong" were those who related to God and the goodness of life and *mankind;* and the Golden Rule *was* the first and last axiom to live by. Maybe all those who tended to complicate life out of fear were adding, not only to the karmic complexities of the earth itself, but also to the karmic complexities of their own lives.

David and I walked on in silence. We walked to the public beach about three miles up the coast where he had parked his car.

It was an old Dodge, green, and in the back seat was a stack of books tied with string. "I brought you some more books, plus a Bible. Just read and see what you think. Want to go eat?" Books? I needed more books?

We sat together in the restaurant above the sea. Whenever we talked, it was never small talk—never, "How was your day?" or "Do you like Brahms?" It was always big talk, as though chat would have been a waste of time. It was unusual for me not to be personal where a man was concerned because the "personal conversation" was usually a lead up to what we both wanted from each other . . . either clues to character or indications of goals in life.

This was different. I wasn't interested in this man in that way. I was interested in what he had to say. I guess all people establish a set of unstated but understood rules of communication when they're together one on one. It's something you don't think about, but it's there and in operation until one of the two breaks what's established and attempts to go on to another level.

David didn't seem interested in breaking what was established either. It made me comfortable, and I instinctively knew that what we had was how it was going to be. Paradoxically, this created an atmosphere in which each encounter with this man who was partially responsible for my deeply questioning our perceptions of reality was a new experience for me.

So, even though we had a delicious Bordeaux wine and a really good beef Wellington, and even though there were candles on the table and we were deeply engrossed each in what the other was saying, and even though some of the other patrons wondered who it was I was with, I never felt inclined to relate to him on a man-woman level, and I didn't really care specifically how he came to believe what he believed. This process was usually an abstract evolution of thinking, anyway. At least, it had been in my case, prompted by a few specific moments that motivated me further. We talked instead about the *need* for faith and a feeling of purpose, about whether the human race had progressed by itself or with some kind of spiritual "guidance," and finally, about the wisdom of being open-minded about all new concepts.

David spoke of how open-mindedness was the mark of real intelligence to him because "only an open-minded person can embrace new ideas and grow."

"I went through a lot of confusion," he said, "when I first started making my spiritual connections. But whenever I felt sort of 'absurd' in the 'real' world around me, I'd stop myself and listen to what my own intuition was telling me was real. I had been conditioned to believe in what I could prove rather than what I could sense. But the more I listened to my own inner voice, the more I got in touch with myself. It finally all became so simple. And now, so many people are doing the same thing that *that* has become what is real."

David didn't seem to be reviewing his belief struggles as any kind of identifiable blueprint for me. It was more just simply what he'd been through. And when he talked, it was with that same calm dignity.

Then, somewhere near the end of the dinner, he asked, "Have you ever seen a UFO?"

I was a bit startled to hear such a question from him. It was one thing to hear "John" discuss God, spiritual truth and extraterrestrials in one breath, and quite another to have a personal friend apparently about to make the same connection.

"No," I said casually, "but I know a few people who have, including Jimmy Carter when he was Governor of Georgia. Carter never talked about it to me, but I saw the report he filed in the newspaper, and it seemed to be professional and unemotional, like most of the reports Jimmy Carter files."

"Right," said David. "What do you think they are?"

"God," I said, "I don't know. Maybe they're secret military weapons nobody will talk about, or maybe they're weather contraptions, or maybe they're hoaxes, or maybe they're from outer space. I don't know. What do you think?"

He sipped his coffee and cognac and wiped the edges of his mouth with his napkin. "I think," he said, "they are from outer space. I think the extraterrestrials in them are highly evolved spiritually. And I think they've been here for a long time."

"For God's sake!" I said. "What makes you think that?" I watched him as he swallowed another sip of coffee. I watched how his eyes blinked calmly over the candlelight. I watched for any expression that would indicate what he was getting at . . . why he should mention such a thing in relation to what we were talking about.

"Well, a lot of people have written about them."

"A lot of kooks have."

"And they're all over the Old Testament. There are all sorts of descriptions that sound like spacecraft to me, and to many others, of course." Again I was reminded of "John," and indeed of my own readings. But David was continuing, "I think Von Daniken is a little kooky, but I believe he's on the right track."

"You mean *Chariots of the Gods* Von Daniken?"

"Yes."

I could feel my "open mind" threatening to snap shut.

"Didn't he do time in a Swiss jail for passing bad checks?"

"Sure. But what's that got to do with what he uncovered? People are full of contradictions and what he did was wrong. He should have found another way to solve his problems because in the end he discredited himself. But not necessarily his work."

After the session with "John" I read all of Von Daniken's work—material that described his contention that many ancient ruins had in fact been constructed by highly advanced civilizations with extraterrestrial help: the Great Pyramid, Stonehenge, Machu Picchu in Peru, the airstrips on the Nazca Plains in Peru, etc.

He also contended that, for example, Ezekiel's descriptions of wheels of fire were spacecraft as well as the pillar of fire that guided Moses and the Israelites for forty years in the desert, culminating with the parting of the Red Sea.

I saw the film *Chariots of the Gods* which alluded to the presence of extraterrestrials all through human history, offering cave drawings and monuments as proof of this contention. What had struck me as I watched the film was the reaction of the audience. They were riveted to the screen and when the film was over, no one got up to leave. They seemed genuinely entranced by the speculations yet unsure how to react. I listened carefully to people as they filed out of the theater. No one made sarcastic remarks or ridiculed the information. In fact, they weren't threatened or intimidated one way or the other. They just filed out silently thinking to themselves until someone mentioned a hamburger. I remember being more interested in their reaction to the film than I was in my own reaction to it.

And now, just as John had done, David tied in UFOs with spiritual intelligence. I listened and questioned him further.

"You mean," I asked, "that angels and chariots spitting fire and things like that in the Bible were really people from another world?"

"Yes, why wouldn't advanced alien beings try to teach us higher spiritual truth? Maybe the God-force is really scientific. I mean, Christ and Moses and some of those people were capable of producing physical miracles, as we call them, that our science can't explain. And too many people are reported to have seen those 'miracles' to allow them to be simply made-up myths. It's got to be that the gifted ones knew something we don't know."

I took a sip of David's brandy.

"Listen," I said, "how did you come to make the connection between the spiritual possibilities of man and outer space?"

"Because," he said, "it makes sense, doesn't it? I mean, there is so much unexplained superior intelligence in ancient history and so much of it relates to religion and spirituality, or at least to the question of God."

"Well, yes," I said, "but that intelligence could have been extremely advanced human civilizations right here on Earth which disappeared or vanished or did themselves in or something. Why does superior intelligence have to come from some other world?"

"Well," he said, "I asked myself that too. But you see there wasn't just one example of superior intelligence. It happened all over the world and at different times. According to Plato and Aristotle and lots of other great minds, Atlantis *really* existed as an extremely advanced civilization. The Incas and the Mayans had as much astronomical and astrological knowledge as we have today, and maybe more. The Sumerians, who lived two thousand years before Christ, had highly developed mathematics and astronomy... I mean, I'll give you some more stuff to read, but it indicates to me that this Earth has been observed and helped and taught throughout its human history by beings that knew more than we do; who knew spiritual as well as scientific, astronomical, mathematical, and physical truths that we are only beginning to fathom."

The brandy was gone. And I felt my mind checking out.

"So, why couldn't humans have learned it themselves?"

David pressed on, downing the ice water which was left. "Because there's too much evidence to indicate that humans had help from 'gods,' from people who were advanced in a *cosmic* sense. Too many of the writings of ancient cultures talk about the 'gods' who went to and from the stars in fiery flying machines bringing 'help and knowledge and promises of immortality.' So I said to myself—why not? No healthy-minded scientist today believes we are the only life in the universe—right?"

"Yes."

"Well, it's worth thinking about, isn't it? I mean, why not take it seriously? It makes sense. It's wild according to some accepted points of view, but it makes sense. Since you're into all this, you might as well go further. Sorry to be so relentless."

We paid the check (Dutch treat) and got up from our table. I was exhausted. By now my earthbound frustration with Gerry looked good. Relentless, David had called himself? *That* was a term usually applied to me. *I* was usually the relentless one with whatever I wanted to figure out. Now somebody was out-relentlessing me.

David gave me his stack of books and dropped me off at my beach apartment.

We had talked about life after death, life before birth, and now we were into life above life!

I thanked him and said goodnight. ✇

Chapter 18

"True fortitude of understanding consists in not letting what we know to be embarrassed by what we don't know."

—RALPH WALDO EMERSON
The Skeptic

❷ I had read concentratedly in the area of channeling and then on the subject of reincarnation, and always for my own spiritual guidance. I concentrated now on a new viewpoint—the possibility of extraterrestrial life and its connection to human life.

I read for days, until my eyes hurt.

A very brief synopsis follows of what I read. Much of this research was important to me in relation to what happened to me later. With respect to the Bible, I use its terminology—that is, angels, pillars of fire, and so on—because these are the words used by the ancients to describe phenomena in the terms understandable in their day.

In the book of Ezekiel in the Old Testament, Ezekiel described what the Earth looked like from great heights. He talked of what it was like to be lifted into a flying ship almost as though by a magnet. He described the back and forth movement of the vehicle as something fast as lightning. He referred to the commander of the craft as "The Lord."

Ezekiel encountered people and ships like that four different times over a period of nineteen years. He spoke of how peaceful the people from the ships were when they *made contact with humans,* going to great pains to avoid causing fear. There was no sign of "hostility or reckless attitudes." He said "The Lord" showed care and respect for him.

In the book of Exodus a vehicle that moved and led the Hebrews out of Egypt to the Red Sea was described as "a pillar of cloud by day and a pillar of fire by night." The pillar hovered over the waters and parted them enabling the Israelites to escape into the wilderness. The "pillar" that led the Israelites for forty years as they wandered in the wilderness gave religious guidance all during that period, and an "angel within" provided Moses with the Ten Commandments. "Angels" are all over the Bible—in fact, the Bible more than suggests that "angels" were missionaries from another world.

During that forty-year period the Israelites were without a source for food or sustenance. But the "pillar of fire" was in charge. The Lord said to Moses, "Behold, I will rain bread from heaven for you" (Exodus 16:4).

The "cloudy pillar" served as a beacon for Israel's journeys in the wilderness. "For throughout all their journeys the cloud of the Lord was upon the tabernacle by day, and fire was in it by night, in the sight of all of the house of Israel" (Exodus 40:38).

The book of Numbers is more specific. The cloudy pillar directed every move the Israelites made. When the cloud moved the people moved, when the cloud stopped the people rested and made another camp (Numbers 9:15–23).

Moses was in day-to-day contact with a being in the "cloudy pillar." The Lord spoke to the people one day saying "Hear my words; if there is a prophet among you, I, the Lord, make myself known to him in a vision, I speak with him in a dream. Not so with my servant Moses; he is entrusted with all my house. With him I speak mouth to mouth, clearly and not in dark speech; and he beholds the form of the Lord" (Numbers 12:6-8).

Until Exodus the Israelites didn't really have a religion. They believed in a kind of promise. But during a forty-year period of wandering in the wilderness, angels implanted the gospel and religion from another world—the Kingdom of Heaven.

A select group of people was instructed in a course of behavior and ethics and worship... Moses, Abraham, Peter, St. Luke, Jacob, and so on. Jacob encountered angels on many occasions. Once he encountered so many he said, "This is God's Army" (Genesis 32:2). The teachings were very concerned that people on Earth learn the values of love, the Golden Rule, and belief in life everlasting.

In the book of Acts, Christ instructed his disciples to take the message of *his* world to all of *their* world.

In the New Testament Christ said: "You are from below, I am from above; You are of this world, I am not of this world" (John 8:23). He said he was in constant contact with beings from his world and he called them "angels." He said the angels were very concerned about the success of their message on Earth.

When I finished reading the Bible notations, I turned to David's other books.

On the Plains of Nazca in Peru there are what appear to be airstrips thousands of years old, and at the same location there are earth paintings of animals, birds, and a figure with a helmet similar in shape to those used by our modern day astronauts. The airstrips and drawings can only be seen from an airplane at a fairly high altitude.

The astrological calendar of Tiahuanaco in the City of Tiahuanaco, 13,000 feet high, symbolically recorded astrological knowledge based on the premise of a round Earth 27,000 years ago. The revolutions of the Earth in accordance with the sun, moon and other planets were all correct.

The Legend of Tiahuanaco told of a golden spaceship coming from the stars.

At Sacsahuaman lies a monument of rock 20,000 tons in weight which was extracted and transported from some distance away and then turned upside down.

Sand vitrifications had been found in the Gobi Desert and at old Iraqi archeological sites, resembling the vitrifications of sand produced by the atomic explosions in the Nevada desert in our times.

Cuneiform texts and tablets from Ur, one of the oldest writings of mankind, told of gods who rode in the heavens in "ships" or gods who came from the stars possessing terrible and powerful weapons and returning again to their stars.

The Eskimos talked of the first tribes brought to the north by gods with metal wings.

The oldest American Indian sages mentioned a thunderbird who introduced fire and fruit to them.

The Mayan legends spoke of how the "gods" were able to recognize everything: the universe, the four cardinal points of the compass, and the round shape of the Earth. The Mayan calendar was so highly developed that its calculations projected for sixty-four million years.

The religious legends of the pre-Inca people said that the stars were inhabited and that "gods" came down to them from the constellation of the Pleiades. Sumerian, Assyrian, Babylonian and Egyptian cuneiform inscriptions presented the same picture: "gods" came from the stars and went back to them; they traveled in fireships or boats of the air, and possessed terrifying and powerful weapons and promised immortality to individual people.

The ancient Indian epic, Mahabharata, about 5000 years old, talked of flying machines, navigated at great heights over vast distances, that could travel forward, backward, upward, and downward at incredible speeds.

In the Tibetan books, *Tantyua* and *Kantyua*, there were constant mentions of flying machines in prehistory. These they called "pearls in the sky." Both books emphasized that the information was secret and not for the masses. Whole chapters in the Samarangava Sutradhara were devoted to describing airships whose tails spouted "fire" and "quicksilver."

Ancient peoples lifted hundreds of tons of stone from one place to another. The Egyptians brought their obelisk from Aswan, the architects of Stonehenge brought their stone blocks from southwest Wales and Marlborough, the stonemasons of Easter Island (known to the natives as the Island of the Bird Man) brought their ready-made statues from quarries miles away.

And the Great Pyramid of Giza stood unexplained.

David's notes said that according to scientific and geological research today, the Great Pyramid is constructed on the exact geophysical land center of the Earth. In other words, if one were to spread the land masses of Earth out flat, the Pyramid would be in the exact epicenter. Its measurements correspond (using Pyramid inches) to the polar diameter and radius of the Earth and also accurately correspond to the measurements in time and movement of the equinoxes and the solar year. And that is only the beginning of the mathematical marvels *built into* the Pyramid of Cheops. Within the halls, rooms and passageways of the Pyramid, the measurements correspond in time to momentous historical events known to the civilizations of Earth, except that they were prophesied rather than simply recorded. The time frame of the great flood was prophesied accurately as well as the rise and fall of man's spiritual and worldly involvement; the birth of Christ and the crucifixion, the ruling of kingdoms by great leaders, outstanding wars between nations and the development of religious and moral movements among people. The two world wars were accurately prophesied in time as well as their respective post-war agreements. Again, I read that Christ's teachings about reincarnation were struck from the Bible during the Fifth Ecumenical Council meeting in Constantinople in the year 553 A.D. The *Catholic Encyclopedia* itself states, in regard to the Fifth Ecumenical Council meeting, that "anyone asserting the belief in the preexistence of souls" would be anathema.

When I finished reading what David had given me I was exhausted. It was true that I had heard much of what I read in dribs and drabs throughout my life, but somehow having it compiled and organized in written form with respected and credible researchers and scientists and archeologists and theologians backing it up—it was different. The accumulation of evidence was too powerful to take casually, much less dismiss. And it certainly wasn't possible for me to comfortably ignore.

I didn't know what I thought about it really. I only know I couldn't stop thinking about it.

I wondered why it was so new to me. Every now and then I'd see a scientist or someone like Carl Sagan allude to the "inevitability of extraterrestrial life in the cosmos" on television. But I hadn't seen anyone present all this overwhelming material at one time, which seemed to point to the need to take our extraterrestrial past more seriously—particularly in relation to spiritual understanding and the birth of monotheism.

I knew that whatever scientific argument one scientist might suggest was usually rejected by another. None of the "experts" seemed to agree on anything anyway. Perhaps this was why there had not been any really unified presentation, much less any unified approach of all the sciences to solving the problem.

And the same was true of the Church. I could just imagine some fundamentalist preacher expounding from his electronic pulpit on Sunday morning that Moses had been guided through the desert by a space craft.

I began to laugh. I sat on my balcony looking out at the minuet of the sandpipers and just laughed out loud. It was absurd. Everything was upside down.

One thing was for sure. As a child and adolescent and now as an adult living in the free land of American democracy, *I had not been educated to think beyond the perimeters of what my traditional teachers had wanted me to know.* Now I had to learn to think for myself. Maybe all of this was crazy, but Columbus wasn't the first person to say the world wasn't flat. And when you came to think of it, how arrogant of us to assume that we were the only rational, reasoning race in the universe.

Eventually David called.

"How're ya doing?" he asked.

"Oh, just sitting around with my head on crooked."

"Well, do you feel like taking a trip?"

Before I thought about it I said, "Sure. Where?"

"Peru."

"You mean the Andes?"

"Why not?"

"Why not? I have a couple of weeks. I don't care where I go. I just want to go somewhere."

"Meet me in Lima at the airport in two days."

"You're on."

Chapter 19

"I am certain that I have been here as I am now a thousand times before, and I hope to return a thousand times. . . . Man is the dialogue between nature and God. On other planets this dialogue will doubtless be of a higher and profounder character. What is lacking is Self-Knowledge. After that the rest will follow."

—J. W. VON GOETHE
Memoirs of Johannes Falk

On the night flight to Peru it was like the old days when I took off whenever I wanted to—free and unencumbered. Spur-of-the-moment adventure—alone and traveling swiftly. I dropped contentedly to sleep.

When I woke up I was over Lima. Somewhere under the soup of smog there was a coastal city. It was worse than Los Angeles. I filled out my entrance card, declared the money I had brought with me and wondered what a South American military dictatorship would be like.

I disembarked at the Jorge Chavez Airport to a chilly morning and an open airport that was made out of cement. I hadn't told anyone where I was going. I hadn't wanted to. I just said I was leaving town on a trip. Most of my friends and my agent were used to that. There were many international travelers on board,

not only returning Peruvians. Obviously Lima was a
center for international business... mostly shady, illegal,
and having nothing to do with helping the plight of the
poor, I thought. There I was again: a rich bleeding-
heart liberal. No one recognized me and when I produced my papers and passport it didn't make any
impression. The customs, police, luggage carriers, airport authorities... everyone... wore uniforms that looked
like leftovers from the Keystone Cops. And the people
acted that way too. I expected rigid Gestapo-like military behavior even though the government was supposed to be a left-wing military group. I didn't know
anything about Peru. I only knew of the Inca civilization,
the Nazca Plains, and the fact that most of Peru had
mountains.

I had packed one fair-sized suitcase with warm- and
cold-weather clothes... a pair of combat boots and lots
of tapes and a tape recorder and note paper. Whatever
was going to happen to me I wanted it down in writing.

Except for the fact that I didn't fill out one docu-
ment in triplicate, nothing untoward happened as I
passed through customs and waited for my suitcase on
the other side. The sun had just come up to take the
chill off the air when I looked over at the wall where
people waited for arrivals. I didn't recognize anyone.
The cement airport couldn't have been more depressing.
The baggage carousel turned and down tumbled my
suitcase. I picked it up along with my hand luggage and
made my way to the street where I would look around
some more and then decide whether to take a cab into
town. I wasn't frightened.

I walked toward the front entrance of the airport
and just as I saw a dilapidated cab that looked as though
it might take me to the local Sheraton I felt someone
take my suitcase out of my hand. Quickly I turned and
looked into the face of David.

"Hi," he said. He had a woolen scarf wrapped
around his neck and a combat jacket zipped up the
front. He was tanned and smiling.

"Hi," I said, "you're Mr. Livingstone, I presume?"

"Anything you say, ma'am. Did you have a good trip?"

"It was okay."

"Welcome to the mountains I love very much. They have saved my life many times. They are peaceful."

I looked into his eyes, not needing to know any more than that.

"Come," he said, "don't mind my jalopy, but I couldn't get a Land Rover. That's the best way to travel in the mountains."

"The mountains?" I asked. "We're going right away to the Andes?"

"Sure. It would be hard to avoid. Peru *is* the Andes. But wait 'til you see them. They're different from the Himalayas but just as gorgeous."

He picked up both bags and led me to an old, red, rental Plymouth which was parked alongside a dirt road adjacent to the airport.

"Did you eat breakfast on the plane?"

"Yep."

"Okay. Then we'll stop and get some provisions before we head straight for Llocllapampa."

The pollution mixed with fog made me cough. I had thought of Lima as a sun-splashed resort city by the sea with perfect climate and people running around in South American muu-muus. This was dank, damp, dingy, and depressing.

David said there was a legend based on fact about Lima. When Pizarro invaded the Inca civilization, by way of a peace offering, the Incas directed Pizarro's armies to make their base camp here in what was now Lima. They proudly showed their conquering masters this territory during the months of January and February, which were the most exquisite months for weather locally and, indeed, anywhere in the world. But that was it. The rest of the year was dismal. As soon as the armies settled in, the weather changed. The Incas professed it to be an accident. But, of course, it never got any better and in no time most of Pizarro's armies had pneumonia.

"Hey, what about those Incas? How come they were so intelligent?" I asked.

"I guess they were easy to help," David said. "Primitive people don't fight miracles, they relax and figure somebody else knows better than they."

"Like who?"

He just winked.

"Oh," I said. "I forgot," and I pointed upward and patted my knee.

David lit up one of his Camels and asked if there was anything special I would be needing because where we were going if there was a kerosene lantern around we'd be lucky.

"I know you're used to roughing it," he said, "but this time there won't be any Sherpas or bearers or anybody to do anything for you except yourself." He suggested toilet paper, basic canned food, a hot water bottle, and anything to keep myself warm. He said there was no heat where we were going either.

I thought of the time I spent in a hut in the Himalayas when I was sure I would freeze to death. My only recourse had been to employ some sort of mind-over-matter technique, so I concentrated on the hottest thing I could think of—the sun. Shivering and chattering I lay down on a makeshift cot, closed my eyes and somewhere in the center of my mind I found my own orange sun. I concentrated as hard as I could and before long I felt perspiration drip from my midriff and finally I had the impression that daylight had come in my head. Every night for the two weeks I spent in the Himalayan snow I used that technique. Now it looked as though I might have to do it again and I was afraid I was out of practice.

The road leading into Lima was paved but clogged with smoke-spewing trucks and dirty cars. People nonchalantly walked around in gray overworn business suits and I wondered what offices they worked in so early in the morning.

"Lima is on the brink of revolution," said David. "The rate of inflation is climbing so rapidly that people find it impossible to live. It's awful. And as usual it's the poor who suffer most. Their salaries stay the same—the prices rise. Anyway—I'm not too interested in how the government here is screwing things up. It would just be a question of time anyway. And it's only symptomatic of what's happening with governments all over the world. Right?" I nodded. "Now to a Peruvian supermarket for basics—okay?"

It felt strange to be in a new place and yet know at the same time that it's being new was not really why I was here.

The so-called supermarket was a little like a small New York privately owned market—not quite a delicatessen on First Avenue, maybe, but I had the feeling the proprietors could raise their prices whenever they felt like it. The meats and cheeses and breads and pastries were housed in glass-enclosed cases and a soft drink called Inca Cola seemed to be David's favorite staple. He bought a case of it and a bottle opener. He opened one bottle right there, shook the fizz out of it and drank it down.

"Between cigarettes and this delicious crap I guess you could say I'm not exactly a health resort."

Remembering my low blood sugar, I bought canned nuts, tuna fish, cheese, and a dozen eggs that I hoped I would be able to hard-boil somewhere. There were many Peruvian pastry delicacies but I couldn't eat them, and I found myself wondering what it would be like if I had a low blood sugar attack in the mountains.

David spoke fluent Spanish. I was surprised, but said nothing, and as he rattled on with the cashier, the shape of his face seemed almost to mold itself around the Peruvian words. He seemed to have the facility to *become* the nationality he was portraying.

"Ah, yes," he said as we left the store. "The world *is* a stage, isn't it, and we are all nothing but actors portraying the scenario."

"You have an advantage," I said. "You seem to know how the script is going to come out."

"Something like that," he answered, lifting his case

of Inca Cola into the back seat. "Only you never can tell
about those actors who haven't read the script." He
winked and opened the door of the used car.

We never did drive through Lima. So I couldn't
say what it was like. I knew there was a Sheraton Hotel
in there somewhere and the Museum of Natural History tracing the civilization of the Incas and even pre-Incas.

We drove northeast further out of town and toward
the foothills of the Andes. David said he had been to
Peru many times and that it was about three times the
size of California and had, because of its varying terrain,
three different climates. He said we were on our way to
a city of about 100,000 inhabitants called Huancayo,
located high in the Andes. We wouldn't be actually
staying in Huancayo because it was too dusty and
crowded. We would be staying along the way in a little
place that barely existed at all except for the fact that
there were mineral baths, some food, a place to sleep
and the most incredible view of the heavens available
on earth. He winked again when he described it and
even though the weather on the outskirts of Lima was
sunless and dismal I began to feel happy. Huancayo was
225 miles away—all uphill...

We stopped in a bazaar just outside the city where
David suggested I buy a poncho made of alpaca wool.
He said the very style of the poncho would come in
handy because it would act as a blanket as well as a
wrap. It was lovely and soft and an oatmeal color I
loved. David said nothing about my Ralph Lauren
leather coat and I was just as glad to cover it up. Along
with the poncho I bought a neck scarf to match. The
price of both items together was eighteen dollars. At
the moment I was sweltering in my blue jeans, but I
had traveled enough to know that where mountains
were concerned nothing was warm enough when the
sun went down.

The road, with native Indians draped in their own
ponchos alongside, began to wind. About forty-three
kilometers outside of Lima we passed a community
called Chosica.

"People come to the lowlands looking for a new life

and end up in a place like this," said David, shaking his head.

There was no grass, no trees, a few cactus, but for the most part the land was barren: the hills surrounding were rock, sand and dust.

Advertisements for Inca Cola were splashed across billboards.

A truck carrying used box spring mattresses, with a picture of Che Guevara on the wheel flaps, passed us. "They admire him here," said David. "Because he died for his ideas."

The people along the road looked Tibetan.

Telephone wires leading to the top of the Andes crisscrossed overhead.

Tiny stalls sold fruit and ice cream and more Inca Cola.

A train transporting coal from above passed us going the other way on the tracks that ran beside the road.

About forty-five minutes outside of Lima the sun broke through the bruise-colored sky and it turned light turquoise. The air became fresher, the trees showed green and once again I was reminded of how badly contaminated our lives had become in big cities regardless of where we lived in the world. Even the smiles on people's faces were more pronounced. I felt happy and was unconcerned that I had no idea what to expect or what might happen to me.

Small communities sprang up with mountain Indians working the fields surrounding them. The higher we climbed the greener it got. We passed Cocachacra. We began to follow the beginning of a river.

"That's the Mantaro," said David. "Wait 'til you see it higher up."

A tunnel railroad wound around the cliffs which were getting steeper now. Burros appeared along the road. We passed a smelting factory.

"They smelt the coal they mine in the mountains," said David. "These are coal smelting communities. They live and die doing just that."

The community was called Rio Seco and behind it

the soil was richer and blacker. The river bed began to
grow greenery. Tea gardens were visible now underneath the volcanic hills.

The river began to tumble over rocks.

There were small square stones with flowers placed
before them jutting out of the ground.

"Those are tombstones," said David. "Here in the
Andes whenever a person dies in a car accident he is
buried on the spot where the accident occurred."

Shrines of bright turquoise were placed in strategic
positions.

We were at 5,000 feet now. I began to feel a bit
sleepy. A woman in a pink striped serape carried water
to her destination which David said must be Rio Seco,
now two miles behind us.

We climbed higher.

Small valleys with grazing cattle were nestled in
between the foothills and soon when the road became
unpaved, dusty and filled with potholes, lumps and
ruts, David suggested we stop at a roadside restaurant
and have some rice and beans. We had been driving for
an hour without stops and he said we had another five
or six hours to go.

The restaurant looked like a Mexican luncheonette
but the food could have been Peruvian gourmet as far as
I was concerned. David ordered us some bottled water
and we settled in to eat rice and beans, stuffed eggs
with hot sauce, and cold boiled potatoes smothered
with a kind of peanut mayonnaise. It was delicious. I
began to breathe a little quicker. He noticed and took
me in the back where an oxygen machine waited, fully
equipped to assist any tourist who might suffer from
altitude sickness. We were now at about 10,000 feet and
since I had danced at a height of about 7,500 feet with
no trouble I didn't think I would be bothered now. But
I breathed some of the oxygen anyway and left the
machine feeling I was flying.

At lunch we talked mostly of Peruvian customs,
how he felt the left wing military government wouldn't
last long and how Peru imported almost all of its gas

and oil from the Middle East when it had a rich supply of its own right under the mountains. David was relaxed, happy that I was too, and seemed less intense than he had been back in Los Angeles. He refused a drink offered by the owner, protesting the altitude and the necessity of keeping his wits for the long winding trip ahead of us. We didn't speak of anything personal, and soon we finished and left the restaurant. On the counter near the door were two jars. One bore the inscription, "Para Llorar," the other "Para Reir." Under them in English it said, "Does your woman love you?"

Back in the Plymouth again and passing a small mining village I noticed a sign saying that we were at 3,746 meters (or 11,238 feet) above sea level. So far I felt nothing really serious. If I did feel altitude nausea David said I could get more oxygen at a nearby mining center called Casapalca. But it wasn't necessary. The greenery disappeared from the mountains and only a red-orange clay earth remained. People pounded rocks alongside the road reminding me of what I had seen in the Himalayas. Many of them smoked. David said seventy per cent of the Peruvian people were Indians and to my eyes their features could have been Oriental or Mongolian. Their hair was blue-black and their eyes like black grapes swimming in suntanned leather faces. The women wore long thick black braids and starched white hats surrounded by black ribboned brims. Their dresses were thick brightly colored cottons.

Mining iron ore and other minerals seemed to be the work around which their lives revolved. Pyramids of mineral earth dotted the valleys where the Indians worked, using hand shovels to fill nearby pickup trucks.

"There is a wealth of minerals in these mountains," said David, "minerals that are not found anywhere else on earth."

He talked awhile about the geological shifts in the earth under the Andes and told me that all over Peru were buried civilizations thousands of years old just waiting to be excavated if the Peruvian government would allocate enough money for that purpose. "But

they won't," he said. "They haven't got enough respect
for the past. That's why they will always be condemned
to make the same mistakes in the future."

Now we passed a chalk mining community called
Chicla. There was a white church and every other
structure was painted turquoise. Even the buses passing us were turquoise. Maybe the people were painting
the color of the sky.

More Peruvian Indians pounded rocks along the
roadside. Just before we entered a railway tunnel the
car sputtered and conked out.

"It's the lack of oxygen," said David. "There's not
enough combustion. Don't worry, it'll start up again."
And it did, just as a herd of llamas was led through the
tunnel looking for all the world like a picture postcard
you'd sign saying, "Wish you were here."

The smoke from our tailpipe was blue now. The
contour of the mountains changed. They were more
horizontal, less vertical. There was snow on their tops.
Wildflowers grew and the higher the altitude the brighter
their colors.

We passed more tombstones along the road, graced
with purple wildflowers.

Passing through San Mateo I now saw eucalyptus
and pine trees. Peruvian peasants dressed like Tibetans
led herds of goats. The women wore iridescent crimson
mixed with orange in their serapes.

There was a Catholic church in every community.

The mountain soil was a deep red now. Iron ore,
David said. Clothes hung on lines in the hot sun which
was getting hotter the higher we climbed. Two women,
wearing white straw-brimmed hats, sat knitting with
long strands of llama wool.

The road was rock now, not paved. A wild hairy pig
walked between two dwellings with a Mobil Oil sign on
one side and Coca-Cola on the other.

The road was dangerously narrow. David said it
was not uncommon for a bus to topple over the edge.

Even though the hot sun was beating down, the
men wore wool sweaters and wool skull caps as though

their basic association with the mountains was cold. All day they gazed at the snowcapped mountains above.

We looked below us at the winding mountain road. And above us at about 20,000 feet on a mountain top waved the Peruvian flag.

The temperature was cooler now. The sunshine brilliant, the air pure and rarefied. Then at 15,806 feet above sea level we came to a sign.

A sign beside a railway crossing called Abra Anticona. It said: *"PUNTO FERROVIARO MAS ALTO DEL MUNDO."* In English: "Highest Railway Point in the World." Just adjacent to that sign was another one. It said: *"EXISTEN LOS PLATILLOS VOLADORES CONTACTO CON OVNIS."* In English: "Flying Saucers Do Exist. UFO Contact Point."

I looked over at David with raised eyebrows. He smiled. "Well," he said, "I'm not the only crazy one, am I?"

"What does that mean?" I asked.

"It means that people see lots of UFOs around here and it's common knowledge and no one is particularly disturbed by it."

I took a deep breath.

"Did we come here to see UFOs? Is that why I'm here?"

"Maybe."

"Oh. My. God."

"Yes," he said. "Exactly."

We drove on. The road became smoother, and now we were descending in altitude. The mountains were dotted with green again and there, running parallel to the road, was a magnificent copper-colored river.

"There's the Mantaro River," said David, "just like I wanted you to see it. Have you ever seen anything more beautiful? Out across the plain ahead is what we call the Mantaro River Valley."

The mountains were like undulating hills. The colors were a mixture of yellows and oranges and falling purple shadows as the afternoon sun descended into what we in films called the Magic Hour.

Puffy whipped clouds hung motionless in the clear sky as I had my first glimpse of an Andean Shangri-La.

David pulled the Plymouth to the side of the road where two men beside an adobe building were patting square mud cakes together with their hands.

"This is it," he said. "This is Llocllapampa. This is where we're going to stay."

"Where?"

"There." He pointed to another adobe building across the street. Except for one other structure about seventy-five feet away there were no other buildings anywhere around.

"That's our hotel," said David. "C'mon, let's get out and stretch."

I couldn't believe what he said. There *was* no hotel. Three women with straw brooms pounded a pile of grain by the roadside while a rooster ran in and out of their skirts.

They smiled at us and waved at David. He spoke to them in Spanish and gestured to me as though he was introducing us. I nodded. He took our bags from the car and told me to follow him.

Through a wooden door separated in the middle so either the top or the bottom could be shut we entered a dirt patio inside the adobe building. There was a paved walkway which led to what turned out to be two rooms. They were next to each other but with no adjoining door. I opened the door to one of the rooms. Across the door was a piece of cotton material on a string. Inside the room was a dirt floor and a low-slung cot. Beside the cot was a crate of some kind which served as a bedside table. There was no electricity and no bathroom. There was a blanket on the bed and a gray-colored pillow . . . no sheets . . . no pillow cases . . .

I turned to David.

"You've got a great imagination."

He smiled. "Yep."

"Is this really it?"

"Yep. It's not much but It's Home," he said. "I'm right next door."

There were some nails hammered into the adobe wall.

"Your closet," he said. "You'd better unpack now if you're going to, because when the sun goes down you won't be able to see a thing."

"I see," I said reluctantly.

"I'll be back in a minute," he said and disappeared into his room, which had exactly the same decor as mine.

He pounded on the thin wall and said the Mantaro River would be our bathroom and he'd take me there in a minute but I should change into something warmer before we went for our first mineral water bath.

This was not science fiction. This was definitely out of one of my old lives. ❧

Chapter 20

*"It is immediately apparent ... that this sense-world,
this seemingly real external universe, though it may
be useful and valid in other respects, cannot be the
external world, but only the self's projected picture
of it ... The evidence of the senses cannot be accepted as evidence of the nature of ultimate reality."*

—E. UNDERHILL
Mysticism

❦ I unzipped my suitcase that had been all over the
world with me and hung up a sweater, my new poncho
and a sun hat. I never forgot to take a sun hat with me
wherever I went, because my face turned into a tomato
after two hours in high-altitude sun. I left my underwear in the suitcase, wondering how I would ever wash
it anyway, and I thanked God (or somebody) that I had
just finished my period and wouldn't have to contend
with that. I looked at my ring watch which somehow
always made me feel secure. I pulled out my tapes,
recording machine and note paper. Sketchily and quickly I jotted down what the place looked and felt like.
With each passing moment of the setting sun I realized
how really cold it was going to get.

David rapped on my door, handed me a towel and
directed me to take my poncho and change into my
combat boots for our first visit to the mineral baths.

Mineral baths in this cold? "Sure," he said. "At first it's murder but then just wait . . ."

We walked from the paved patio back onto the road. The surrounding mountains were splashed with purple shadows. Barnyard animals that I couldn't see gurgled and clucked at each other. A mangy dog waddled up to us wagging her tail followed by three puppies. The men patting the earth squares were gone for the evening and right across the street from our "hotel" was an adobe building called FOOD. That meant the people inside would cook for us. Loudly through the door I heard a scratchy radio broadcasting a soccer game. Inside, Peruvian Indians laughed and cheered to themselves and then shuffled back and forth in between tables that had been set up for the evening. Soup steamed on a gas stove and an old Indian woman with no teeth asked if we'd like some. "No," David said to me. "Let's eat afterward. We'll get heartburn from the mineral baths if we eat now."

I wasn't particularly hungry anyway, but I asked if someone would boil some eggs for me just so I'd have some food on hand in case I needed it. David asked the Indian woman to take the eggs out of the Plymouth. She smiled and nodded.

He led me around toward the back of the building and using a flashlight from his back pocket we went down some stairs. They were steep, and in the fading light I was afraid I might trip. I might be in Shangri-La now but some day I'd have to go back to dancing. I heard water flowing below. Then spread out in the sunset before me was the glorious Mantaro River. It rushed over the mountain rocks and splashed against the over-hanging trees embedded in the high banks. There were level green knolls of grass leading down to the water where a few Indians hunched in their ponchos sat gazing at the sun settling behind the mountains. Even in the fading light I could see that the river was orange.

"Come," said David, leading me to what looked like an adobe enclosure covered with a tin roof. "It's not much to look at but wait 'til you feel it inside." He unbolted a crude wooden door, went in and from another pocket took a candle, lit it, and placed it on a wooden bench inside the enclosure. Next to the bench deep in the ground was a gurgling pool of sparkling water.

"This is one of the famous Andes mineral baths," he said.

I looked down into it. It wasn't just the candlelight that made it sparkle. It seemed to be the water itself. A light film of steam hung over it. I knelt down on the earth floor and ran my hand through the water. To my surprise it felt warm and bubbly . . . bubbly and stinging and effervescent . . . like champagne.

"The minerals make it bubble," said David. "And it's great for aching bones and muscles. You'll see."

When I drew my hand out of the water it was freezing.

"I'm supposed to go all the way in that water and not freeze to death when I get out?" I asked, laughing.

"Well, for a few minutes it's cold as hell but after that you'll be warmer than if you didn't do it at all."

I stood up awkwardly. I wished I could go in with all my clothes on. Now how was this supposed to work? Was I supposed to peel off my clothes with him standing right there or what?

"You go ahead," said David. "I'll wait outside. Call me when you're ready."

Slowly I took off my poncho and hung it on one of five nails protruding from the wall. I wondered how many people had done the same thing in the candlelight. Then I took off my sweater and slacks. I wondered what they did after they got out of the water. I wondered how I could hang each garment so I could put them back on quickly when I was ready to leave. Down to my underpants and socks, I ripped them off quickly because by now I was shivering. The hell with it. I left everything in a little pile on the wooden bench wondering how it would look to David when he came back in.

The candlelight flickered against the cold stone walls. I stepped quickly to the bubbling pool of water in the ground and slowly I put my right leg in. I hoped I would find a bottom and I did. It was slightly slippery. Tangy bubbles settled onto my skin. I slid in all the way up to my neck. It felt as though I had just stepped into a giant deep dish pie of warm bubbling soda water. It felt wonderful.

The water was so buoyant I felt I was floating. In fact, it was difficult to firmly find the bottom. It felt as though I was walking in the midst of the water, somehow upright. There was a square hole in the opposite wall where the water drained out to the river outside. Apparently this was a constantly fed pool from underground somewhere.

"Okay," I yelled to David, "I'm in now and it's great."

"Sure," he said, coming through the door, "wait 'til you feel it really go through your skin."

David turned around, pulled off his jacket, sweater, shirt, underpants and boots and socks in about five seconds and said, "Now *you* turn around." I did.

"Okay," he said.

I turned back around. He was standing under the water across the small pool from me.

I breathed deeply and tried to relax. "You'll have to bear with me awhile," I said. "This is all so sudden, and I know I've done a lot of things in my life, but I have a feeling that none of it was like this." I felt ridiculous.

"Yep, you're right."

"Yes," I breathed again. I didn't even want to ask what he meant.

"Look," he said, "swish your arms up and down like this in the water and feel how the bubbles stick to your skin."

I swirled my arms up and down and around and it was like two swizzle sticks going through freshly poured champagne. The swizzle was like self-generating heat. It wasn't the same as the sulphur baths in Japan. They were more mild and calm. These waters had zing and punch and a verve of their own.

David stood quietly with the candlelight flickering

off the opposite wall. His blue eyes seemed lit themselves and small drops of water fell from his chin. I wondered what I looked like to him.

I couldn't think of what to say so I said, "Do you come here often?"

David laughed. "Yep," he said. He stared into the candle. "Want to try something?" he asked.

I thought, Oh shit, here it comes. "What do you mean?" I asked, looking around casually.

"See the light of that candle?" he asked.

"Yes," I answered.

"Okay, focus on the light real hard and take a deep breath."

"Take a deep breath?" I asked.

"Yes, take a deep breath."

I breathed deeply, almost choking on some spit. I had been taking deep breaths all day. "Can I just let my arms go?" I asked, wanting to appear as though I was willing to try anything.

"Sure. In this water they float. In fact, it would really be hard to sink in this water."

I thought, that's a relief. At least I wouldn't drown if worse came to worst. I let my arms go as though they were unattached, smiling in the candlelight. I felt them rise slightly beside me.

My God, I thought. Now he'll just leap across this pool and scoop me under my arms and because of this goddamn buoyancy I'll never get them down.

"Now just concentrate on the candle until you feel *you* are the candlelight."

Jesus, I thought. He must be kidding. Until *I'm* the candlelight? I can't even be *me* right now, whoever that was.

I stared at the flickering light. I tried not to blink. I took another deep breath. My heart was pounding. I was sure he could hear it reverberate through the water. I just stood there staring into the candle as he had suggested.

Quietly David said, "Hey, Shirl. What are you afraid of?"

"Me?" I asked.

"No," he said teasingly. "The woman standing behind you."

I felt really ridiculous now. I thought of all the guys who had said, "Hey, I just want to lie down with you and relax. I don't want to *do* anything."

"Hey," said David, "if that was on my mind all I'd have to do is suggest it, right?"

Jesus, he was direct.

I coughed. "Well," I said. "Well, I hesitate," I said.

"Well, you don't have to hesitate. I just want you to try something, and it isn't what you think. Besides, I don't even want to."

I felt myself get indignant. He didn't even want to?

"Why?" I asked. "Why not?"

"What do you mean, why not?" he asked. "That's not what we came here for. If you thought it was, you'll just have to be patient and give me time."

I laughed out loud, making an echo on the walls.

"Come on," he said, "concentrate on the candle and breathe deeply."

"Okay," I said, "I guess I might as well. After all, we've had a couple of lifetimes together, right?"

He laughed. "Right."

It was clear he thought I was a jerk.

I tried again to gaze freely at the candle.

"Okay, breathe deeply again," he gently directed me.

I tried to breathe deeply again.

"Okay," he said. "Now concentrate on the light of the candle as though it were the center of your own being. Make the candle *you*. Only think about the candle—nothing else."

I concentrated and breathed deeper. I guess I'll really have to do this, I thought. Besides, he's right. I'm a jerk and he's really nice. I felt my mind begin to relax. I concentrated with more relaxation. My eyelids felt a little bit heavy until I could tell that my eyes were half closed, but still the candle was visible.

I heard David's voice faintly in the background of my mind.

"That's good. Great, you're doing great."

I liked the sound of his voice above the water. It seemed to skip along with the bubbles. I felt my breathing slow down. Slowly, I was aware that my heartbeat was pulsating in rhythm with my breathing. Somehow the rhythm of the two seemed in sync. Time slowly slipped away until I became unaware of it. The candle continued to flicker, but now it began to be the center of my mind. My whole body seemed to float too, not only my arms, but all of me. Slowly, slowly, I *became* the water and each tingling bubble was a component part of the water. It was a marvelous double feeling. I was totally conscious, aware of myself, yet part of everything around me. I remember being aware that every single bubble was a part of all of the water that surrounded me, almost as though the water wouldn't be what it was without each bubble doing its part to sustain the whole of it. I felt the cool sides of the walls housing the warm water pool even though I was lost somewhere in its midst. I felt shadows and flickers and a slight breeze. But mostly, I felt the inside of myself. I felt the involuntary reflex of my own breathing. It seemed to be a moving entity oblivious of my control. Then I felt the interconnection of my breathing with the pulse of the energy around me. The air itself seemed to pulsate. In fact, I *was* the air. I was the air, the water, the darkness, the walls, the bubbles, the candle, the wet rocks under the water, and even the sound of the rushing river outside. Then I felt my energy vibrate to David. Since I was part of everything around me, that meant David too. At that moment I stopped myself. I could feel myself make a conscious decision not to go that far. Again my hesitation, my fear or whatever you want to call it, stopped me, and I stopped the flow of relaxation and the attempt to become "one" with everything.

"That's okay," I heard David say, "that was good. How was it for a first attempt at breathing meditation?"

I stretched my arms out of the water and asked what time it was.

"It doesn't matter about time," he said. "What

matters is that you forget about it for a while. You *breathed*. You really breathed. Breathing is life. Don't you feel like you've had a rest?"

Yes, I did. Definitely. I asked him if I had been hypnotized.

"No, just a kind of self-relaxing expanded awareness," he said. "You can learn to rejuvenate like that instantaneously. Breathing is an involuntary act, and if you can learn to regulate it, you will stay young longer."

Shit, I thought in a kind of dream, Elizabeth Arden should teach this in her beauty courses. I could hear David talking to me, but I was still spaced out from my own breath. He was talking about animals, and how the ones who lived the longest were the ones that breathed the least. Something about giant tortoises only breathing four times a minute and they live to be three hundred years old. I remember thinking if I had cold blood I'd only breathe four times a minute too. But I had warm blood and I was beginning to feel shivery.

"So, are you interested in living a long time, eh?" he asked.

I shook my head. I felt the champagne bubbles in my brain.

"Living a long time? I don't know. Are you?"

"Me?" he said.

"No," I said. "The man standing behind you."

He smiled. "Am I interested in living a long time?"

"Yeah."

"Yeah," he answered. "I am, but I don't think I will."

There was something in the way he said it that made me shiver. The shiver surprised me.

"Well, nobody could live long in this cold. I'm cold now. What do you say?"

"I say," he said, "let's get out of here."

He turned to face the flickering wall. I stepped slowly out of the water. My teeth clacked together as though they were false and my arms and hands shook so hard I could barely reach for the towel on the nail in the wall. Then as hard as I could I rubbed my arms, legs, feet and torso until I could feel the blood come to the surface and I actually began to tingle with a warm afterglow. My clothes felt cold next to my skin but soon my body heat reflected inside the wool of the sweater and socks.

"I feel wonderful now," I said. "That water is really something."

"Take the flashlight out of my pocket and wait for me outside," said David. "I'll be there as quick as I can get dry."

The cold mountain air must have registered somewhere around fifteen degrees, but it was fresh and clear. I walked around the side of the pool shelter and looked out over the river and the dark looming mountains above. Life was a novel, I thought to myself. Two months ago I never could have predicted in my wildest imagination that I would be here doing this. And I was really loving it. I was also learning that trusting the best instincts in myself had its virtues. You could actually space out on them.

I felt suddenly hungry and when those pangs came I knew I should eat immediately or my blood sugar would drop.

"Okay," said David, fully dressed, rubbing his hands together and smiling. "Let's go up and get some grub. They'll have hot milk waiting for us and some Indian stew made of meat and vegetables and mountain herbs."

He blew out the candle, stuffed it into his pocket and said we'd need it later in our rooms. He also suggested that I use the river for the bathroom now because later it would be much too cold to make the trek.

I squatted behind a rock and used some Kleenex I had stashed in my pocket. Climbing the cold stone stairs, I wondered how the cold would be when I tried to sleep.

"Don't worry about sleeping," said David, once again seeming to read my mind. "It'll all come in its own time."

If he had said that an hour before I would have assumed he meant something else.

The radio soccer game was on full blast when we

walked into the FOOD building on the road above. Runny-nosed children scampered back and forth in between the tables that were set up for tourists who might be exploring the area and want to eat. One younger woman cooking had a child at her skirts and another strapped to her back. She wore the customary white starched hat with the black ribboned brim even though it was night time.

David called for some hot milk and stew and we talked about food. I told him how much I loved "junk food" and he told me how bad it was to eat. I told him I knew that. I loved it anyway. He talked about how important it was to take care of the body because at the same time you'd be taking care of your spirit. He said it was just a question of chemistry. I said I wasn't very good at that either. He gave me a run down on food-combining and I said, yes, I had heard most of it before. As he talked, I reflected on how he had been all evening. He seemed compelled to teach me everything there was in as fast a time as possible. He was telling me I should relax, yet he himself was driven. He was criticizing my junk-food habits, but he had them too. Sometimes he sounded almost pompous and presumptuous. Sometimes he didn't seem to really be enjoying the life he said I should relax and enjoy more.

It was funny; I was hacking Gerry about letting himself go so he could know more who he was and David was doing the same thing with me. I wondered what Gerry would think if he could see me now. I thought of my theme song, "If They Could See Me Now." I wondered what the audience in Vegas would think if I came out and gave them a few jokes about spiritual discovery in the Andes. I really seemed to be two people—or ten people—I didn't know. Yet was I an actress because I was more closely in touch with some of the roles I had played in other lives?

The woman with the child on her back came to our table. She was carrying hot milk and stew. I scooped it up as though eating might go out of style.

It was delicious, spiced with mountain herbs I had never heard of. I sopped up the natural juices with the

thick homemade heavy bread rolls. They reminded me
of my happiest time as a child camping out in Virginia
when the world and life seemed simple.

"Tomorrow," said David, "we'll take a long walk.
I'll show you some of the territory, and you'll see for
yourself why I love this place."

He led me across the road to our hotel. The stars
were so close I felt that I could reach out and pluck
them like plums. I could almost hear the surrounding
mountains sway under them. The Andes were not like
the Bhutanese Himalayas. They felt lower and more
spread out. The environment wasn't as isolated, and
because of the pervasive Peruvian Indian culture, I
didn't feel as insignificant as I had high above the world
with the Bhutanese lamas.

Our rooms smelled dank and dusty, and I wondered who else had slept there. There was a good
five-degree drop in temperature when I walked inside.
David handed me the candle, said he had another for
himself, and said goodnight.

"By the way," he said, "just a little tip about
sleeping in a cold climate—if you sleep with no clothes
on under your poncho, you'll find it much warmer."

I couldn't understand. I was intending to put on
everything I brought.

"No," he said, "the body generates its own aura
heat. Try it. You'll see what I mean."

I said goodnight. I didn't want to hear any more
from him. I took off my clothes under the poncho. I
crawled in under the wool blanket on the cot and
prayed (so to speak) that I would get warm. My feet
were ice. I waited. Since the alpaca wool was soft, it felt
nice. I waited some more. I felt I was watching my own
pot boil. I calmed my mind and my chattering teeth as
much as I could. I thought of my electric blanket by the
ocean and how I had loved to sleep in a cold rainstorm
with the windows wide open and the blanket turned up
high. Right that minute, as I lay in the wilds of the
Andes, that electric blanket was my favorite part of an
advanced civilization. I thought of Gerry again. It was
nice being without him. I thought of how impossible it

would be for me to describe what I was up to, to him. I wondered where he was. I wondered if he was *really* seeing it. I thought of my show. Where were my gypsies tonight?—my dancers . . . at Joe Allen's having cheeseburgers and gossiping about how the big stars were not nearly so all-around talented as they were? I thought of what it was to be a star when you really weren't all that sure you deserved it.

Soon I realized my muscles were relaxing from the warmth of the space between my body and the covers. It was the *space* that was warm, not the covers. I suddenly understood that most of what we didn't understand in our lives was what we couldn't *see*. The invisible truth was the truth that required the most struggle to find. *Seeing* wasn't believing—not at all. *Looking* was what it was more about.

With a kind of relaxed shiver I fell off to sleep, with only the sound of silence. Then somewhere behind the building I heard pigs snorting.

Chapter 21

*"No theory of physics that deals only with physics
will ever explain physics. I believe that as we go on
trying to understand the universe, we are at the
same time trying to understand man. Today I think
we are beginning to suspect that man is not a tiny
cog that doesn't really make much difference to the
running of the huge machine but rather that there is
a much more intimate tie between man and the
universe than we heretofore suspected....the physical
world is in some deep sense tied to the human
being."*

—DR. JOHN A. WHEELER

❧ The sun rose over the mountains about five-thirty
A.M. It didn't stream into my room because there were
no windows but the contrast from the cold of the night
was so pronounced I could feel the warmth of the first
rays even through the walls. My poncho lay comfortably
around me. I had been warm all night.

I stood in my bare feet on the cold earth floor and
thought what contradictory logic it was getting dressed
now when the sun was out, and undressed during the
cold night. I knew the mountain air would be fresh and
sharp and because of the altitude the sun would burn. I
put on my California sun hat and walked outside. I
could smell morning smoke from across the road and as

I rounded the Plymouth I saw David sitting on a mud wall watching the men from the day before pat their square bricks into what would ultimately be the foundation of a house they were building.

"Good morning," he said. "How was it last night?"

"Just like you said. Nude meant warmth. I wouldn't have believed it but there it was."

"That's beginning to become a habit with you, isn't it?"

"What is?"

"You're finally believing because it *is*."

"Yeah, well. What's for breakfast?"

"They boiled your eggs for you. So all you need now is a bag and some salt. Let's get some hot milk and rolls."

We walked into the food room and the woman with the baby on her back smiled openly, with a kind of tacit understanding that the two-room love affair that David and I were conducting was just another strange North American custom.

"They don't ask personal questions around here," he said. "Anything we do is anything we do."

We sat next to a window and I saw the women from the evening before continue to pound their grain.

"They are separating the wheat from the chaff," said David with a wink. He certainly did wink a lot. "We'll have bread made from those very wheat kernels in a day or two."

In the morning light I could see that the tile roof on our adobe hotel was red and around the women were roosters with feathers of the same color.

David leaned back in his chair and watched me. I guess he had decided to grow a beard because he hadn't shaved and probably couldn't have if he wanted to. He really did have a handsome face.

"Did you sleep well, did you dream?" he asked.

"I can't remember. I was mostly pleased with being warm enough." I didn't feel like being analyzed.

We munched our rolls and hot milk and I peeled an egg and ate it. In a place like this a person didn't need much except maybe more of themselves.

"Can we go for a walk?" I asked.

"Sure. Great idea."

We stepped outside into the sunlight. The air felt thin and crisp against my face. My heart raced slightly with the altitude. I stretched my arms out beside me and breathed and lifted my face into the sun.

I loved mountains more than any other part of the Earth. To me they had been through so much and seemed so patient and resigned and wisely silent. They represented every extreme I could think of—height, depth, bottom, top, grandeur, insignificance, struggle, attainment—everything. And regardless of what adversity befell a mountain it seemed to tower with its steadfast resilience when it was over, even if it erupted from inside itself.

"Let's walk down by the river," said David. "Want to brush your teeth?"

I had my toothbrush in my back pocket and as we walked down the stone stairs and passed the mineral pool bathhouse David ran ahead of me, skipping with his arms outstretched almost like a kid from kindergarten during recess. He skipped across the grassy river bank tilting his head from one side to another in sheer childish glee.

"I love it out here!!" I heard him yell to the river. "You river—you are rushing so fast—why? Where are you going that you have to be on time!"

I laughed with a kind of amazement and ran up to him. "I love the water," he said, "excuse me. Here, over here is another mineral pool for drinking, or tooth-brushing, or washing." He ran with great leaps to the water and knelt down, put his head under and came up laughing and sputtering in the sunlight. His salt-and-pepper hair dripped like a bowl around his face and he smiled with such playful abandon that I felt like a child too.

I knelt beside the pool and looked into it. Patches of white sulphur film swam on top. A slow current from beneath fed fresh running bubbles into the center.

David cupped his hands and drank. "You have to

get used to the taste but it's sensational for the system; cleans out the impurities and settles your digestion."

I dug out my toothbrush, dipped it into the water and tasted it on my tongue. It was like medicinal salt.

"You're not sad today, are you?" I asked him.

"No, I'm never sad when I'm outside. It's too real here to be sad. Cities make me sad because people care too much about the wrong things. When you're in touch with this, you're in touch with people." He shook his wet hair into the air and sprawled out on his back with his head on his hands looking up at the sky.

I finished brushing my teeth, stood up, stretched in the sunlight and we began to walk.

I opened and shut my eyes blinking into the cloud-puffed brilliant blue sky. God, it was beautiful. And it was even more beautiful when I thought that beauty simply existed for the sake of itself. Beauty didn't need a reason and couldn't be explained. It just was. It didn't have anything to do with anyone else. It didn't need to be shared to be appreciated. Beauty was beauty. And it was necessary like food and water.

I felt David walking beside me relaxed and unassuming.

"Feel better?" he asked.

"Yeah, I feel good," I said, partially wondering at the same time what it would feel like to feel totally good, feel totally myself . . . to feel that I knew myself completely. I felt like a walking cliché. So what else was new? Wasn't everybody looking for the same feeling— to know themselves? Three blue birds sat on a tree limb looking down at me as we passed under them. They didn't even blink. Their audacity made me chuckle out loud.

The Mantaro River bubbled and rushed beside us. I picked up a tree branch and began to drag it behind me. I liked the feeling of having nothing to do but drag a tree branch.

"David?" I asked, breaking what I could feel was a reverie of his own, "do you think there is any such thing as human nature?"

He looked up and took a deep breath. "I don't think so. No," he said. "I think we humans are taught most everything we feel. I think people can do and be and think anything... it depends on what we learn."

I dragged the branch behind me thinking of the time I had spent in China. It was that trip that had made me come to the same conclusion. The Chinese had acted brutally and cruelly with each other in their bitter past because that was the behavior of the times, the mode of the day, the attitude to be observed in order to sustain the pecking order of the class system.

But Mao had said the Chinese people were a blank piece of paper on which something beautiful could be written. He had believed that human nature was basically a question of education ... you could educate people into observing behavior patterns that were more democratic, more fair, more kind. In fact, he had used a kind of militant sledgehammer approach in the education of fairness. People were forced to be fair through education and reeducation. They were all required to participate in the self-criticism sessions on every level. No one was excused from participation. It was a gigantic, monumental effort in group therapy directed toward changing the patterns of the past. And it seemed to work. Privacy and the right not to participate were not respected, but then the country was in such big trouble everyone realized they had to pull together. So to me, the overwhelming characteristic of the New China had been the people working together to change what they believed to be their basic natures.

Modern China now said a handful of chopsticks held together tightly was more unbreakable than one pair. And as they held together, they were allowing themselves to totally reevaluate the value system they had held sacred for centuries. They seemed to understand that they were revolutionizing the priorities that they had thought were immutable. And the big lesson to them seemed to be what they were learning about themselves.

I often thought about what it must be like to find out that you are not necessarily competitive or territorial or jealous or materialistic. Maybe the real human conflict wasn't about what we really believed we were or were not, but what we actually could be if we allowed ourselves the option of trusting the possibilities of our own spiritual potential. And if our own potential was to be more spiritual, then where did the new Chinese come in? I could find nothing spiritual in the New China. In fact, they seemed to ridicule spiritual concepts, almost afraid that spiritual notions would thwart their revolution.

I could see the Chinese revolution going the way of all modern day revolutions if they negated the need for the spiritual recognition of man. I was beginning to believe that what was wrong with all of us was our refusal to live with the knowledge that God—the word we use for a concept of incredibly complex spiritual energies—was the missing link that should be part of our daily lives.

Now Buckminster Fuller's theory about most of what transpires within the human activity of *reality* being utterly invisible, unsmellable, and untouchable began to make sense. He said that ninety-nine percent of reality could only be comprehended by man's metaphysical mind, guided by something he only sensed might be the truth. He said man *was* metaphysical mind. And the brain was only a place to store information. He said only man's metaphysical mind could communicate. The *brain* could not. That man was a self-contained microcommunicating system, and humanity was a macrocommunicating system. And that *all information of everything, including God,* was continually being broadcast and received through electromagnetic waves, only we weren't aware of it because we were only using one percent of our capacities to perceive the truth.

But what would help man to understand, not only what he came from, but where he was actually going? How could the State answer the deep, gnawing, longing questions of our origins and our purpose? How could the State be helpful in putting us more closely in touch with why we were alive when it was afraid that in doing so its power would be dissipated?

I could see why the communists had never gone into India. It would be impossible to sway the deep spirituality of the Indian people. They would never condone the State replacing their spiritual philosophy even if it meant eating better. Their spiritual beliefs were the oldest on earth. The Indians had been taught and conditioned to be in touch with their spiritual natures since Krishna walked the earth so that it was a part of everything they did or didn't do. A communist regime would have a tough time getting the Indian people to go along with the revolutionary materialism of Marx. Even Mahatma Gandhi couldn't get the cows out of the houses or off the streets because the Indians still believed in the transmigration of souls (which was the animal forerunner to reincarnation into human forms). Maybe they were even right about that for all we know.

It was astonishing to me how the unraveling of mystery worked. As long as there was one loose thread, it was possible to unravel the whole ball of wax. As long as the human race continued to be basically unhappy in its struggle to understand the Great Mystery, the impetus would be there to thwart all authority that stood in its path . . . whether it was the Church, the State, or the revolutionary society itself. No matter where we looked, the answer seemed to be in a force that was more knowing, more wise, more understanding, and more benevolent than we ourselves. And before we could understand that force, we would have to understand ourselves. We then became the Great Mystery. It wasn't, who is God? It was, who were *we?*

❧ David and I walked upstream along the rocky banks of the orange river. The early noon sun was hot and shimmering. I was perspiring under my poncho. I took it off and David carried it for me. My California sun hat suddenly seemed my most valuable possession. The rubber-soled combat boots were solid and heavy against the jagged rocks. My feet were comfortable. When my feet were comfortable, I was comfortable.

I sat down on a rock and made some notes. David waded into the river.

Peruvian mountain people dotted the sides of the river either washing their clothes or lying on the ground— mostly in the sun. Their sense of time seemed slow and unhurried—almost careless —and their body movements corresponded. Sometimes they smiled as they ambled past us, but usually they just acknowledged our presence with a nod. David greeted them with his friendly Spanish. He never really seemed foreign anywhere.

"There's an outdoor sulphur pool not too far up the river," he called to me. "Do you want to wash your hair or something? It's great to take the baths in the sunlight."

It sounded great. I got up wondering if I would be able to recall the emotional carefreeness I felt here in the Andes. I wondered if I would be able to remember how close this was to supreme peace the next time I was caught in crosstown traffic in New York, or when the lights didn't work properly during a dramatic number in my show, or when my latest picture flopped at the box office. Or Gerry . . . would I let myself be rankled and frustrated over the human obstacle course that had become our relationship? Would I be able to understand his drawbacks, and see my own, with more perspective if I conjured up the image of a moment on the Mantaro River banks when the sun was hot and my thoughts soared?

I continued to trail my branch as we walked further upstream toward the sulphur pool. I heard sharp crystal birdcalls pierce the rarefied mountain air. I wondered if it would ever be possible to *see* music and *hear* the colors in a rainbow.

"What's on your mind?" asked David.

"Oh, I don't know," I said. "I was just wondering if there was some kind of technique a person could use to feel inner peace and happiness when all hell was breaking loose in their own little world."

David shrugged his eyebrows. "I don't know how it would work for you, but somebody once described a technique they used that they called 'The Golden Dream.'

For example, if you are trying to fall asleep and your mind is bouncing around with all kinds of so-called problems that won't quit—here's what I do. I think of what would make me *at that moment* the happiest person in the world. I picture all of it in detail—what I would be wearing, who I would be with, what it would sound like, what kind of weather would be going on, what food I would be eating, what I would be touching . . . all that kind of stuff that would make me happy, in detail. Then I wait. I have the whole picture in my mind—created by my own will and fantasy, and it becomes so real that I *am* happy. I feel myself begin to relax and actually vibrate on a kind of even frequency, and in no time I'm off to sleep—or 'on the astral plane,' as I like to term it."

I listened, picturing myself doing what he said. It seemed very possible.

"So that's the Golden Dream, eh?" I said.

"Yes," said David. "Good title for a song."

"Yeah. Much better than 'The Impossible Dream.'"

"So," he went on, "when you concentrate on what would make you happy, you actually produce an electromagnetic frequency which operates internally and literally soothes you into a feeling of inner peace."

"So it's really just plain mind over matter, isn't it?"

"Sure," he said, "but I really think something more is involved. For me, I think it would be exhibiting faith to myself and faith in myself. In other words, if I have enough faith in something, particularly through concentration or meditation, or whatever you want to call it, then I am unconsciously giving off enough positive energy which could ultimately result in its attainment."

"Even if what you want is unrealistic?"

"Who knows if it's unrealistic?"

"You mean faith moves mountains?"

"Yeah, probably. I think the positive mind is limitless. So I guess that would include mountains. That's apparently something like what Christ was doing. Only it's more than just faith, or meditation, or concentration. He had the *knowledge* of how to do it."

"And where did the son-of-a-gun get that knowledge?"

"He said it was from God. But he also said He was the Son of God. So I think He was telling us that through God He had learned. That's what all the Indian avatars say too. They don't say *they* are the reasons they can materialize bread out of stones or cures out of disease. They say *God* gives them the power and the knowledge to carry out His works."

"You really are a believer, David. Aren't you?"

"I believe," said David, "that most of us don't really know ourselves well enough to know what we want. And by knowing ourselves better we would be better in touch with God, or the Creative Source."

I was huffing and puffing now as we trudged in the noon day heat. The altitude was getting to me.

David moved slightly ahead of me looking for a footpath that he knew led to the sulphur pool. I was ready for the buoyant water. I wanted to sit, and soak, and think about my dream which I was suddenly aware I was unaware of. I had no dream. I couldn't imagine what would make me *specifically* happy. I couldn't meditate on the details of the smells, the sights, the touch or the sounds of such a dream because I didn't know what my dream was.

He led me up the mountain to a path which ran parallel to the river. About half a mile further on we came to a wooden hut that housed the beginning of some stone stairs which led down into a niche inside the mountain. Walls of mountain rock loomed up around us as we descended the narrow stone stairs. At the bottom was a bubbling sulphur pool. Three old women waded in the bubbles wearing their starched hats and colorful native dresses. When they looked up and saw us they covered their faces and turned away.

"The mountain elders are very reserved up here," said David. "They have a thing about nudity and they need their privacy, so let's turn our backs when we reach bottom and I think they will quietly leave."

Across the pool on the other side a young man lay sprawled in the water with his legs over the rocks. He was completely dressed in blue jeans and a shirt.

"Is that his concession to the elders?" I asked David.

"Sure, otherwise he'd have to wait for them too. Besides, his clothes are no problem to him. A short walk home and they'll be dry."

David took out another hardboiled egg, peeled it and handed it to me. "It's not good to eat this before a sulphur bath, but anyway."

The old women waded out of the water and climbed the stairs nodding to us stoically as they left. The young boy stayed where he was. We walked to the edge of the water. White clumps of sulphur sparkled in the sunlight and gentle steam wafted above the water as the warmth met the mountain air. David put down my poncho and the bag of eggs.

I stretched in the sun and watched the young boy. He didn't make a move to leave, just stared into the water.

"Well, what should we do?" I asked. "Get undressed or what?"

"Hmmm. Let's see," said David. "Let's leave on our underwear. That'll make it easier for everybody."

I took off my slacks, socks and combat boots, leaving my blouse 'til last because I wasn't wearing a bra. Then with self-conscious flurry I whipped it off and walked into the water. The young boy continued to stare into the water, and David was busy getting undressed himself. Nobody really cared whether I was half nude or not.

The water was warm and tingly just as it had been the night before but the experience of feeling it in the sunlight now was incandescent. First of all the top of the water looked like dancing silver. There was something about the way the sun played on the clusters of white sulphur that made the water look like silver liquid underneath. The rocks on the bottom were slippery with moss and algae but the buoyancy kept me upright. Somewhere near the center of the pool I found a comfortable rock to sit on and let myself in up to my neck. Now the reflection of the silver liquid nearly blinded me at eye level. I was happy I had my sunglasses and my hat. How ridiculous, I thought. Here I am engulfed in such ravishing natural beauty and I feel I have to protect myself from bad effects. I pumped my arms up and down under the water until my entire body was covered with sulphur mineral bubbles. They clung to my skin with a stringent kind of prickle, stinging ever so slightly but because of it, seeming to make my blood rush faster. I could feel the pool being fed from an underground source. The water rushed gently to the surface in a warm stream. The surface of the pool was warm from the mountain sunlight. And the temperature of my body fell somewhere in between. David stepped into the pool. He wore jockey shorts. He had muscular straight legs, except that his left one looked as though it might have been broken and reset. It was unnoticeable in street clothes. His torso was trim but not particularly muscular and his shoulders were narrow rather than broad. He didn't look like a man who worked out with weights but he did look in good shape.

He smiled slightly as though he knew I was checking him out but he said nothing as he waded in and knelt up to his neck. He breathed deeply and shut his eyes in pleasure at the tingly warmth of the water in the mountain air.

The young boy didn't move. He seemed in a trance. The liquid silver could probably do that to a person. I asked David.

"Yeah, it can," he said. "That's why it's so relaxing. The mountain people use the waters as much for their spirits as their bodies. It's just too bad they won't take off their clothes."

As the water began to take effect slowly, I realized I was getting heartburn. It began as a small knot somewhere in my upper chest region and spread.

"It's just the sulphur and minerals bringing out digestive defects," said David. "That's why it's better not to eat before. But it doesn't do any harm. Just makes you aware that your digestion is upset."

He retired to the opposite side of the sulphur pool to think and meditate. He sat quietly on the underwater rocks and gazed serenely into the water at eye level. I lifted my closed eyes to the sun. Heavenly, I thought. I looked over at David. His eyes weren't blinking and his face was expressionless. A fly crawled across the bridge of his nose. He looked totally at peace, and as if he just weren't there. I watched him for a long time. The boy with the blue jeans left. The three old women waited at the top of the stairs.

I drifted over and put my sun hat on a dry rock. Then I dunked my hair into the water and rinsed it. I could feel the sulphur make my hair soft. In and out of the water I lifted my head, leaning backward. I felt so exhilarated, filled with elation. I remembered how I wished I could rush into the sea giving myself up totally to it. But just rushing my body into the water wouldn't have been enough. I needed to plunge my head and face under in order to feel that I was free of reluctance . . . that's what I wanted to be . . . free of reluctance . . . reluctance about everything . . . it didn't matter. I wanted to feel totally open and embracing as though there was nothing to be suspicious about. I looked over at David again. That's the way his face looked . . . completely oblivious to anything negative . . . serene. He looked as though he could have been part of the water . . . he *was* the water—only his form was human.

I wondered how long David would meditate in the bubbling water. He hadn't moved. Carbonated bubbles clung to his unmoving arms under the surface of the water. I wished I could go under the way he seemed to be doing. I wondered what might be going on inside of him as he sat so peacefully inert.

I wondered if his soul could leave his body if he wanted it to. I wondered whether he was his soul or whether he was his body. No . . . the body died . . . the soul's energy lived eternally. So, that must mean we are our souls—the body only houses the soul.

David opened his eyes slowly. He blinked up at the sun and wiped his chin.

"Jesus," he said, "I was meditating! How long have I been under?"

I said I didn't know, maybe over an hour. Time didn't matter anyway. In fact, it probably didn't exist.

David laughed and nodded. "What's on your mind?" he asked.

Oh God, I thought, how could I condense everything into words? "I don't know," I said, "just thinking and wondering. Wondering if a baby is born knowing everything and if little by little it forgets."

"Yeah," said David. "Being in the body can be a drag. I have a much better time out there," he pointed to the sky and gently moved an arm through it. "Come on," he said, "let's go for a walk. I have something to tell you, but I don't know how. Sometimes it's easier to think when you're moving."

He climbed out of the water.

One old woman waited at the top of the stairs for us to leave.

We dressed quickly in the warm sun. David stopped, handed me a peeled egg and said, "Take it easy with yourself. Have patience. It will all be fine."

We climbed the stairs, said goodbye to the woman, apologizing for the amount of time we had spent in the water, and began to walk back along the orange water of the Mantaro River.

David walked ahead of me and stretched out his arms. He lifted his face up to the sun and sighed. "Oh," he said, "I hope you can begin to feel some of the happiness and inner peace just waiting to be touched inside you."

I was taken aback by the direct personal quality of what he said.

"All of this stuff *is* personal," he said, sensing my reaction, "because what we're missing is ourselves. You're beginning to put the pieces of yourself together."

I lifted my face upward to the sun and thought of the few times I could honestly say I had experienced a sheer and complete feeling of happiness. Most of the time I had aborted the feeling by reminding myself of the negatives that persisted either during that moment or in my life in general. Like right this moment. The hot sun on my face filled me with unabashed pleasure until I remembered that I could get sunburned if it lasted too long. I laughed at myself. So what if I got a red nose and it peeled later? So what?

David began to skip. He certainly loved to skip. I skipped with him. Our knapsacks bounced on our shoulders and our knees buckled under us when we skidded on pebbles. I found myself laughing with him. I laughed and laughed and the moment I felt a twinge of negative thought, I drove it from my mind with a mental sweep. Quick flashes of Gerry, the pictures I had made... Hollywood, Hawaii, New York... the world... dancing people I knew, people I wished I didn't know... and when the darting flashes turned negative, I would overwhelm them with that same inner light that I experienced in the Himalayas. What was it I had read? First we are in the light, next the light is in us, and finally we and the light become one.

Past the small streams that emptied into the Mantaro, we skipped and walked and skipped again. Blue birds and sparrows darted in and out of tree branches. A hand-woven swinging bridge swayed under us when we crossed back and forth across the river. Time passed but time stood still. I could honestly say I felt happy. Now I could honestly say I didn't care what time it was. Time wasn't feeling. It wasn't action. It was only time. If only I could keep the negative thoughts of my other world— my real world—out of my head.

We raced into Lloclapampa perspiring and exhausted, put our knapsacks in our rooms and in the afternoon light we sat in the "eating" hall and had warm milk and cold rolls. Outside, the woman with the child on her back pounded wheat from chaff while three men from the village chewed coca leaves and packed dirt and straw into square blocks for what would be their new home. ✿

Chapter 22

"I cannot believe for a moment that life in the first instance originated on this insignificant little ball which we call the earth.... The particles which combined to evolve living creatures on this planet of ours probably came from some other body elsewhere in the universe."

—THOMAS A. EDISON
The Diary and Sundry Observations

🐲 Next day the morning was crisp and for some reason seemed hopeful and new. I looked at my ring watch. It was my favorite piece of jewelry. I had been around the world with that ring watch. It said 9:00 A.M., July tenth. I wondered how the weather was in London. I visualized it somehow. I saw rain and murky streets and people dripping with umbrellas. I saw Gerry coming out of a subway walking toward Parliament. I wondered if my visualization was real or fantasy.

I put on my combat boots, slacks, blouse and sweater and walked outside.

Across the street David was sitting on the stone wall.

"I thought we'd go into Ataura," he said, "but first let's get you some more eggs. Not much of a gourmet menu up here, is it?" He winked and did a hitch step as he disappeared into the restaurant.

The lady with no teeth and the baby came out with a basket of vegetables which she took to our car.

"We're taking her too," said David, handing me some hot milk and two peeled eggs. "She needs to sell her vegetables and doesn't often get a lift."

She smiled with toothless delight and got into the back seat. I wished I could get her fitted for some real-world dentures.

The morning light across the Andes was different from the Himalayas. The shadows fell with broader strokes and were more horizontal because the mountains were more spread out. The mountains looked more like humped plains.

Golden slashes of wheat waved gently in the morning breeze. Sheep and cows and llamas ambled lazily together on the roadside interspersed every so often with toddling babies whose mothers carried other children in orange-pink pouches on their backs.

I ate my eggs. David spoke in Spanish to the woman who sat in the back seat. He translated for me. She was talking about wild flowers that could be ground up into a paste, heated and placed on the sinuses to relieve pressure. She said there was a medical use for every herb in the hills and we could buy them all in Ataura. Her baby slept so soundly it looked like dead weight in her lap.

I lifted my arm and hand across the back of the seat. The woman saw my ring watch. She touched it and her hands were warm. She said something in Spanish. David said, "She wants your ring. She thinks it's beautiful and wants it."

Immediately I felt my mind clutch. Would I give my favorite piece of jewelry and my connection to the real world (because it was a watch) to this lady that I didn't know? I watched David watch me.

The woman took my finger in her hand and removed the ring watch. I didn't resist. She clutched it in her hand, then looked up at the sun.

"What would make her happy?" I asked David. "Ask her, would you please? What would make her really happy?"

He did. She answered, "Rings and things."

I said, "That would make you happier than happiness?"

"Oh, yes," she said with conviction, "because it would mean my family was comfortable." She turned the ring over on her finger posing her hand out in front of her and smiling. "What is that?" she asked next, pointing to our box of Kleenex. "Is it like toilet paper?"

I handed it to her, first demonstrating how the pop-up box worked. She seized the box and turned it over and over examining each edge. Then slowly she pulled out the first tissue. When the tissue under it replaced it she seemed startled. But she didn't make a game out of it; she conserved the tissues. She folded her hands across her baby on her lap and looked at the ring watch. I didn't say anything. I watched the scenery, feeling ashamed that I was afraid she would keep it. Why couldn't I just sweepingly say, "It's yours. I can get another one later." But I couldn't. It represented personal attachments and memories. But it wasn't just the ring watch. It was any "thing" that I had had a personal experience with. The monetary value of the "thing" had nothing to do with it. It was the emotional attachment. It was almost as though "the things" were extensions of an investment in love. Those "things" were always there when I wanted them. They never went away. They were permanent. All I had to do was reach out and touch them and they were there. I could depend on them. They made me feel safe because behind them were the people whose love I wanted the most. Was that then the basis for greed? Was it mostly a manifestation of the need for human love that we somehow never got enough of? Was a security blanket or a teddy bear the beginning of the acquisitionary replacement of love? I gazed out at the morning feeling David feel me thinking. Up ahead of us, looming into the white clouds, were high mountains covered with ice and snow.

"Those are the Huaytapallana Ice Peaks," said David.

I looked out at them. They seemed above the real world—white and graceful and stark. I wondered what

the weather was like on the mountains. I wondered if
Shangri-La lay beyond. I wondered what it would be
like to try to get there on foot.

"Have you been to the Ice Peaks?" asked the
woman.

"No," I answered. "Have you?"

"Oh, no," she said. "But many people have seen
the flying discs that come from behind the peaks. Do
you have flying discs in your mountains in the United
States?"

I turned around in my seat and looked into her
eyes. They were innocent and casual.

"Yes," I said. "I guess so. But I've never seen one."

"They leave marks when they land," she said. "And
if you come too close they get frightened and go away.
They come out at night, when it's too cold for us to
watch them. Lots of them go back and forth across the
sky."

I took a piece of Kleenex out of the box and blew
my nose.

"What are they, do you think?" I asked.

"I have no opinion. I only listen," she said.

"Well, what are they doing?"

"Scientists come here to look at them. And they
say we are nothing compared to those discs."

"What do you think the discs are doing?"

"They come from Venus."

"From Venus?"

"Yes, the scientists told us. They said they were
studying our planet."

"Are you afraid of them?" I asked.

"No. A friend of mine saw one land and he walked
over to it. But just when he got up to it it flew away. He
thought the people were afraid of him."

"Why?"

"Because he is bigger than they are."

I waited for her to say more. She didn't. She just
looked out of the window. It wasn't that she didn't want
to talk. She just wasn't much interested in the subject
and had apparently exhausted its possibilities. Or perhaps she was just being polite in satisfying a stranger's

curiosity. In any case, she held the baby's head and embarked on an animated conversation about the sale of her vegetables and how prices were getting so high. She said she had heard that we used some chemical medicine to grow our vegetables bigger and wondered how she could get some.

We drove on over the spreading terrain. I tried to absorb what the woman had said. The sun was directly above the Ice Peaks now, making them glisten.

At an intersection three policemen stopped us and asked David where we were going and why. They peered in at us. Seeing that foreigners were driving they cautioned us about the riots in Huancayo (where we were not going) and waved us on.

More people appeared along the roadside the closer we got to town. Every now and then we'd see a man dressed in a black western suit.

"They are in mourning when they're dressed like that," said David.

The woman talked about her children. She said she had five of them. She said she didn't want any more so she and her husband stopped having sex. When I mentioned birth control methods she had trouble understanding and had no knowledge at all about her own body. She was young, in her thirties, and so were her friends, who were all having the same problem. None of her friends had sex anymore either, in an effort to keep their families from expanding.

More women with magenta-striped pouches on their backs appeared walking toward Ataura. They wore their customary white wide-brimmed hats and skirts with white piqúe petticoats, looking as though they were costumed extras in a movie being shot on location. There were dogs everywhere, and as we entered the town the first thing I heard was a Neil Sedaka record playing on a juke box. We parked the car and got out to walk. The woman walked away with my ring watch and her baby. I stared after her. David watched me.

The street bazaars sold everything from bedding to freshly ground coffee and old records. The sun was hot now but in the shade of the buildings it was cool.

Pictures of Christ with a candle underneath hung in
every shop. People sipped a sweet corn cola called Maiz
as they ambled about. Dogs scampered through the
fresh fruits and vegetables. Laid out on the streets in
the sun for sale were rope, shoes, plastic tubs, beans,
peas, and colored materials. Young boys rented comic
books to read. A woman braided rope she had just
bought.

An old man dressed in a pair of beat-up slacks,
sneakers, a brown felt hat with a flower over his left ear
and a gray tattered sweater stood next to a restaurant
juke box. He moved gently, but out of rhythm, trying to
keep time to an Elvis Presley record. An empty Inca
Cola bottle protruded from his back pocket as he shuffled over to someone in the restaurant and begged for
food which he immediately dumped into his brown felt
hat. Eating soup at a table across from him sat a man
who was clearly drunk, shouting obscenities at the wall.

Down the street young people waited for a movie
theater to open. *The Ten Commandments* was on the
bill and a turquoise wrought-iron gate separated the
people from the box office.

Our lady caught up with us and directed us to the
herb stall. Laid out on a blanket were small piles of
herbs which she said would cure most any ailment a
person could have. Tara for asthma, valeriana for the
nervous system, *Hircampuri* for the liver, digestion,
diabetes, bile and heartburn. I took some of that to
make tea and there was a tree bark called *Sangrednada*
which was good for ulcers. I should have bought that
too.

Three women sat on a curb. One was nursing a
baby with her hand in the lap of a friend, while the
third petted a dog gnawing on a bone between them. A
man rubbed powdered sulphur on the brim of his white
hat to make it stiff. Beside him was some cheese made
of boiled milk called *quesillo*.

Inside a flower market, a fairyland display of gladiolas,
daisies, Spanish carnations, rooster's crests, chrysanthe-
mums and jonquils dazzled my eyes. Children, eating

Peruvian popcorn made with sugar, walked among the flowers.

Our lady took her vegetables off to sell. She still had my ring watch. I tried not to notice. I knew I would see her later. David and I walked until we were hungry. We sat in an indoor-outdoor restaurant having rice and beans topped with onions and a hot sauce called *rocoto* which must be the spiciest condiment devised by man.

"Do you like it here?" I asked David.

"Yes," he said, "it's real. The people have no pretensions. They are what they are. They're simple."

"Maybe when people are comfortable," I said, "they hurt each other more. Maybe we should all stay poor and struggling."

"No," he said, "I don't think so. That would negate progress and the drive for a better life. No, the answer is something like my credo. Do you want to hear it?"

"Sure."

He cleared his throat and, as though he was reciting at graduation class, he said, "Work hard. Don't lie. And try not to hurt anyone. That's it. That's how I live. I remind myself of that three-pronged philosophy every day. I've educated myself not to forget it."

"Do you get depressed and lonely?"

"Sure."

"How do you keep going?"

"I guess you could say that happiness is knowing what you believe in."

"But the lack of self-doubt is what makes some people self-righteous and dangerous."

"Yes, but a person who is self-righteous wants everyone else to think as they do."

I thought about that for a moment.

"Do you think I do that?"

"What?"

"Want things my way?"

David put down his fork. "From what I pick up about you, I would have to say yes."

I felt as though he had slapped me. My eyes welled with tears.

"What's wrong?" he said.

I tried to hold the tears back, but I couldn't. I could feel them run down my cheeks and David's soft blue eyes looking through to my insides. And at the same time, I was flooded with insight.

David reached over and mashed a tear on my chin. "That one traveled a long way down," he said. "It's the same journey we all have to travel before we realize who we are." He paused. "Is that what's going wrong with you and your friend?" he asked.

I tried to talk clearly. "My friend?"

"Yes," said David, "there must be some man you're involved with that you're going off to meet in strange places all the time."

"You mean like I'm doing with you?"

"Well, yes," he said.

"I guess what you said about me is fair, and I guess our problems are inevitable. I want him to *look* at what he's doing and he won't. Not really. I guess I do want him to see things my way. If only he would *really* look, he'd find his own way. But he won't. It's frightening to him. And I guess I have to accept that. If he *wants* to ignore the truth of himself, I guess I must allow him that privilege, mustn't I? He has the right, I guess."

David reached across the table and took my hand.

"You, on the other hand," he said, "have a mind like an oil drill. You're one of those people who may hassle others but you'll also get to yourself. You *have* the self-courage or whatever you want to call it to take a good honest look and you will be ruthless with yourself once you see what you're doing. In fact you shouldn't be too ruthless. As I've said before—be patient with yourself."

Why did gentleness make me cry?

"C'mon," said David. "I went through the same thing, you know. You have to, to get to where you want to be."

"Where do I want to be?" I spluttered.

"Where you live, don't you? Where you deeply

and basically live is what you are trying to reach, isn't it? Isn't that how it feels?"

"It feels like everything I've lived has been a sham, a glossy eight-by-ten. And it turns out that most everything I lived and believed was a myth."

"Like what?"

"Well, I thought when I died that was the end. I believed that what I saw was what there was. I believed there was nothing more and nothing less than here and now and that was all I had to deal with. I believed that the life the human race led was real and physical. Now I find we've been playing parts in some spiritual play, with an ongoing script. So when I start thinking about how I've played my part, I'm not too happy."

"Well, we all feel that way, don't we? Besides, what are you worried about? You'll get to play another part after this and another one after that. In fact you'll keep on playing parts until you finally get it right!"

I laughed and sputtered and ate some more beans and hot sauce.

"This hot sauce is the worst," I said. "It makes me cry."

"Well, life is like hot sauce. As soon as you start enjoying it, it makes you cry. It's *accepting* the combinations that is the key. And you can't accept any of that stuff until you accept yourself. And to accept yourself you have to know yourself. To know yourself is the deepest knowledge of all. Christ said it: 'Know thyself.' And then be true to it. Because *you* are a microcosm of the cosmos."

I leaned back and sighed. My legs were stiff from sitting. I needed to stand up and stretch and walk.

David paid the check and we went outside. People were packing up their wares to be ready for sundown. In the mountains the sun dictated all commerce, activity and behavior.

We walked around for a while. David had some Inca Cola at a candy stand and I had a tangerine. The lady with the vegetables and my ring watch had disappeared, either hitching a ride from someone else or staying in town.

David and I got in the car and started back to Llocllapampa. The early evening light was clear and purplish blue. The stretched plains outside of Ataura were dotted with people trudging home for the night. Dogs barked in the distance and a baby or two cried. David was quiet as he drove. I thought about the truth of what he had said. That I wanted life my way, and on my terms. That whoever I was involved with should look as closely at themselves as I was trying to look at myself. He hadn't said it as an accusation, but more that I would have to admit it if I wanted to move on. He had implied also that my strident compulsion to insist that others analyze themselves was not altogether unfair because it forced a degree of progress in them, but I should respect their inability or reluctance to do that if they didn't want to.

I, in fact, was having a problem looking at the truth myself, so why couldn't I respect the fact that others might experience the same pain? Gerry really must have gone through hell; loving me and caring so much about what I thought, but at the same time feeling it impossible to look at himself in a light that he knew would please me. He had often told me he felt so inadequate in living up to my expectations. I could see what he meant. No man could live with that kind of challenge. He had to be his own man, not the man I wanted him to be. And, if it wasn't enough, it wasn't enough.

The sun was completely gone now. Life in the mountains revolved around the sun. I felt my stomach settle into a kind of an easy place. When it was easy, I was easy.

David seemed to be mesmerized by the road. He stared straight ahead saying nothing. Then he turned to me.

"Shirl?" he said. "There's something I need to tell you. About a girl called Mayan."

"Sure," I said quietly. "Whatever you want."

He drove on for a moment or two. Then he said, "Ask me some questions so I can lead into it, okay?"

"Okay," I said, liking the game. "Let's see. Did you have a love affair with her?"

"Well, yes," he said, "but it wasn't what you'd call a regular type love affair. It was more like a cosmic love affair."

I chuckled to myself thinking that all love affairs seemed cosmic when you were having them.

"Well," I said, "I can understand that. What did she do? I mean did she have a profession?"

David lit up one of his cigarettes and opened the window to breathe deeper. "Well, actually she's a geologist. She was up here on a mining expedition."

"Here? Oh, I see. So you had your love affair up here in the sulphur baths and along the banks of the bubbling Mantaro?" I realized how sarcastic I must be sounding but I really did it so David would feel comfortable with the teasing.

He didn't react. "No," he said, "I was up here with two other guys just bumming around when I met her."

"Oh, a mountain pickup?" I said, going too far.

He still did not react. "Well, no," he said. "It wasn't like that. I was out walking alone one morning and she came driving along this very road in an old Pontiac. She stopped and got out. When I first saw her I thought she was the most beautiful woman I had ever seen. She seemed almost translucent. I mean her skin was shining. I didn't notice what she was wearing— jeans, probably—but the way she moved was like flowing. And I remember I couldn't take my eyes off her face. I don't know. It was the whole effect. It just knocked me for a loop, and yet I felt perfectly and wonderfully peaceful. *At peace.*"

As David described his feelings I noticed that his face relaxed. All the muscular tension that was usually operating with quick awareness in him dropped away. He sounded as though he had been instantly hypnotized.

"What else did she look like?" I asked.

"Small," he said. "Real small and petite, with long thick black hair, this marvelous very white transparent skin, and dark dark almost almond-shaped eyes. Not

Oriental eyes, I mean not with those lids, but with a tilt, a slant to them. She walked over to me, almost as though she knew I'd be there. We began to walk together. And the strange thing, although it didn't seem so at the time, is that we didn't say anything to each other. It was as though we didn't need to. I had never experienced anything like that before and I didn't give it much mind. I felt almost that she knew what I was thinking anyway."

David stopped, remembering.

"Yeah," he continued, shaking his head with memories. "Yeah, so after a while I thought I should say *something*. So I asked her what she was doing up here, and she said she was with her people doing some geological studies in the mountains. I asked her what people. She said she'd tell me later. That sounded okay. I asked her where she was from. She said she'd tell me that later, too. So I didn't ask her anything else. Then she began to ask me all about myself. But for some reason I can't explain I felt there was no need for her to do that."

"How do you mean?" I asked, feeling that David was in some other world as he recalled this extraordinary meeting.

"Well," he said hesitantly, "you know that feeling you sometimes get when you meet someone new that they really know you and understand you? Well, it was like that. I felt that she really seemed to know all about me and she was just kind of giving me time to get used to the idea."

David looked ahead, thinking to himself.

"And you?" I asked. "Did you feel that you knew her?"

I thought he was going to tell me that he was feeling he had known her in another life or something.

"No, not really." He hesitated. "So then," he continued, "well, we walked together, and soon she began to talk about all kinds of stuff... the world, governments, different attitudes in different countries, God, languages. I mean it was Greek to me. I wasn't into any of this stuff at the time, you understand."

"So it was quite a time ago?"

"Yeah. Long time. I was beginning to think she was some kind of international spy only I couldn't figure out who for. She talked about the negative energy of some of our world leaders and how people needed to believe in themselves, that the most important relationship was between each soul and God. I asked if she was a Jesus freak. She laughed and said in a way she was a lot freakier than that but that if we had really understood what Christ was talking about no one would call it freakish. She talked and talked. We had dinner, and she talked. I loved talking and listening and being with her but I just didn't know what to make of most of what she said. After awhile I asked her where she was staying. But she wouldn't tell me. I didn't press it. Soon she smiled and said she had to leave but that I'd see her again. She showed up the next day and found me. We went for another all day walk and she talked more. Always important stuff. I couldn't figure out what was going on and told her so. She said she'd tell me when the time came, but if I felt I was learning from her I should just relax and learn.

"I took a walk in and around these hills every day. And every day she found me, regardless of where I walked. We talked about so many things. Then one day, we were sitting by the river and she began to talk, very specifically, about the human soul and what it was. Before I met Mayan I couldn't have cared less whether there was life after death or whether God was alive and well and living in Orange County. And souls? . . . Jesus. But I listened to her and after awhile I realized she sounded as though she was giving me some sort of important scientific information. She said I should write it down because she said I was capable of absorbing it and one day I would pass it on to the right person who would see that it was noticed . . . maybe that person is you."

"Me?" I asked, startled. I was thoroughly absorbed in his story about this Mayan and didn't see myself as a part of it at all.

"Well, maybe. She said I should record everything

she was teaching me, which I did, and she said I should commit it all to paper so I could look at it and show it to others."

"Oh, did you write it down?"

"Yes. Would you like to read it?"

"Well, sure. But I think I'm still missing the point. Why didn't you give me that stuff about her along with all the other reading material you gave me?"

"Well, because of who she is."

"Who she is? What do you mean?"

David actually blushed. Then he clammed up. "Ask me some more questions," he said. He sounded a bit strained.

This was more than a simple tale of boy-meets-girl in the mountains. This was some kind of therapy.

"Okay," I said. "Mayan. That's an exotic name. Where is she from?"

David choked on his cigarette. "You mean what country or what city?"

"Well, yeah." I couldn't understand the problem. "I mean, from the way you described her she sounded very exotic. Might she have been from Polynesia?"

"No. Further than that."

"Further—what do you mean, further east? Is she from Japan or China or something?"

"No, not further east, further up."

"Further up?" I was beginning to sound like the straight man in a vaudeville act.

"Yes, further up and further out."

"David," I said, "now you're the one who's far out. What's going on here? What are you talking about? *Tell me*. This is a stupid game. You've had enough lead-in— just tell me. Where could she be from that's so hard to say? Another planet?"

David turned around and took both hands off the wheel and held them in the air. "You got it!" he said. "You guessed it. You're right."

"What, for God's sake?"

"What you just said."

"That Mayan was from another planet?"

"Yes, yes, yes, yes! That's what I found so hard to

tell you. It's true though. I swear to God, it's true. And she proved it to me several times over, which I'll tell you about."

I felt myself shut my mouth. I took one of David's cigarettes from the pack and lit it and inhaled. I opened the window on my side and blew the smoke into the night air. Then, holding the cigarette, I scrunched down into the seat and put my feet on the dashboard and smoked. I remember in detail every move I made because the thing that was mind-boggling to me was that I felt he was sincere. I know it must sound crazy, but I actually felt that he was not nuts or hallucinating or making it up.

We drove on quietly. I didn't say anything. Neither did David. The night was clear and dry and cold. The stars hung like zircons in the sky. I looked up. Had I really heard him say what he said? He was a man I trusted. He had been so much a part of my growing spiritual understanding. I at least believed he believed what he had said. In fact I'd heard about quite a few people who claimed to have had contact with extraterrestrials but I had never been in the position of having to evaluate their sincerity. I left that up to interested scientists or psychologists.

But now it seemed I would have to make some kind of judgment about a friend. I stared at the crystal stars and remembered the Christmas telescope I had received as a child after months of begging. I remembered the nights I had gazed through the telescope into the heavens, feeling somehow that I belonged there. Wasn't that everyone's haunting desire? Were the heavens a fundamental reminder that we as humans belonged to the magic network of the cosmos? That we were all an integral piece of a gigantic universal puzzle which was not so clear to us yet because of our limited three-dimensional consciousness? Did David and others like him desire to understand so fervently that they actually believed they had "contact" with a piece of the cosmic puzzle? I smoked my cigarette and then breathed deeply, aware of the contradiction that I desired pure air at the same time that I was polluting my own lungs.

Llocllapampa was dark and peaceful when we arrived. Next to our "hotel" some piglets truffled around in an old rubber tire enjoying mush grain which was their dinner, while their mother looked on patiently.

The woman with the child had not returned. Her mother had cooked a kidney stew in wine sauce for the evening meal. The hot thick rolls were freshly baked and sweet churned butter spilled around the edges. Two kerosene lamps hung from a coat hanger on a beam above us giving light to our table. The radio blared with the soccer game as the family's young children walked in and around our table watching us eat. The older woman used a gas stove to cook on, which was fueled by a propane pipe on the side of the road. The stove and sink and refrigerator were up against one wall of the restaurant and barely had any light over them.

"Beautiful night tonight," the older woman said to David. "It would be a good night for the astronomers."

David stretched his arms over his head and sighed. Then quite casually he asked her in Spanish, "Have you ever seen a UFO?"

"Oh yes," she said, "many. And my uncle has seen them fly right into Lake Titicaca and disappear. He was frightened at first because he thought maybe he was going loco." She pointed to her head. "But then several of his friends told him they had seen the same thing. He felt better."

David sighed deeply again as though he were relieved at what she said. She went to the stove and dished out some stew for us. I followed her.

"What do you think they are?" I said, feeling like one of thousands of tourists who must have asked the same question.

She put the stew on the table for us. "Extraterrestrial aliens," she said. "Everyone knows that."

"Do you think they're friendly?" I asked.

"I don't know. I think so," she said. "They live high in the mountains and they fly their discs way under the mountains so that no one can find them."

She brought us some hot rolls to go with the stew

and asked if we had enjoyed Ataura. I nodded and smiled. But she didn't seem particularly interested in pursuing the preposterous nature of her previous subject of conversation: like our friend in the car, the extraterrestrials in her landscape were unimportant, a curiosity that did not affect her life. Daily living, making ends meet, had a lot more significance for her.

Now, having observed the conversational amenities, she simply set our table and went about her after-dinner chores.

I looked at David across the steaming stew. I wasn't hungry.

"That's the way they all act up here," he said apologetically. "They're just used to it. They wonder why people like us are so intrigued. They laugh about the astronomers who come to study and wait. They say the discs will never come out when *they* are here. They say the disc people like to be alone, and that's the way the mountain people treat them. The mountain people don't know why they're here, except a lot of them say they are mining minerals in the mountains."

"And they're not afraid of them?"

"Don't seem to be. They say they've never hurt anybody, in fact, they say they run away."

"And lots of people have seen them?"

"Shirley," said David, "everyone I've talked to up here has a flying-disc story. *Every single one.*"

I looked into his eyes. They were calm and I would have to say relieved.

"David," I said, "where can I find your Mayan?"

He looked at me and let his shoulders drop away as though a big load had been removed from his back.

"I can't *find* Mayan," he said quietly. "I miss her terribly and keep coming back here hoping she'll turn up. She changed my life. Everything I think now is because of what I learned from her. She is the reason I found such peace in myself. And I want to impart it all to you."

I looked out the window of the building called FOOD into the dark night of the Andes mountains.

"David," I said, "whatever I could say about what I've suddenly found myself involved in here would be truly—to coin a cliché—a masterpiece of understatement."

I got up from the table. We walked under the low-slung gateway to our "hotel."

"But thanks, David," I said, "thanks for trusting me and for telling me about it."

His hand squeezed gently on my shoulder. In the dark his voice caught in his throat.

"G'night," he said. "Don't let the bedbugs bite."

I kissed him on the cheek and went into my dark and dank sleeping room and fell asleep immediately because I was frankly a little bit frightened to stay awake and think about what was going on. 🙶

Chapter 23

"*Looking at the matter from the most rigidly scientific point of view, the assumption that, amidst the myriads of worlds scattered through endless space, there can be no intelligence, as much greater than man's as his is greater than a blackbeetle's, no being endowed with powers of influencing the course of nature as much greater than his, as his is greater than a snail's, seems to me not merely baseless, but impertinent. Without stepping beyond the analogy of that which is known, it is easy to people the cosmos with entities, in ascending scale until we reach something practically indistinguishable from omnipotence, omnipresence, and omniscience.*"

—Thomas H. Huxley
Essays Upon Some Controverted Questions

The next morning I stepped into the sunlight refreshed as though I had slept for a week.

David was waiting. He had some of our famous hot milk and rolls for me and we drank and ate as we began to walk.

I looked out across the mountainous plains toward the Ice Peaks on the horizon. "So what else hides up there besides all the UFOs the locals chat about?" I asked, gently choking on a roll.

David laughed. "Well, since you ask—Mayan said

the valleys in between the peaks are unreachable by
land. That's why it's safe for them. When she first
described it to me it sounded like *Lost Horizon*."

"David," I said, "umm—did Mayan say exactly
where she was from?"

"Sure. The Pleiades."

"Well. Did you ever question her claim that she
was an extraterrestrial?"

David laughed and spit out part of his roll.

"Are you kidding? I thought I had gotten ahold of
some bad pot. Or she had. Of course I didn't believe
her. In fact, after she told me I was openly hostile to
her. Then one day very early in the morning, sunrise,
as a matter of fact—long before anyone else was up—
she instructed me to go to the base of one of the
foothills over there and watch the top of a specific peak.
I did. And you know what I saw?"

"What?" I wasn't sure I wanted to know.

"I looked up into the sky and exactly over that
peak came one of those flying discs I had heard the
peasants talk about. I thought I would crap. From then
on she had no problem with me. But I have to tell you
she scolded me for forcing her to use the 'seeing is
believing' technique. She said I should have been more
intelligent and open-minded."

"You mean gullible like me?"

"Well," he answered, "I told you in the beginning—
real intelligence is being open-minded. That doesn't
make you a fool."

"No?" (Why did I feel like one?)

David glanced at me. "No," he said very firmly.
"Listen, Shirl. What's happening to you *is* mind-blowing.
Just the way it was with me. And it's happening awfully
fast. There's no way to really say these things without
going all the way. That's why it seems so heavy. Look,
there's a lot of outside proof of unidentified spacecraft—I
mean from sources like the Air Force, radar tracking
stations, literally hundreds of *multiple* sightings, that is,
people who've seen them at the same time and place
and *with* others—so we can go along with that, right?"

"Right."

"Okay. If there are UFOs, somebody's got to be controlling them—in person, or by remote. And if not Earth people—and everyone seems agreed these craft do things our technology does not know about—then it's got to be extraterrestrials."

He peered at me to see how I was taking this. "It's a pity everyone needs their own private proof," he went on, "because from what Mayan told me, the extraterrestrials are *superior* because they understand the process of the *spiritual* domain of life. She says science, really highly advanced science, and spiritual understanding, are the same thing. Even Einstein was saying that. So, if you've gone as far as you have with the spiritual stuff, why not try to make the connection with higher technology? If it doesn't feel right, forget about it."

Forget about it? My God, who in hell could forget this kind of thing?

David saw me thinking... "open-minded" as he would say.

"Look," he said, "you don't have a problem with the reincarnation stuff, do you?"

"No," I said, "not really. Not after all I've read on the subject and experienced myself. I mean, when I play a role, I put on the emotional cloak of another person. So, I can see that the soul might do the same thing every time it re-embodies."

I was reminded of the many, many actors and actresses I had met who expressed bewilderment at where they got their inspiration when confronted with roles entirely alien to anything they had personally experienced: many times we based feelings we were supposed to act out on events in our own lives, but more often than not we were asked to dredge up feelings and reactions that we had never been familiar with, and as far as we knew, were outside our frame of reference. Yet the miracle of inspiration carried us to some deeper understanding, and when we were especially good, there was a faint resonance under our consciousness that reminded us that we had in fact emotionally been there before.

Maybe actors really were in effect the spiritual
re-enactors of the soul's experience. Maybe that's why
it felt familiar to me.

My mind drifted again to those haunting summer
nights lolling on the hot grass with my telescope. It was
as though I *remembered* the "feelings" I had had when
I was looking at the stars. They felt familiar. It was as
simple as that. Was I remembering an acquaintance
with the knowledge of life there? Had I, or for that
matter had everyone on Earth today experienced the
familiarity with "helpers" from other celestial places
during our long struggle through the traumas of time?
John and McPherson and Ambres had said as much.
But who were *they*? Shit, I thought, it's perfectly
straightforward—they are disembodied spirits who believe the world has always been visited by extraterrestrials.
David is an embodied spirit who believes the same... My
mind leapt to the Bible and I wondered if Ezekiel and
Moses, for example, had been in the same circumstances centuries ago that David believed he found
himself in with his Mayan today? It was easier then, I
thought. Wonders and marvels were practically an ev-
eryday affair—*everybody* believed in such things then.
Oh God, I thought—just like the folks around here...

I asked David if we could just sit in the sun for
awhile. We found a grassy spot nestled in the mountain
rocks and stretched out. We breathed deeply for a few
minutes and lay down looking up at the sky.

I tried to put everything out of my mind and just
"be." I felt David do the same. Birds chirped and the
river water gurgled and splashed. A small black dog
ambled by, left his signature on a bush, and trotted
happily away.

About half an hour must have gone by. We didn't
speak. It was nice to feel peaceful. Then I heard David
say something. His voice was slurred and sleepy. Or
maybe it was I who was sleepy.

I looked over at him. "What?" I asked.

He sighed, turned over on his side, and looked at
me. "Want to talk about Mayan?" he asked. "Because
she had a lot to say about you."

"About *me*?" I felt foolish. "Look, David. I don't know any Mayan. I mean, she's *your* problem."

David grinned. "Oh, she's no problem—although she may have created a couple for you."

"What do you mean?"

"Well, that's why we need to talk about her."

I thought a moment. "Okay if I record this?"

"Sure."

I took out my tape recorder and pushed the record button. If this was really happening, I wanted to be able to prove it to somebody. I checked the moving tape and proceeded. "Well," I said, "now what's this all about, David?"

"In the first place, do you remember a guy coming to your door—oh, maybe ten years ago, with three stones from the Masai chieftain you knew so well?"

My memory raced backward. Yes, I remembered someone ringing my doorbell in Encino about two years after my African trip, sometime in the mid-sixties. He didn't identify himself. He made no impression on me at all, but he handed me three colored stones which he said were magic amulets for health, wisdom, and security. The Masai chieftain had met him on safari and had asked if he was from America. He had said yes, and the chieftain then had asked him if he knew me. He said no, but he had heard of me. The chieftain had simply said, "Will you give these to her?" And the guy said yes, somehow he would.

Then it struck me.

"How the hell do you know about that guy?"

"Oh, it was me," David said.

"*You?*" My voice rose to a strangled squeak.

"Yes. Now calm down, Shirl. As a matter of fact, I didn't know myself at the time what it was all about. All I knew was the man gave me the stones for you and asked me to deliver them. I simply thought 'far out' —and did it."

"And then what?" I said belligerently, feeling somehow invaded.

"Well, a good deal later, Mayan told me about it. I mean what it meant. She said I had been directed to you because we'd known each other in previous lives, and some day you'd want proof of it."

"Well, why all the goddamn secrecy? Why couldn't you tell me who you were all this time?" And even as I asked I knew the answer.

"You weren't ready, were you? The whole point was to deliver the stones—even before *either* of us knew what it was about. Then Mayan had to convince me. And now I have to convince you . . ."

"I guess," I said slowly, "if proof is needed, it makes sense. But what's the point? What does it all mean?"

"What it comes down to, Shirley, is that you're to be a teacher. Like me. But on a much wider scale."

"A wider scale?"

"Yes."

"What do you mean? I'm no teacher. I haven't got the patience. I'm a learner."

"Yes, but you like to write, don't you?"

Oh my God, I thought. Am I *supposed* to write a book about all of this? Did I subconsciously plan to do that? Was that why I took my tape recorder with me everywhere and wrote notes at the end of every day?

"She thought that with your particular mental bent you could write a very entertaining, informative account of your personal excursion into these matters and maybe teach people at the same time."

Jesus, I thought, did this make sense? My other two books had been a personal account of my travels and thoughts through Africa, India, Bhutan, America, politics, show business, and China—was I now supposed to write an account of my past lives, God, and extraterrestrials?!? I laughed at the logical absurdity of it.

"Who would believe it if I wrote for publication about all this?" I asked.

"You'd be surprised," he said. "There are more people out there doing this than you realize. Everyone is motivated by a desire to know the truth. *Everyone*."

"The truth? *What* truth?"

"The simple truth," he said, "of knowing yourself. And to know yourself is to know God."

"You mean *that* is the Big Truth?"

"That's it. The point, Shirley, is that it *is* simple. God is simplicity. *Man* is complexity. Man has made himself complex. But he yearns toward understanding, toward the truth behind that complexity. And those who begin to understand it, *desire* to share their understanding."

"But that would be only *my* understanding. That wouldn't necessarily be the truth."

"No," David said, "there is only one truth, and that is God. You can help others understand God through themselves by sharing the account of how you understand God through *yourself*.

I felt a kind of clutch in my stomach and in my heart. It was true that I loved to share my adventures with my writing. But to say I would now write about how *I found God* was ridiculous to me. I wasn't even sure I believed in this thing called God. I was interested in people. The idea of having had past lives interested me because it offered an explanation of who I was today.

"David," I said, "look, my own personal identity and how I came to be who I am is something I feel comfortable with, but I can't say I *believe* in God."

"That's right," he said. "You don't *believe* in God. You *know* God. Belief implies acceptance of something unknown. You have simply forgotten what you already know."

I sat in the sunlit silence, my mind battering at itself. I had forgotten what I already knew.

David seemed to sense my flash of fear because he continued, "You certainly picked the wrong line of work if you are afraid of public humiliation, didn't you?"

He caught me off guard.

"What do you mean?" I asked.

"Well," he said, "you set yourself up for a fall every time you walk out on the stage or act in a film, don't you?"

I hadn't quite thought of it that way, but he was right. I had terrible stage fright and it wasn't based on whether I'd be good or not, it was based on what the people would think of me. There was a big difference.

"Did it ever occur to you," he went on, "that you chose a public profession so you would *overcome* your fear of humiliation?"

I had often thought the same thing, but never really admitted it to myself. I longed for anonymity, wanted to be the fly on the wall, was much more interested in asking questions than being asked, and whenever I was involved with the public exposure of my profession, I couldn't wait for it to be over so I could become a recluse again and go away somewhere and think and write.

Yet, I kept on being a public personality as though I was slowly, little by little, trying to squeeze the fear out of myself. And it had gotten better recently too. In fact, the more I learned about my internal self the less self-conscious I was of what others might think. I had always longed for the feeling of being carefree and totally unconcerned with what others thought of me. In fact, I think I had orchestrated a public personality so distinct in that regard that people really did believe I didn't give a damn what anybody else thought. I remembered telling my press agent once that I wanted to appear totally free-spirited.

So I said to David, "Do you think I *planned* to become a so-called 'free-spirited' public personality so I could get away with writing what you and Mayan have been talking about?"

"Maybe," he said. "Maybe that's the karma you chose for yourself. Why don't you just put it on the back burner for now?"

On the back burner? I was trying to stop my mind from lurching over itself. I felt as though I was grasping way beyond what I could understand. It was a feeling of groping in a darkness with only the help of clichés as lanterns to light the way . . . phrases like inner knowingness, higher consciousness, high vibrations, inner peace, enlightenment, et cetera, et cetera, et cetera. I was feeling none of those things. Instead, I was feeling set up. Was David setting me up to write about all of this?

"David," I shouted. "For God's sake, you say this Mayan is an *extraterrestrial?* Well, okay. Jesus, if you want to believe it, that's your affair—but I think the whole thing sounds like a tub of shit!" It was more than I could stand.

I was suddenly overcome with suspicion, feeling absurd that I was directing honest questions, as though the discussion was credible at all, to a person who claimed to have had a relationship with an extraterrestrial. It was just suddenly too damn much. I felt more than a little hostile. In fact, I wanted to be even more than harsh. Write about this stuff? I couldn't even think about it anymore. I felt my brain would explode. I had reached my limit of open-mindedness.

David continued to sit peacefully. Then he rolled over on his stomach, apparently unconcerned and uninvolved with what was transpiring. I could feel my pulse accelerate and I began to calculate how long it would take for me to get down from the mountains and onto a plane back to the sane world I understood.

My mind and hostility raced on as though I was having an inner dialogue with myself over my own stupid open-mindedness and the awful truth that I might be one of those suckers born every minute as P.T. Barnum would say.

David breathed calmly.

"David!" My voice was harsh. "Are you there or not?"

"I am here," he answered immediately. His voice was soft, with an annoyingly patient tone.

"Well?" I said loudly and defensively.

He raised up on an elbow. "Well, what, Shirley? You seem to have accepted the idea of reincarnation, you are at least partly convinced that there are UFOs and hence something that flies them. Now what can possibly make you think the human race has an exclusive on life in the cosmos?"

I didn't know what to think. I began to feel physically uncomfortable. My skin itched. The sun was suffocating. *I did not want to be there*.

Finally David said, "Try to be calm. Breathe deeply and concentrate on that. I know it's a struggle. I went through the same process. What you're suffering from is overload. Overload with everything. Just proceed at your own pace, and try to proceed peacefully. You'll make more progress that way."

"Progress?" I screamed at him. "You are upsetting everything mankind believes in, replacing it instead with some kind of outrageous metaphysical twilight zone mumbo jumbo, and *this* you call progress?"

"It's funny," he said. "They think *our* priorities are mumbo jumbo. *We* are still in the Dark Ages. Certainly the behavior of the human race would seem to bear me out. The fact is, we are still basically rather primitive."

"Well okay," I said, "all *right*. I know that, goddammit. But man is probably only animalistic anyway. That explains why we act the way we do. So why do you espouse all these ideas that we are better than we are?"

"Ah," he said, not in an I-told-you-so manner, but more as if *I* had proved his point. "That's the rub, isn't it? You are upset because *I* believe in you more than you do. And that challenges you to improve beyond what you believe you are capable of."

My God, I thought. That's what I had been doing to Gerry. I snorted out a breath that turned into a chuckle at the way I brought my cosmic outrage down to a personal example.

"Feeling better?" David asked. "I know that when you understand, you understand quickly."

"Oh shit," I said. "I don't know. I don't know what you're talking about."

"Yes, you do," he said gently.

I got up and began to pace around David. I wanted to nudge him with my foot. No—I wanted to kick him.

"Don't be afraid," he said. "Remember you are on the right path or you wouldn't be here."

That made me laugh. Oh Christ, I thought.

"It's all only a question of time anyway," he went

on. "But as you can see, just looking around at the world—time is running out. It's a struggle, I know. But that's life."

I laughed again.

"And remember you have already been through this struggle in many lifetimes. So relax. You can do it again."

I knelt back down on the ground beside him.

"But if I've been through this so-called spiritual struggle before, why am I going through it again?"

"Because," he said, "there are other aspects of your soul's progression you need to work out. Patience and tolerance, for example. It's not enough to intellectually understand the spiritual aspect of man. You have to *live* it. Understand?"

"What do you mean? Like Jesus Christ or somebody?"

"Right. He worked out his soul's progression to near perfection. Others can too. That, in fact, was Christ's message: all people can accomplish what he accomplished—know your potential, that's all it takes."

"What about these extraterrestrials of yours? Are they doing it too? Do they *need* to?"

"Certainly," he answered. "Every living soul in the cosmos needs to. *That* is the purpose of life. That's all they are trying to teach...know your complete potential. The extraterrestrials are still learning about themselves too. But the spiritual aspect of ourselves is what is missing on Earth."

I looked up into the sun. My skin had stopped itching and once again the sun rays felt good. I sighed to myself and looked over at my tape recorder. It was nearly to the end of the sixty-minute tape.

"Mayan always says," David's voice was a murmur, "love God, love your neighbor, love yourself, and love God's work for you are part of that work. Remember that. And something else. She told me not to forget to tell you one thing. She said that in order to get to the fruit of the tree you have to go out on a limb."

He stopped. I shut off the tape recorder and passed out on my back.

But I have that tape. I have listened to it again and again and heard David repeat the very words that McPherson and Gerry both used. ❧

> *"The UFO phenomenon is a challenge to mankind. It is the duty of scientists to take up this challenge, to disclose the nature of the UFO and to establish the scientific truth."*

—DR. FELIX ZIGEL
Moscow Institute of Aviation

❧ I lay there for a long time. Then I felt David move. I turned over and looked at him. He opened his eyes all the way and shielded them from the sun. A tear dribbled from one eye. He looked as though he had just woken from a deep sleep.

He sighed heavily and stretched. "Christ," he said, "I was out. I'm sorry, but I felt so peaceful in the sun I let myself go way under."

He churned his arms in the air and brushed his eyes again. "It's so warm and beautiful."

I just looked at him.

"What's on your mind?" he said, wiping perspiration from his chin. "How long have you been lying there like that?"

"About an hour," I said. "And I have something to say."

Some quality in the tone of my voice must have caught him. He sat up. So did I.

"This is unbelievable," I said. "I feel like a horse's ass. The hell with open-minded intelligence. I think I must be a first-class gullible jerk."

David looked at me with sadness. "You mean about Mayan," he said.

"I mean about the whole damn thing!" I said, almost in tears with outrage, exasperation and a much deeper feeling—of fear that my rage was mistaken . . .

"I know," he said. "Jesus, do I know. I went through all of that too. But then after awhile I just couldn't ignore that what she said 'felt' right. You know what I mean? I mean I know you can make fun of feelings and everything. But when you come right down to it 'feelings' *are* everything. I mean even scientists have to have a 'feeling' about something before they set out to prove it. I just 'felt' that she was telling the truth."

I sat staring at him with my arms dangling onto the grass. Then I stood up and looked down at him.

"David," I said, "how do you know you weren't just projecting some need you felt deep in your subconscious and it manifested in your believing what this person named Mayan said about herself? Maybe you *needed* to believe it—so she picked that up and just told you what you wanted to believe."

David looked at me, astonished.

"But I *didn't want* to believe it," he said. "I told you. It took two trips back here and months of talking to her before I was even civil to her when she tried to tell me about this stuff. I hated what she was saying. I mean, she said she nearly gave up on me. She said I was almost too hostile to tolerate. And she was right. She upset all my beliefs and even my sanity for awhile. I liked my fast cars, and fast women and my life in the fast lane. The last thing I wanted was to give that stuff up and become spiritual. I wasn't even unhappy. I wasn't looking for anything. But after awhile I had to admit that what she was saying made sense."

"What made sense, being a person from the Pleiades?"

"Well no," he answered. "Not that. Her spiritual message made sense. All of her teachings and explanations of the reincarnation of life and cosmic laws and justice. *That's* what made sense. I couldn't run away from it."

I watched him closely. He seemed to be so genuine.

"I don't want to convince you of anything, Shirley," he said. "What you believe is up to you. I just feel you should seriously consider the possibility of what I am saying. It doesn't make any difference to my life one way or the other. I already know what I believe."

I stood with my arms unmoving against my sides.

Another antique-yellow colored train came through the mountains. I wanted to jump into the freshly mined cargo of coal and dunk myself until I was black with its residue. *That* would be real. I wanted to dance to every Peruvian juke box I heard. *That* would be real. I also wanted to skip on top of the orange bubbles of the Mantaro, unconcerned that I might sink. I wanted to march to the Huaytapallana Ice Peaks and project myself over them so I could see for myself what was on the other side.

I got up and started to walk. David stayed where he was.

I walked for the rest of the day alone. My thoughts clanged together like thick new chains...full of confusion, fear, sadness, and hurt. Then I would experience bewildering eruptions of joy. What was going on, what was happening to me?

❖ Was David only believing what he needed to believe? I thought back to California. Did Kevin Ryerson and Cat need to believe in spiritual entities? Were Sturé and Turid and Lars and Birgitta so agonized in their lives that they all needed to believe that this incarnate spiritual entity really guided them? Certainly they did not seem agonized, and David had never met any of these people, yet they were all thinking the same thing—from the reality of Karmic cosmic justice to the existence of extraterrestrial spirituality. ❖

Chapter 24

"Take our own bodies. I believe they are composed of myriads and myriads of infinitesimally small individuals, each in itself a unit of life, and that these units work in squads—or swarms, as I prefer to call them—and that these infinitesimally small units live forever. When we 'die' these swarms of units, like a swarm of bees, so to speak, betake themselves elsewhere, and go on functioning in some other form or environment."

—THOMAS EDISON
The Diary and Sundry Observations

❧ I went off by myself the next morning, rambling and thinking—or not really thinking, just letting all the new experiences wash through me without trying to sort things out. Absorbing really new thinking, getting a new view, a totally different set of perspectives on life, is a process that takes and needs time—just time—to percolate through. We are so accustomed to the things we have grown up with that we don't even remember the necessary silent times, the shut-out-the-world times, the solitary times of one's growing up. And maybe one always needed some solitude. I sure as hell did right then.

It was late afternoon before I got back to David. "Let's get to the sulphur baths," I said.

"Sure."

As we headed that way David reached into his pocket and handed me a bracelet of what looked like silver. It was just like the one he wore all the time. "Mayan gave me this," he said. "I want you to have it. Wear it on your wrist all the time you are here. It will help make things more clear."

I put it on wondering what he meant.

"What's it made out of?" I asked.

"Oh," he said, "I don't know. It's hard to say. But it works."

"What do you mean? It makes what work?" I couldn't understand what he was talking about.

"Well, when I wear mine, I feel my thoughts are somehow more amplified so that I think with more clarity."

"How come?"

"I don't know exactly," he said. "It's something to do with what she calls the third force."

"Mayan gave you the bracelets?" I asked.

"Yes. Let's get on down to the bathhouse. I can think better there and I'll try to tell you what she told me."

"Okay."

The temperature was beginning to chill as we made our way to the pool house through the afternoon light; the sky was so clear and crisp that I could see the moon hovering in the daylight like a gigantic heavy gray ball. I felt my head vibrate. Some of my confusion lifted. The sky was real. The chill was penetrating. The moon was actual. Of those facts, there was no question.

David carried a candle and I carried my tape recorder. At night, my soft woolen poncho meant as much to me as my hat did during the day. I thought of immersing myself in the lukewarm sulphur water. Already my muscular aches were subsiding. The "waters" were helpful; that was also a fact. Hanging our clothes on the nails of the musty-smelling walls, we quickly undressed and inched our way under the water. It bubbled around us almost like a language. Maybe that was how water talked. Churning our arms around us, we touched the mossy rocks underneath with our feet, and again I was pleasantly surprised at how buoyant the bubbling water was. I felt I couldn't sink if I wanted to. I wondered if I'd be water-logged before this adventure ended.

The bathhouse was dim. David struck a match, lit the candle, turned it upside down to drip wax onto the earth floor above us and placed the candle securely in the drippings as they dried on the cold stone.

"Relax a little," he said, "you're wound up tight as a drum. I have to tell you more of what Mayan taught me. It's a mind-blower." As though my mind hadn't already been blown enough.

I reached over to the tape recorder and turned it on.

"First," said David, "let's review your high school chemistry and the makeup of the atom."

"I didn't take chemistry," I said. "I always knew I wanted to be in show business, so it didn't seem useful."

"All right—no problem. You know that the proton is the positive charge of energy and the electron is the negative."

"Yes."

"And you know that each of these charges carries energy equally balanced."

"Yes."

"And that the negative and the positive attract each other and the alike charges repel each other."

"Yes."

"You know that the electrons rotate around the protons constantly and at great speeds. In fact, the electrons and neutrons rotate around the protons in relatively the same way that the Earth and other planets in our system revolve around the sun. In other words, this atom is a miniature planetary system."

"Yes, I remember reading that. Quite exciting, I think, that the atom is a microcosm of a planetary system. It makes you wonder if the whole universe isn't in one drop of water."

David's face lit up. But he didn't stop.

"Now," he said, "there is a force at work that acts as the cohesive element enabling that miniature planetary system to rotate. This energy is what Mayan called a Divine Force—a force that is the organizer of all matter in the cosmos. It organizes the atom. Everything in creation is made up of atoms—trees, sand, water, whiskers on kittens, planets, galaxies—everything. Everything that is physical is made out of atoms. You might say this Force is the ultimate Source, the thinking element of nature."

"Wait a minute," I said, "hold it. A *thinking* element?"

He stopped a minute and looked into the candlelight. Then he said, "Look, Shirley, let me tell you that later, okay? Just listen for now and if it doesn't make sense, forget it."

"Okay," I said. "You brought it up. Take your time. So this Source is the 'thinking' element of nature. Then what?"

"Okay," he said, "now let me break down the components of the atom. You understand that one simple atom is made up of protons, neutrons and electrons, right?"

"Right."

"And for the moment, you understand that this Source is the cohesive glue that holds the electrons and protons and neutrons together?"

"Well, if you say so," I said. "You mean it is a kind of ocean in which everything floats?"

"Good, yes," said David, "that ocean holds the atoms together, the planets together, the galaxies together and the Universe together—together in harmony."

"This is what Mayan told you?" I asked, beginning to feel a strange stirring in my head.

David nodded. "Bear with me."

"Okay." I swallowed.

"Okay." David went on. "The Source, or 'ocean,' as

you call it, is made up of balancing and contrasting polarities."

"Polarities?" I asked.

"Yes," said David. "Polarities of positive and negative, yin and yang, or as scientists refer to it today, 'quarks.'"

"I've heard of that," I said.

"I'm not surprised. Some of our scientists suspect this energy is there but they can't measure it because it is not molecular. They say there's an energy that fills interatomic space, but they don't know what it is. Even *they* call it the cohesive element of the atom, which they term as 'gluon.' They know it is not matter, but rather units of energy."

"Well, specifically, what is it you are getting at?"

"Mayan says it is this subatomic energy that makes up the Source. Therefore the Source, that form of energy, is not molecular. Now I'm going to tell you the hard part to understand, but the part that is the most important. This energy is the energy that makes up the soul. Our bodies are made out of atoms; our souls are made of this Source energy."

I could feel a nervous perspiration begin to seep out of my scalp. Could the soul be made of an energy force as real as the physical? Was that why the soul lived infinitely? My mind tumbled over and over. David's words rescued me.

"Our science doesn't recognize the existence of the soul, so it can't recognize the scientific makeup of the Source. If and when science does get to establishing the Source, it will be acknowledging spirituality as a physical reality."

"Why? David, can't you see what a colossal assumption that is? I mean, who *says* this Source, if it exists, is necessarily the soul force? It could be anything—part of a fourth dimension, or space, or time—anything at all. And it seems to me to make damn little difference, at this point, whether we know for a fact, or don't know, what the soul is made of. I mean, if we have to take its basic existence on faith—and we do, there isn't any *proof*—then what's the point of breaking down its

components—why the hell not take its composition on
faith? Why even ask any questions about the mechanics
of the thing? Mechanics only have meaning because
they can be proved. The soul can't be *proved*, and so as
far as I'm concerned, it doesn't need to be. But don't
try and sell me mechanics on faith."

David chuckled. "Mayan said that that's what's
wrong with our science. It doesn't allow for the existence of forces that seem to dwell in the simple spiritual
realm. That's why they don't really know what electricity *is*—they know it exists only because it has physical
results."

"But you really believe the soul is a *physical*
force?"

"Yes, exactly. But it is a significantly different *kind*
of force from the physical atomic and molecular forces
that comprise the body. It is a subatomic force, the
intelligent energy that organizes life. It is part of every
cell, it is part of DNA, it is in us, and of us, and the
whole of it—everywhere—is what we call 'God.'"

I was perspiring now and feeling dizzy. No matter
how I protested it, I can only say that this sounded real
to me. I don't know why. I can't explain it. I felt I was
remembering something somewhere way underneath
my mind in a place I had never touched. What David
reported Mayan as saying triggered *recognition* in me,
like suddenly coming into focus on something familiar
that you've been staring at without seeing. I felt what
he was saying was true because I had known it
somewhere, sometime, before. Not the structure of it,
so much, as the sure knowledge of a meaningful awareness
that exists outside of, or rather *in addition to*, and as a
part of, the life we know.

"You see?" he said gently. "This is it. This Source
fills and organizes all life. It is the beginning and the
end; the Alpha and the Omega. It is the God of
Creation. And it is very much in Us."

I stared at him. I couldn't talk. There really was
nothing to say.

I thought how arrogant it was to imagine God as a
human, with a physical form like ours, created in our

own image. No wonder we negated the spirit. Even our religious concepts of the soul were based mostly on physical images. And science couldn't admit the possibility that a spiritual form might actually exist.

"So you see," said David, "when Christ said God is everywhere, in a sense he was being literal—what he meant was this life-guiding spiritual energy is everywhere. Life, then, is the combination of the molecular structure which is physical matter, and the Source which is spiritual energy. The physical form dies. The spiritual energy lives forever."

I clutched my arms around my midriff. Then I wiped the perspiration from my scalp and clutched myself again. I said out loud: "Energy cannot be created or destroyed, just transformed," as though I was reciting high school physics.

"Right," said David. "All is energy. But science only deals in what it can see and prove. Molecular properties are easier to find than energy units. And the soul is an accumulation of energy units. It has its own free will and when its accompanying body dies, it simply individualizes itself until it makes its karmic decision as to what new form will house it. Hence what we call reincarnation. Hence life after death. Hence the life before birth."

I was silent. I wanted to think. I wanted not to think. I wanted, above all, to rest. I breathed deeply. A kind of bile rose to my throat. I stared at the flickering candle. My head felt light. I physically felt a kind of tunnel open in my mind. It grew like a cavern of clear space that was open and free of jumble. It didn't feel like thought. It felt actually physical. The flame of the candle slowly melted into the space in my mind. Once again I felt myself *become* the flame. I had no arms, no legs, no body, no physical form. I became the space in my mind. I felt myself flow into the space, fill it, and float off, rising out of my body until I began to soar. I was aware that my body remained in the water. I looked down and saw it. David stood next to it. My spirit or mind or soul, or whatever it was, climbed higher into space. Right through the ceiling of the pool

house and upward over the twilight river I literally felt
I was flying . . . no, flying wasn't the right word . . . it was
more gentle than that . . . wafting seemed to describe it
best . . . wafting higher and higher until I could see the
mountains and the landscape below me and I recognized what I had seen during the day.

And attached to my spirit was a thin, thin silver
cord that remained stretched though attached to my
body in the pool of water. I wasn't in a dream. No, I
was conscious of everything, it seemed. I was even
conscious that I didn't want to soar too high. I was
conscious that I didn't want to soar too far away from
my body. I definitely felt connected. What was certain
to me was that I felt two forms . . . my body form below
and my spirit form that soared. I was in two places at
once, and I accepted it completely. I was aware, as I
soared, of vibrational energy around me. I couldn't see
it, but I felt a new sense of "sensing" it. It felt like a
new dimension of perception, somehow, that had nothing to do with hearing or seeing or smelling or tasting
or touching. I couldn't describe it to myself. I knew it
was there—physically—yet I knew my body was below
me.

Was this what all those people interviewed by
Elizabeth Kubler-Ross had experienced? Had my spiritual energy separated itself from the physical form? Was
I floating *as* my soul? I was consciously aware of my
questions as I soared freely above the Earth. I was so
conscious of what I felt that in those moments I understood how irrelevant my physical body was. I was
experiencing the separation, I guess. Experiencing the
two entities—and very much more besides.

I watched the silver cord attached to my body. I
had read about the silver cord in metaphysical literature.
It glistened in the air. It felt limitless in length . . . totally
elastic, always attached to my body. My sight came
from some kind of spiritual eye. It wasn't like seeing
with real eyes. I soared higher and wondered how far
the cord would stretch without snapping. The moment
I thought about hesitation, my soaring stopped. I stopped
my flight, consciously, in space. I didn't want to go any

higher. As it was I could see the curvature of the Earth, and darkness on the other side of the globe. The space surrounding my spirit was soothing and gentle and pure. I began to perceive waves of energy connections and undulating thought energy patterns. The silver cord wasn't taut or stretched. It only floated gently.

I directed myself downward, back to my body. Slowly I descended. Slowly . . . down, down . . . gently through the space I wafted back to earth. The energy vibrations subsided . . . the rolling sensation of the undulating thought waves disappeared above me and with a soft fusion of contact that felt like a puff, I melded back into my body. My body felt comfortable, familiar, but it also felt restricting and cumbersome and limiting . . . I was glad to be back, but knew that I would want to go out again.

The silver cord melded into the flickering candle-light and I shook myself free of the concentration and looked over at David who was smiling.

I didn't really understand what had happened. I tried to explain it to David.

"I know," he said. "See how realization is a physical act?" he said. "What you *real*ized was your soul and your soul left your body. That's all." But he was clearly delighted.

"You mean I was astrally projecting just then?" I asked.

"Sure," he said. "I was doing that this morning right here while you were off walking. I take trips all over the place. I save on fuel costs," he grinned. "In the astral world you can go anywhere you feel like, meet all kinds of other souls too. It's just that when you return to your body and wake up you often don't remember where you've been. Something like dreaming."

"So is that what happens when you die; your soul just rises out of your body and floats and soars into the astral world?"

"Sure," said David, "except you're only dead if your silver cord snaps. The cord snaps and breaks off when the body can no longer sustain the life force. It's really very simple. I can't tell you specifically how it is

to die, but I can tell you that the principle is the same
as astral projection, only there's no body to return to."

I began to shiver slightly in the water. I wanted
more hot milk ... something familiar. I couldn't go back
to a warm cozy room or bask in a really hot soapy tub. I
could only keep going forward regardless of how uncomfortable it might be.

"I guess I should get out of this water," I said,
feeling my teeth begin to chatter.

"Okay," said David. "Let's go get some milk and
food."

I rubbed my skin hard until it tingled and whipped
on my clothes like a quick change artist. Outside David
hugged me hard as though I had graduated or something.

All my perceptions were upside down ... that is all
of my worldly, conditioned, perceptions were topsy-
turvy. My new perceptions were becoming more clearly
simple. What I had experienced had a dreamlike quality to it but it wasn't a dream. It was more like a new
dimension.

A cloak of calm settled over me as we had our hot
milk and stew with the woman with no teeth and her
children. The soccer game from Lima blared loudly on
a shortwave radio interspersed with reports of wide-
spread riots in Huancayo about an hour further into the
mountains. The announcer said they were "inflation"
riots. People were throwing rocks and debris into shop
windows protesting the high cost of living. Even here
in the Andes people couldn't afford to live because their
wages couldn't accommodate the prices. David said
there would probably be a change in government soon,
whether by coup or otherwise, but it probably wouldn't
matter anyway because it would be the same problem
all over again.

When we walked outside to cross the highway to
our "hotel," it was dark. We stumbled over some large
rocks. David said the protestors used the line of boul-
ders as a technique to prevent traffic from making it to
Huancayo where its 100,000 residents were already
subject to a curfew after nine o'clock. The rocks prevented
government troops from rushing to the rescue too.

I had a kerosene lamp which gave off a kind of gaseous, smelly heat. But at least there was some warmth as I walked into my room and collapsed on the bed. The cold earth floor smelled musty and when I wrapped myself in my poncho, I wondered how open I would be to learning if I were more comfortable. Was it necessary to live with basic discomfort in order to learn basics?

"Okay," said David, "have a good sleep. Relax. Maybe I'll see you on the astral plane!" He winked and quietly left.

I stared into the silver fragment of the kerosene lamp until my eyes hurt. I lay on the makeshift cot— listening to the silence of the rocky mountains. I could hear the pigs snorting outside.

My brain swirled and leapt and crawled around inside itself. I was exhausted. I wanted to leave myself. Did I want to run and hide and forget everything I had experienced up here? I had been a grabber at life, wanting to feel, touch, experience everything I possibly could. I couldn't imagine not being avidly involved in the daily scrabble. Yet did I really want my old life back, the familiar agony of searching for purpose and reason, my fears, jealousies, struggles in driving toward whatever was true in reality? Did I long to have back again everything that had made me unhappy, or ecstatic, simply because it was familiar? Would I ever be able to relax again in the belief that life and reality were simply what I could see, touch and hear? That death was death and simply the *end*? Did I want to go back to the "safe" feeling that without proof, nothing was worthy of faith?

I heard a soft tap on the wall separating my room from David's.

"Relax, Shirley," David whispered loudly with a laugh in his voice. "I can feel your brain and it's keeping me awake."

I laughed too. "You got me into this," I said, staring at the gray slab wall beside my head. "Now you say I'm keeping you awake..."

"Try to sleep. You need it."

"Sure. How? How do I fall asleep when I know I'm

going to live a million years? I'm not sure I've even liked this much."

"Concentrate."

"On what?"

"On your golden dream, remember?"

"Yes, I remember."

Only I didn't. I couldn't think of anything I could call my golden dream. And *that* was harder than anything.

Chapter 25

I spent the next few days walking and thinking.
Sometimes David came with me, sometimes not. Sometimes I wanted to go home, back to America, back to
the familiarity of my old world with its fast-paced
involvement, its clanking relationships, its unrealistic
romance, all the rushing with no seeming purpose—the
events, the news, the arts, movies, hits, flops, sweat,
hard work, black humor, competition, new fashions,
profits, color TV, and success. I missed it all. I was used
to it. I had survived in its colorful confusion, and I
missed it. But I didn't want to be unfulfilled in it
anymore either. I watched the woman with no teeth
wash her clothes by stamping on them with her feet.
They came out clean. The clothes, I mean. (Probably
the feet, too.) That's what I wanted to do with my
life . . . stamp on it until it came out clean. *Could* I go

333

back to my old world now? Would I be two people? Was I more than one person anyway? I stopped and laughed right there. That was the whole lesson, wasn't it? I was all the people I had ever lived. I had probably been through versions of this brain drain more than a few times before.

David watched me go through the emotional pull with calm understanding.

"I had to do the same thing," he said one day, sitting on a rock staring into a mountain daisy. "Just know yourself, remember? And in yourself is the universe."

One night after stew in the FOOD building, he asked if I wanted to watch the sky for a while. The food made us warm and gave us a feeling of reinforcement against the cold.

"Let's try it," he said. "If it's too cold, we'll go inside. Straw is warm if we bury ourselves deep enough."

So, using a shovel belonging to one of the coca-chewing workmen, we dug a fairly deep rectangular hole in the soft earth just behind our "hotel." Then we piled mounds of straw into it. We lay on top of the straw and piled even more on top around us. It seemed warm enough to relax. If I thought I was warm, I was warm.

David gazed up into the sky. He had a kind of longing expression on his face.

I lay in the straw wondering how I would feel about Peru when I left it. I had a curious habit of getting homesick for every country I had ever been in—even the Soviet Union which I didn't like very much. Some spark in me was always touched when I went to a new place and I was usually haunted by it when I left. I wondered how many countries I had lived in in my other lives. I didn't understand why I couldn't remember.

The stars above us looked two feet over our heads. I shivered a little but the grandeur made the chill ridiculous. David lay quietly beside me. We looked into the sky for about an hour.

Then I looked over at him.

"I'm glad I came," I said. "Thank you."

Soon after that we fell asleep. If the space discs came out it was irrelevant to both of us. We needed rest. We woke up with the sunrise and walked in the dawn shadows for about two hours. We didn't talk much. And later, when we ate our rolls and hot milk, our conversation was about how reassuring it was that no one or nothing ever dies. In the afternoon, we walked some more ... up and down the sides of mountains and along the Mantaro River. We bought Mantaro yogurt along the road. We skipped and ran. We waded in the cold river and splashed with the orange water. I felt totally and completely in the present, and when I took a nap in the late afternoon sun, stretched out on the hot grass, my mind and heart felt as though gentle waves of liquid velvet undulated over and around me.

I began to feel (rather than to think about) a new way of looking at life and myself. I felt as though I was giving up an old self. A self that had believed that guilt, jealousy, materialism, sexual hangups, and doubt were part of being human. I had once come to terms with the performance of those emotions, felt reasonably resigned to them, and now I was having to undo the resignation and venture into a new kind of life-thought that required that I not only work out the negatives, but that if I didn't I would have to pay for avoiding it with my own karma later on. Since my life would apparently not be over when I died, I was stuck with it right smack into eternity. So I might as well get started now. Such a concept had been alien to anything I ever imagined. I thought about my life and relationships back home.

I remembered Gerry's sudden revelation one day when he said that I had romanticized him to such an extent that he couldn't possibly live up to it. It was my way of programming the relationship so that it couldn't possibly work. Romantic notions did that. They made life impossible to live—realistically or otherwise, because romantic notions were impossible to sustain.

I found myself thinking of Gerry in a different way. I looked at him in a more objective light. Much more realistically and from *his* point of view.

David and I talked about it, although I never

identified Gerry. But David helped me with understanding my own feelings. As we talked, it slowly dawned on me that I had always used my loving, protective, cocoon relationships with men *to hold myself back*. To keep from being really free and expansive, I had woven a web of soothing safety around myself and the man in my life. The *us*, therefore, had been more important to me than *me*. I was protecting myself from my own potential in the name of love.

David and I walked miles every day across the plains of wheat and along the Mantaro River banks. We sat and watched sunups and sundowns. When my conflict got me down, I talked it over with him and he reminded me to examine the reasons for it, my conditioning, my contradictions and that the choice of breaking through to a new freedom and learning process was mine.

Sitting in a relaxed sunlit mood on a hill somewhere, or in the bubbly sulphur water, he came back again and again to his talks with Mayan.

In one session, she had spoken of the need for all women to believe in themselves as women, the need to be secure in that. "Women have the right, even with the independence already achieved in the United States, to be even more independent and free," she said. "No society can function democratically until women are considered equal on every basis, *particularly to themselves*. And you will never attain such a thing other than through your own self-effort. In fact," she said, "nothing is worth having, except that which is won by 'self-effort.' The souls of human beings, particularly women, are chained to the earth through the comforts of home and land and limited love, and until you learn to break those chains for higher knowledge, you will continue to suffer."

She had reminded David that women are cleverer than men—which he repeated with a straight face. He sure took Mayan seriously.

In another session, Mayan had described science as the handmaiden of God. But she said that science had so advanced technology on Earth that it had outstripped our ability to cope with it to the point where technology had become totally life-threatening; that we actually needed to dismantle our nuclear fission plants and concentrate research resources on solving the problems of dangerous technological wastes of all kinds. Even technology, she said, is not a bad thing—it is how you use it and what you use it for: as an example she had cited the sun as a limitless source of energy which we should learn to store and utilize. Then science, through technology, would serve both man and Earth.

Mayan continually emphasized that in all of the cosmos, nothing was valued as highly as one living soul, and in the value of one living soul lay the value of the entire cosmos. She said that humankind follows a spiral projection upward, that although it may appear we are not progressing, that is in fact not true. With each rebirth and afterlife reflection, humankind finds itself on a higher plane, whether we realize it or not. And, she said, with each individual soul's progression, the machinery and the movement of the entire cosmos is affected, because each individual soul is *that* important.

She said that man has a habit of reducing his understanding to the perceptions of his own mind, that it is difficult for us to break through our own frames of reference and allow our imaginations to take quantum leaps into other dimensions, transcending the limits imposed on us by lifetimes of structured thinking.

🐾 We had been in the Andes now for two-and-a-half weeks. It seemed two-and-a-half years. To say my point of view had been altered was obvious. I could feel it in everything I thought. I felt as though my own potential was opening up. Now, I thought, if I could only hang on to it when I returned to earth! And I wondered whether my new point of view would also change my life.

We took side trips to Ataura every few days for tape batteries, paper, pens, and just to see crowds of people. We didn't see any rioting, but police were everywhere. When I shopped in the small, dusty food markets, the fruit and vegetables were not fresh and the prices were outrageous. Fifty-nine cents for an apple. Small tape recorders were $450.00 and prices for other electrical hardware appliances would have been exorbitant even for a thriving economy: no wonder there were incipient rebels all over the place. Prices were astronomical and salaries low. There were few Americans visible, mostly college students on treks through the Andes.

At the Sunday fair in Ataura people came from hundreds of miles away to sell wares that included everything from antique Victrolas to goats. We ate rice and beans, and I didn't care whether the onions sprinkled on top gave me heartburn or not. We continued to hear people in shops and restaurants talk about UFOs. David translated and it seemed that each person had had some kind of UFO experience, describing cigar-shaped craft out of which flew discs, or just discs alone.

Nearly everyone had a story about the Huaytapallana Ice Peaks. Either they seemed on fire at certain times "with the sky lighting up," or formations of craft were seen above them. There didn't seem to be much fear running through the related experiences, only awe. And everyone who had seen a UFO believed the craft belonged to beings from outer space.

We were sitting in the heartburn cafe on my last day in the Andes. I was scheduled to leave for New York from Lima at six o'clock the next morning. Looking out at the Ice Peaks, David got up, plucked a daisy from the vase on the table, put it behind his ear, and went to buy a Spanish newspaper. I saw his face drop when he read the headlines.

"There's been a big blackout in New York City," he said, "and lots of people went 'free shopping.'"

"Free shopping?" I asked.

"Looting," he said.

"My God," I said, "was anybody hurt or killed or anything?"

He read on. "No," he said, "the system just broke down. Like it does everywhere. Now there'll be a big clamor for more law and order and racism will be a big thing again, I guess, because most of the people who went on the shopping spree weren't white."

My mind flashed to my friend Bella Abzug. She would be gearing up her campaign for mayor right about now. I wondered if she'd win or whether she should have stayed in the House of Representatives. She lost the Senate race by half a percentage point and most people believed she was the front runner for mayor.

I told David what I was thinking and how I loved Bella and how I hoped she'd be effective if she won.

"I like her too," he said. "You always know where you stand with Bella. I guess I could say the people who don't like Bella are the people I don't like."

I nodded, thinking of her strong personality and of how I might help her in her campaign if I were in New York.

"God, I wonder if Bella will really win," I said. "I wonder if the Liberal wing of the Democratic party in New York will fragment itself again, or whether they'll really let her win this time."

David chewed on his daisy. "Want to ask someone?" he asked.

"What do you mean?"

"Well, there's a woman up here who's a famous psychic. She's been uncanny with me. Let's go ask her about Bella."

"What the hell," I said. "I might as well know what I'm getting into when I go back to New York."

David drove to a house on the edge of town nestled into the side of the mountains. It was modest and white stucco. There were wild flowers growing against the walls.

A young girl answered the door and welcomed David as though she knew him. He explained that we'd like to see her mother. She nodded and said her mother had been working on her Sanskrit texts all morning.

"Sanskrit?" I asked. "What is a Peruvian woman in the Andes doing with Sanskrit?"

"She doesn't understand either," said David. "She's never had any education in Sanskrit, doesn't consciously know how to read it or write it, but she goes into a trance and the automatic writing starts to flow through her fingers. Something like the way Mohammed wrote the Koran, except that he was illiterate."

"You mean," I asked, "that some kind of inner voice inspires her to write down stuff she doesn't know anything about?"

"Yes," said David. "She says she has no control over it. It commands her at all sorts of odd hours. So she finds herself, even in the dark, writing long passages of spiritual teachings in a language that she doesn't recognize."

"Have these passages been verified?" I asked.

"Oh sure," he said, "she's known to be one of the world's renowned experts on Sanskrit, but nobody understands how. Historians and language scholars on Sanskrit from all over the world have verified that what she is writing is real. She says she doesn't want to understand it as long as it helps people."

We waited in a clean and Spartan hallway for Maria.

When she appeared, I was struck by how plain and middle-class Peruvian she looked. A print dress clung to her broad hips and she waddled as she walked in scuffed shoes with thick heels run down on the outside. Her face was open and friendly and her hair bore the remnants of an old permanent.

She greeted David with an embrace and, holding my arm, ushered us into her well-kept living room with a glass-topped coffee table and furniture from Sears and Roebuck, Lima branch.

She spoke only Spanish which David translated.

"How can I be of help?" she asked.

David looked at me. "Do you want to ask her about Bella?"

"Sure."

I ran through the background on Bella once more and he translated to Maria.

She reached out her hand and said, "Could I please hold something that you wear all the time?"

"Why?" I asked.

"Because," she said, "I need to touch your energy vibrations."

I reached up and took off my diamond heart necklace that I wore during the filming of *The Turning Point* and had worn ever since.

Maria fondled the necklace in her right hand and closed her eyes and seemed to "feel" its vibrations.

"You are a good friend of the woman in question," she said.

I nodded.

"And she is in a competition to win a position of leadership in your New York City." She was making statements rather than asking me.

I nodded again.

Maria's eyes opened.

"No," she said, "I don't see her winning this competition. I see instead a man with a bald head and long fingers."

I looked over at David in confusion. I didn't know who she could be talking about. She clearly knew nothing about New York politics and was operating on some other kind of imagery.

"Are you sure?" I asked. "There must be some mistake. I don't know who you are describing, and I know the people who have declared their candidacy. So, something doesn't fit."

"This person has not declared himself yet," she responded.

I felt a drop of perspiration trickle down my midriff and changed the subject.

I asked her about the movies I might make. She answered by saying I had already made a good one which would win awards and was beautiful because it revolved around the world of the ballet (*The Turning Point* had not yet been released).

I sat quietly for a moment.

"I also see a man standing by a window," she said.

"He gazes into white snow and understands that it is impossible for you to be together."

I blinked and coughed softly to myself.

"He has thought a great deal about it, but cannot see his way clear to be with you. I hope you understand what I refer to."

I didn't want to talk anymore about myself.

"What about Bella?" I asked.

Maria looked over at me with sad, round eyes.

"Your woman will not win," she said. "She won't even be in the running. A bald man with long fingers whom no one has yet considered will be victorious."

I stood up with Maria. She obviously had other things to do. I thanked her. She was warm and sad. She hooked my necklace around my neck for me and said she would be happy to see me again if I wanted. She embraced us and we left.

I was upset with what she had said—mostly because she had seemed so sure.

"How could she be so definite?" I asked David as we headed toward the car, a slight drizzle of rain falling, slowly making the mountain town a mass of mud.

"I don't know," he answered. "Just wait and see. Maybe she's wrong. But I have to admit that's rare." He shivered a little and gestured toward the car. I walked with him, unable to think of much to say. He started the car and we headed for Llocllapampa. David was silent and I respected my reluctance to break into his thoughts, but I wondered again about the string of "coincidence" which had marked the growth of the very special and dear relationship we shared. Every word he spoke now took on hidden meaning. *Why* had he come along in the first place? He had absolutely nothing to gain from knowing me—in fact, ten years ago he had come and gone as a stranger, leaving the Masai stones with me to remind us both, it seems, that that was not a simple accident.

I thought of all I had learned because of him . . . the adventurous wonder of his Mayan, whoever she was . . . the world of the spirit she and he had introduced me to . . . their reminders that the big mysteries of life were there to solve if we would only look... of the books David had suggested I read... of the dozens of people here to whom UFOs were commonplace. I tried to piece it all together: the sessions with Ambres, with McPherson and John, worlds apart but saying the same thing... the continual connections of God and spirit and love and karma and other worlds and Cosmic Justice and basic kindness and spiritual enlightenment and Jesus and flying machines and the Golden Rule and advanced civilizations and "gods" who came in chariots of fire and people throughout human history who had performed unexplained miracles.

Was it all beginning to make sense? Perhaps humans *were* a part of an overall cosmic plan that had been in effect for thousands and thousands of years? Could it even be that people who claimed to have had trips in spacecraft were telling the truth—even though their stories ended up in the *National Enquirer*? No, that would really be too much... But what was I going to do about all this? Would anybody believe me if I were to write about it? Was that why David had come into my life? He had said I would be able to risk humiliation if I really believed what I had learned. But then he said my credibility wouldn't be damaged if people believed I was sincere. Well, I was. But I had this horrible jellylike feeling about *what* it was I was sincere about...

On toward Llocllapampa we drove. I thought about packing my suitcase quickly so we could enjoy the sunset before leaving for Lima. But when we got there, a Peruvian man dressed in a uniform was waiting outside our hotel. David turned to me and said, "A friend of mine will drive you down the mountain. He doesn't speak English, but he's reliable. You'll make your plane for New York. I'm going to stay here for a while."

My stomach fell to my feet. I wanted to cry. "Wait a minute," I said, "just like that? I'm leaving and you're staying here? I want to talk some more. Why are you staying?"

He looked at me. "I don't have to get back. You do. That's all. Just think about everything that's happened over the last few weeks. Absorb it slowly. It's just the beginning for you. You need time alone now. I would think you'd better get back to your real life just to ground yourself. You have your notes and your tapes and a million books to read and investigations to investigate. Do it. You've thought a lot and learned a lot. Now it's better for you to be on your own."

The tears welled in my eyes. I didn't know what to say. He reached over and took my hand. "Look at that sky," he said. "Is that freedom or is that freedom? Now go on and pack."

I eased myself into my cold dark room for the last time. As I stuffed my clothes and tapes and notes into my suitcase, I longed for another mineral bath. I wouldn't hear the pigs snorting in the mountain silence that night. I wouldn't brush my teeth in the orange river in the morning. I wouldn't walk in the mountain afternoon again. I wouldn't be with David anymore. I hadn't really speculated about the future at all, and suddenly it was in my lap.

🌀 When I finished packing, I walked out into the setting sun. The lady with no teeth was waiting at the Plymouth with my ring watch. I looked at David: he shrugged and smiled. I took the watch, put it in the palm of her hand and closed her fingers over it. I nodded and smiled over her voluble delight and turned back to David.

Very gently he pinched my chin and kind of waggled it a bit. I grabbed his hand in both of mine and held on hard. "Am I supposed to go now? Just like that? Just *leave*?"

"Yes." Holding my hand he walked me to my side of the Plymouth. I looked around at the purple-hued mountains. With one arm he hugged my shoulders as he opened the car door. "We'll see each other again. I promise. Trust me. Remember we've been together through many lives, right?"

I scratched the back of my neck and tried not to

cry. I climbed in as his friend put my suitcase in the
back seat. David slammed the door and leaned in to
me.

"I love you," he said. "And remember nothing is
more important than love."

I felt an unbearable ache in my throat. I could
hardly speak for fear of losing complete control. "Yes," I
choked. "I don't understand but I love you too."

"Good," he said. "Now go get 'em. That's all . . . it's
simple. Be yourself, don't be afraid, and love the world."

His friend turned on the ignition and stepped on
the gas. We pulled away from the town that wasn't a
town. I didn't look back, but I could feel David waving,
his left shoulder slumped as he stood watching us go.

❀

". . . what marvellous deepening of emotional
power may be gained with the recognition of
the idea of pre-existence . . . we learn that we
have been living in a hemisphere only, that we
have been thinking half-thoughts, that we need
a new faith to join past with future over the
great parallel of the present, and so to round
out our emotional world to a perfect sphere."

—LAFCADIO HEARN
Kokoro

❀ The man driving said something in Spanish and I
nodded and smiled and was relieved I couldn't talk to
him.

I tried to ease the ache in my throat by drinking in
the familiar countryside. Down the Andes we wound,
past the mining towns, past the herds of llamas, past
the women dressed in wide-brimmed white starched
hats, past the UFO signpost at the railway crossing.
The air became dustier, less rarefied, thicker, easier to
breathe but not as heady. The sun fell behind the
mountains behind us. Chugging up the other side of

the steep winding roads we passed empty trucks that would be full of coal and iron ore and rock when they descended again a day later.

My mind tumbled with images: bubbling sulphur water, hot languid mountain grass, the orange river, the peasant mountain people chewing coke leaves for energy, confusing talks with David in the sunlight. I dozed.

I woke with a jolt at a break in the road. Night had fallen completely now and the Peruvian stars glistened like chunks of low-flying crystal. My Peruvian driver drove stolidly on.

Driving into Lima was like entering a backward world. I tried not to look. Squatters' huts lined the roadside. People walked aimlessly. Factories spewed dirty smoke into the already filthy night air. Clouds hung over the city, wet and thick and putrid, obscuring the glistening beauty of the other world above.

I felt a chill and put on my Ralph Lauren butter-leather coat to prepare for New York. The man stopped in front of Varig Airlines and helped me with my suitcase. I thanked him and thought better than to give him money. We shook hands and he smiled and drove off in the old jalopy that had been like a home in the mountains.

I checked in and went right to the plane. Two hours out of Lima, at an altitude of 35,000 feet, I saw an electrical storm on the horizon that looked as though the Kingdom of Heaven was clashing against itself. The lightning splashed the sky pure white like blazing daylight for as far as I could see. The colossal power of the electricity made me cower in my seat feeling as insignificant as a flea. Nothing seemed to be as powerful as nature. Except, according to David, and Mayan, and John, and Ambres, and McPherson, and Cat, and Cayce, and—I now realized—many, many others, nothing was as powerful as the *collective* human mind, that infinitely elastic web of strength called human consciousness, and represented by the communal energy people referred to as their souls. It seemed to me that there were endless worlds for me to explore. And I *wanted* to, I really wanted to know.

Maybe one could never physically prove whether the soul existed or not. I wasn't sure that that even mattered. Perhaps reality was only what one believed it to be anyway. That would make all perceived realities real. Maybe that was the lesson I was learning—learning *to think with unlimitedness* . . . to believe that anything is possible . . . to believe that one can do anything, soar anywhere, *become everything*. Maybe one human soul *was everything*. And such a reality was up to each of us to relearn.

Maybe the tragedy of the human race was that we had forgotten we were each Divine. And if we re-realized that, we could dispel fear from our lives. In dispelling fear, we could dispel hate. And much more. With the fear we would rid ourselves of greed and war and killing. Fear was the root and circle around which our lives revolved—fear of failure, fear of pain, fear of humiliation, fear of loneliness, of being unloved, of ourselves, fear of death, ultimately fear of fear. Fear itself was insidious, infectious, seeping in from one point of unreality to permeate all our lives. Perhaps our belief in death was the gravest unreality of all. If we could truly know that we never really died, that we always got another chance, that no pain, no humiliation, no loss, was ever final, total and forever, maybe we could understand that there was nothing to fear. It could be that human beings were using their talent for complexity as an excuse to avoid the responsibility for being what we really understood we were from the beginning—basically part of what we called "God," and without limitation, masters of our own divine potential.

I sat quietly tense, held in place by the seat-belt—man's answer to the electrical storm exploding around us. The airplane shook and bobbed violently in the stupefying display of dazzling, raw, natural power visible from every window. What was night outside had become a thunderously electrified daylight, flash after blazing flash revealing clouds and colors and an astral terrain of currents and rains whirling and raging around our small craft. No one spoke. No one screamed. As far as I could tell, no one cried. We had no choice. It was

moments like this, I thought, that forced one to think
and stretch one's awareness beyond what we had been
taught. It was moments like this, maybe too few and far
between, that acted as a catalyst for our understanding
a little better the internal control of which we were
really capable. No one in the airplane could fight the
storm. No one could overcome it. No one could really
even understand it. It just *was*. And this elemental
crisis had brought us all together, sharing without a
word having been spoken.

I determined to relax, beginning with my feet.
Then I worked my way up, through ankles, legs, arms,
hands, solar plexus, and chest. It worked. I began to
feel I was part of the bobbing, creaking plane. My
breathing came more evenly. My heart stopped beating
so fast. The perspiration on my midriff and forehead
cooled. Then I stopped and realized I had controlled
my fear by using the mind to control the body . . . a
positive mind insisting on not being afraid. And what
was controlling my mind? I can only say it was my soul.
My soul knew it was going to be all right, no matter
what happened to the body. My soul—my own,
subconscious, individualized piece of the universal
energy—believed it was a part of everything, even of
the crashing, tumultuous storm outside. My soul knew
it would survive, that it was eternal, that it was ongoing
and unlimited in its understanding that this, too, was
part of the adventure we call life.

At peace and exhausted, I fell asleep. 🌀

Chapter 26

*"This day before dawn I ascended a hill and look'd
    at the crowded heaven.
And I said to my spirit, When we become the
    enfolders of those orbs, and the pleasure and
    knowledge of everything in them, shall we be
    fill'd and satisfied then?
And my spirit said, No, we but level that lift to
    pass and continue beyond.
You are also asking me questions and I hear you,
    I answer that I cannot answer, you must find
    out for yourself."*

—WALT WHITMAN
Song of Myself

When I arrived in New York I met with Bella
immediately. It was her birthday and her campaign staff
threw a fundraising party at Studio 54.

Bella knew I had been in Peru, and I told her I had
been meditating in a hut in the Andes. She had read
my books and believed I was capable of any kind of
weird adventure. In any case, it was not the time for a
talk together. I told her I had a good rest in my mud
hut and she laughed, rolling her eyes, and then plunged
into her campaign strategy just to return to a familiar
kind of insanity.

I watched intently, waiting for something that would

confirm or deny what Maria in the Andes had said.
Bella's losing campaign for the mayoralty of New York is
now history. She never even made it to the runoffs. Ed
Koch, that tall, balding fellow with the long fingers,
won, hands down.

I wished I had asked Maria more questions.

❧ With the accumulation of the events that led up to
my trip to Peru and the events in Peru itself, I began to
lead a life beneath the life that was obvious to most of
my friends. I made my films, danced and sang in my
television specials, and toured with my live show. I was
still reasonably active in the women's movement, politics and human rights, but I found that I really preferred to travel and think.

The relationship with Gerry cooled, and ended.
With my new perspectives, it did indeed feel like
something from another life . . .

I loved traveling because it helped me gain a more
accurate and objective view of the world as well as of
myself. I went all over Europe, Scandinavia, Southeast
Asia, Japan, Australia, Canada, Mexico, and to many
cities in America.

And the more I traveled, the more I learned about
the spiritual dimensions of life that I was growing to
understand. My own convictions were taking shape and
being confirmed wherever I went.

I found that the theory of the progression of souls
through the process of reincarnation had become part of
new age thought systems, not only in California, but all
over the Western world. Over casual conversations it
would come out. And whenever I pursued it more
seriously, I found that people were thirsty to compare
notes on their feelings about past-life recall and spiritual consciousness. They usually concluded by saying it
was good to have a serious dialogue on such theories
with someone who didn't believe they were crazy.
Some of the people were just regular citizens in their
respective countries. But others held high-level posi-

tions of influence in political and journalistic circles. The latter were careful to hold their beliefs close to their vests and felt saddened by the need to do so.

Yet I did not want to be talking to myself, as it were. I wanted and needed opposition, criticism, questioning. I searched for it first in my reading and found the strongest skeptics were among those with the most serious beliefs. I don't know why it surprised me. People to whom spirituality and higher consciousness are truly important most particularly do *not* want to be taken in by fakes, charlatans, self-deluded prophets, or parlor mystics. I found that searching experiments had been conducted, sometimes over periods of many years, and certainly in all areas of psychic phenomena.

The literature on the whole subject was vast—almost overwhelming—dating back to the ancient Sumerian cuneiform tablets, and down the centuries through Egyptian records, the Greek oracles, Hindu scriptures, the Druidic tradition, Essene literature, the records of secret societies such as the Free Masons, and many more; all the way to the writings of Carl Jung and even more recent parapsychological investigations. The quest, and the point of view, was always to recognize the potential for expanded consciousness in man in order to enable him to live more fully and peacefully *with and through* his spiritual dimension.

Along with my reading, I questioned many different kinds of people about their beliefs. Time and again the strongest prejudice I encountered was firmly entrenched in the minds of those who thought of themselves as intellectual pragmatists. These were people who had a kind of knee-jerk reaction to mere words like psychic, astral, spiritual dimension, and could not get beyond a conditioned reflex.

After a while, I began to see that there was another kind of rejection of spiritual values, a rejection which was a real need in certain people. They had come to terms with this world just as it is, accepting the wonder and joy that life on earth offers, accepting as well the horror, pain, and agony. Courageously, such people embraced the whole, willing and eager to go the limit, but always within the compass that this life is all there is. A whole additional dimension which might—or might not—be crucial to their ills and joys was just the additional straw they could not, did not, want to cope with. Again, it was a view I could well understand. Enough is enough, after all. And yet . . .

And yet everywhere I went, I continually encountered a deep need for spirituality and expanded consciousness, a need for people to come together, to share their energies in *something* that worked. I found people had had experiences similar to mine: people involved with trance channeling, past life recall, growing spiritual awareness, and even contact with UFOs. I found spiritual communities, such as Findhorn, were springing up all over the world. I visited and stayed at several.

I wondered whether coming into the Aquarian Age (as the astrologers and astronomers called it) also meant that we were coming into an age of Love and Light. Those were the two words most often used to characterize the feelings attached to the new age discoveries. Some of the world's leaders spoke in spiritual terms— Pierre Trudeau urged a "conspiracy of love" for humanity. Zbigniew Brzezinski spoke of an "increasing yearning for something spiritual" in a world of technology where materialism had proven unsatisfying. The spiritual urge, then, knew no politics, as I supposed it never had. Nor was the urge to transcend the material plane of existence new, either.

I went back and read more about the American transcendentalist movement. Some of the people involved in that movement were Ralph Waldo Emerson, Henry Thoreau, Bronson Alcott (father to Louisa M., of *Little Women* fame) and dozens of others. They had been rebels against over-intellectualism and the linear custom of believing only what one could see or prove. They found this both limiting and ultimately wasteful since within these bounds man's full potential could never be developed. They believed that the real essentials were invisible, untouchable—*but not unreal.*

In fact, interestingly enough, even the American Revolution itself was conceived and initiated by men whose belief in the spiritual world was an integrated part of their lives. As I reread some of that period of American history, I realized how much we had forgotten, how *metaphysically* bold those revolutionaries had been. Our forefathers—Thomas Jefferson, Thomas Paine, John Adams, Benjamin Franklin, George Washington—all were transcendentalists.

The significance of their beliefs emerged all over the Great Seal of America, on the reverse of which the legend reads, "A New Order of Ages Begins," along with the third eye which also appears at the top of the Great Pyramid of Giza on the dollar bill! All of this symbolism was designated by our transcendentalist founders at the birth of the United States.

I began to read more about these men and realized how deeply they threatened the older orders of the time with their new thinking. The transcendentalists drew not only from Quaker and Puritan traditions, but also from German and Greek philosophers, as well as from Eastern religions. When they were accused of having contempt for history, they replied that humankind should be liberated from history. They believed that all observation was relative. They saw *through* their eyes, not *with* their eyes.

All pointed out that *inner reform must precede social reform*. Continually they emphasized the need for personal transformation, but as the American Revolution moved into the Industrial Revolution, the transcendentalists found themselves increasingly isolated and misunderstood. Technology and machines were on the minds of Americans.

They came to be known as occultists and began to operate more within their own circles. By the end of the nineteenth century, the worst fears of our founding fathers had been realized. We were now fully on the path of materialism—our spiritual heritage overwhelmed by industrialization, history books barely mentioning our mystical beginnings.

But, as is more fully developed in Marilyn Ferguson's "The Aquarian Conspiracy" published in 1980, the spiritual support system of our revolutionary forefathers had taken hold in art and in literature.

William Blake, for example, considered the American and French revolutions as only the first steps toward a worldwide spiritual revolution.

Just as Blake had been influenced by the German mystic, writer and philosopher Jacob Boehme and by Emanuel Swedenborg, Blake now influenced writers, artists and politicians for years to come: Nathaniel Hawthorne, Emily Dickinson, Herman Melville, John Dewey, Thoreau, Gandhi, Martin Luther King—all deeply believed in metaphysical dimensions that would ultimately explain the mystery of life.

I read and read and talked more and more freely to people about my experiences in spiritual search. Many others seemed to be searching also for a balance between their inner lives and their outer lives. Many of them attended spiritual channelings, seeking answers from the "other side."

Studio executives, bank presidents, journalists, actors and actresses, musicians, writers, househusbands and housewives attended the spiritual channelings that I had been introduced to. No one questioned the validity of the process anymore. They only wrestled with the information they received—past-life information, psychological information, dietary information, medical and scientific information: information about Atlantis, Lemuria, the creation of the cosmos, extraterrestrials . . . everything one could think of to ask. The spiritual entities (not in the body) became their friends and confidants. People discussed their personalities, their humor, their understanding, as if they were physically present.

As I talked with the hundreds who came to these sessions, I realized they were more comfortable and open with each other than with those in their lives who had not recognized the need for spirituality. This was not a religious feeling. Not at all. It was simply that to be without spiritual awareness was like being without arms and legs. Some had skeptical questions when they found the going rough. But all of the people I talked to just kept going. They told me about the predictions that had been channeled that had come to pass. They told me how some of the past-life information had altered their perspectives on their present lives. They told me how vacant the lives of friends seemed to be who did not share their search—to whom they could not speak in spiritual terms.

They were not at all close-mouthed when I questioned them, but all said they found it difficult to relate to others who did not understand. They went about their daily lives with the knowledge and support that they had each other, but mostly they derived great happiness and joy from the fact that they were getting more in touch with their own spiritual selves. Some of their relationships and long friendships eventually foundered because their spiritual beliefs and values could not be shared and they could not abide the cynical and intellectual limitations of the past. Some said they found it necessary to lead two lives—for fear of threatening those they loved.

At the same time science was having its own struggle. I read in *The New York Times* that scientists had been forced to come around to the "big bang" theory of the creation of the universe. It looked as though the theologians had been right after all. The Bible had called the shot and the scientists were having to admit it. The universe had been created by a colossal explosion all at once, "in one moment of time," about twenty billion years ago. The astronomical and scientific and biblical accounts of Genesis all coincided now, much to the dismay of most scientists, who found it "irritating," to say the least. The universe was expanding in some places as fast as one hundred million miles an hour. That meant *there had been a beginning*.

So the question the scientists posed was, "What came before the beginning?" They were concluding now that, "There must have been a Divine Will constituting nature from nothingness."

So perhaps a theological explanation might hold an answer. Scientists had been able to trace the origins of humanity on the planet, the chemical ingredients of life itself, the formation of stars out of primal mists: but now they had hit a solid barrier. An article (by the scientist Robert Jastrow, Director of NASA's Goddard Institute for Space Studies) said, "For the scientist who has lived by his faith in the power of reason, the story ends like a bad dream. He has scaled the mountains of ignorance, he is about to conquer the highest peak; as he pulls himself over the final rock, he is greeted by a band of theologians who have been sitting there for centuries."

❧ It seemed as though the whole world was rushing toward a confrontation with itself. In the last hundred years we had progressed farther and faster than in all the time preceding, most particularly in the areas of technology, matched only by the various scientific disciplines, fairly bursting with new discoveries. And this rapid growth was very much ongoing. People now living remembered a wholly different world, one they had experienced in their childhood, when life moved at the pace it took to walk to your neighbor's for company; while others, now living, had been raised in the age of television and telephone communication, a computer-wise generation to whom reading was difficult and writing awkward.

The energy packed into this period by the acceleration of discovery on all fronts had altered time. We were experiencing a form of time dilation, the kind of adrenaline-induced, stretched-out feeling that occurs in a moment of sharp crisis: but this dilation, this crisis, was on a massive scale, confronting us daily in every aspect of our lives. No wonder that more and more people were turning to the dimension of the spirit, seeking a wholeness that had been lost in the maelstrom of energy vibrating through their lives. The more intense their living became, the more they needed to control those energies.

Now, it seemed to me, this search, this sense of spiritual dimension, this turning to a source for inner strength was inevitable, a process of humanity catching up with itself, an acceleration of spiritual discovery beginning to match the energy of discovery in other areas. More, spiritual discovery seemed to me an essential component if we were not to become disoriented by the other energies we were releasing. We needed that centered calm, the inward certainty that relaxes and concentrates our vitality so that we can direct our own energies, not have them merely react with an adrenal response to outside stimuli.

As my spiritual interests and experiences increased, I wrote more and more about it. At first, this was mainly for myself. It helped me to clarify what I thought, and besides, I have always liked to write about what I was up to. What I had always liked now had an added dimension. My whole life was beginning to light up for me, but sometimes I'd wonder how readers would respond to what I was putting down on paper if I were ever to put it into a book. (By now, I needed no spiritual guides to inform me on the likely reactions of many intellectuals I know—of all those without even the leaven of personal friendship to soften their views. Nor could I really hold it against them. But I was sick and tired of dead-end philosophy—and I didn't want to give up on the human race.)

As for myself in the here and now, I had arrived at some kind of crossroads. I still had to deal with my private fear of writing about this material from the new point of view of belief. So what could a person do when confronted—although it had been a gradual confrontation—with understanding that the life they had led up to that point was only *part* of the truth? I never had been one to shut off about anything. I wasn't about to do so now. As far as going public was concerned, I had gone public on politics, on women's rights, on social change, on war and on what I believed to be injustice. I *was public*. That was my character. I was not used to holding back what interested me or what I believed in. I had thought a lot about that during every phase of my

life. I had grown up in public. I had made my mistakes
in public. I had been right and wrong in public. I had
laughed and cried in public, been in love in public,
written in public, apologized in public, and now, I
thought, I suppose I will have to say what I think about
human and extraterrestrial spirituality in public. Well,
so be it.

I talked it over with Bella, as I had a tendency to
do about things that counted. I had long since told her
everything that had happened in Peru. She knew that I
was continuing to pursue my new concepts; that I was
working with channelers, healers, and meditation; reading classics; visiting psychic centers and the like; and
trying to expand and raise my own conscious awareness
of dimensions that might be presently beyond our
understanding.

Now I tried to explain that the political solutions
she was involved in seemed to be resulting in the same
failures they had in the past, and that maybe it was
time for all of us in the world to take a look at life from
another perspective. We were sitting in an all-night
restaurant in Manhattan after having seen yet another
movie that exploited violence and fear.

"We can't go on like this," I said. "We're all scared
and frightened. We can blow the planet apart any day.
Life in any case seems to be falling apart around us, and
the only solutions we can come up with are more law
and order and more military spending."

"So?" she said, with one of her penetrating looks.
"So? What's your solution?"

"Well," I hesitated. "Well, look. For starters, I
think we have all become slaves to our own fear. We
keep *expecting* that we'll run into bad trouble to the
point where we almost get a sense of satisfaction when
things do turn to crap."

Bella put her hands in her lap and stared at her
midnight salad. "Yeah, well," she said, "so things turn
to crap. That's what politicians have to deal with."

"Could it be that they're so busy coping with the
mess that they don't take the time to figure out how to
turn it off?"

Bella shrugged. "This isn't something you can argue from generalities. You've had enough to do with politics to know that. So what is it you're getting at?"

"Fear, Bella. Fear. Fear of death; fear of self-made holocaust; fear of the future, or fear that we won't have one because we are literally, for the first time in history, capable of destroying the world; fear of much smaller things like losing our jobs, or our families, or the regard of friends and neighbors . . ."

"Now, wait a minute. Being afraid is perfectly natural—in some situations it's downright healthy. Mankind wouldn't have got where it has without fear."

"Okay, right. But by the same token, mankind wouldn't have got where it has if it had always let fear dictate its actions. I'm not saying it's wrong to be afraid, but that it's dangerous to let fear control our lives. Plus the very important fact that, to me now, most of these fears are unnecessary."

"How come?"

"Well, frankly Bella, to me, being certain about the actual existence of the soul, I mean as a reality, has made all the difference. It's not something I came to easily. But that's where I am now, so I believe that everyone has, or rather *is*, a soul, of divine origin, and one that has lived many times before and will live again."

"Oh," she said, twisting her hands, "we should just sit back and leave it all to cosmic design or something?"

"No," I said. "I wouldn't put it that way. I guess that it is really a question of tending to one's own self and the people we come in contact with as kindly and tolerantly as possible, knowing that what we put out will come back. I guess I'm saying that each of us has to start with ourselves, because that's all that we can really control in the first place."

"Does that mean you're opting out of involvement in politics, the women's liberation movement and everything?"

"No way. On the contrary. If anything, I'm going to be even more concerned and involved."

"So, what's different then?"

"What's different is how I *feel* about it. I'm looking at the whole thing from a new perspective, one that doesn't include fear. Fear is what has turned us all off, alienated us from ourselves and from each other. So many people are indifferent, apathetic—my God, you know yourself what a struggle it is to get the voting population to the polls. A helluva lot of people are simply too afraid to care, or believe that it wouldn't make any difference if they did. They don't realize that it is *themselves* they don't *dare* care about; it's *themselves* they're opting out on. Instead, they bitch about what the other guy is doing. It always comes back to the individual. Yet they're the ones who, out of fear, shut themselves off. All other life, on earth anyway, flourishes with 'feelings.' Feeling, *caring*, has become our most precious missing dimension. As far as I'm concerned, non-believers in spirituality, the soul, reincarnation, whatever, can start right there, by letting their imaginations help them to care; and if they never got any further, the world would still be a better place. But what I myself really believe is that if each of us could rid ourselves of fear by honestly understanding our own spirituality, by acknowledging it and achieving a higher awareness, that the ripple effect would be astonishing."

"I don't know what you mean. Give me an example," said Bella. "I mean, with the world going the way it is, *who* is an example of that?"

I thought a moment, and almost involuntarily I said, "Anwar Sadat, for one, or Martin Luther King, or Buddha, or Christ, or Mother Teresa, or Gandhi. All these people personally believed in a higher cosmic design which enabled them to take up a positive belief in human potential. They emphasized the positive. Also, Thomas Jefferson, Thoreau, Voltaire—and a lot more."

"Yeah," said Bella. "But what are you saying they believed in?"

"A kind of higher harmony; that they were part of a larger design that was not related only to *this* life experience."

"Are you saying that they all believed in reincarnation?"

I sipped my red wine, remembering all that I had read on the founding fathers of the American revolution; their involvement with mystical sects and teachings, and the existence of the soul.

"Not necessarily," I said. "But Jefferson and Washington and Ben Franklin—in fact, most of the men who signed the Bill of Rights and drew up the Constitution, said they wanted to form a new republic based on spiritual values. And those values they believed in went all the way back to the beliefs of Hindu scriptures and Egyptian mysticism. That's why they put the pyramid on the dollar bill—in fact, the dollar and the Great Seal are full of spiritual symbols that link way back to long before the revolution. And all those pre-Christian beliefs had to do with reincarnation."

"Show me the research," said Bella.

"Of course I will. I just mention it because they were our original politicians, yet none of the people in politics these days seem to even know the origins of their democracy. I can see that they're distracted because everything is in such a mess, but if some of them did acquaint themselves with what our forefathers actually intended, if they could identify with the early principles, that might influence how they vote now and what priorities they find most important. They might even manage to stop the destructive course we're on."

Bella lit a cigarette and tossed the match into an ashtray. "So you believe that humans fit into a larger plan than most of us think we do. Our ideas and beliefs are off the mark and that's why we've screwed up the world so badly?"

"Right. Except it's not 'most of us.' Most of the world's people do believe in reincarnation, in a larger plan. It's Westerners who leave out the important part."

"And that important part is what?"

"The pre-existence of the soul—the fact that we have lived many times and will live many more as the laws of cause and effect work themselves out."

Bella considered awhile, pulled on the cigarette, blew out a deep breath. "Listen," she said, "I was educated in the orthodox Jewish tradition and a deep belief in a spiritual being is not foreign to me." I had never heard her say that before. "But," she went on, "believing in the soul is one thing. Believing in reincarnation of the soul is another. You might be right in what you can sense and what you believe, but I can't go along with it. I'll tell you one thing though—I wish I could."

I felt tears well up in my eyes. "Why, Bella?"

"Because," she said slowly, "then I could believe that everything was going to turn out okay, even if I did nothing about it. I wouldn't have to fight so hard to make things better. Maybe I need the challenge. But, my darling, if people like me didn't fight to do our part it just might not turn out well. You see?"

I blew my nose. "I guess so," I said. "Yes, I see. It could be that all of us have our own roles to play, but the challenge would be there anyway, I think. Or maybe this time around, it's necessary to you to perceive it that way. I know that *I* must have been many different people in many different times. That's why I feel so at home in so many places in the world. I usually feel I've been there before. And I'm just learning to trust these feelings that my intellect might say were ridiculous. The point is, if all this happened to me, then it has to have happened to others. In some strange way we may all know each other. How many times have you met someone and had an instant recognition of what we even call 'a kindred spirit'?"

"Well, yeah." Bella sounded careful. "And you are saying that, from your point of view, you believe that we are all part of each other—and also part of a larger design?"

"Right. That's where disincarnate beings come in. If I lived many lifetimes, then what was I doing between each lifetime? I mean, where was I? If my soul energy went to spend a while in the ether, as the mystical texts suggest, then what would be the differ-

ence between me in-between lifetimes and Tom Mc-
Pherson now who says he is an entity speaking through
Kevin? I mean, maybe there are all kinds of dimensions
of reality of which the earth plane is only one."

Bella looked at me searchingly. "What I'm trying to
understand," she said, "is how you got into all of this.
How did all this happen? I know you and all those other
famous and intelligent people who believe as you do
weren't bananas. So what is going on?"

I leaned back in my chair. "I don't know, Bellitchka.
Maybe life is a cosmic joke on us. We take it all so
seriously. We try to legislate morality instead of living
it, and go around judging everybody who thinks differently than we do when maybe there is no such thing as
one reality. Maybe everything is real—earth plane,
astral plane, plain plane, I don't know. I just know that
from what *I* have learned, felt, and read, I can't ignore
it. And why should I? Some of the greatest minds this
planet has ever seen believed in what I'm just beginning to understand. So I'm going to go on investigating,
not only because I'm just plain curious but because it's
also making me happy."

Bella smiled. "Okay, that I can go along with. So
tell me what difference all this is really making in your
life. That's what I'm concerned about."

I thought a bit, trying to find the words that would
reassure my friend. Finally I said, "Bella, it's strange,
but *knowing* that there is a law of cause and effect in
operation makes me very aware of how precious every
single moment of every single day can be."

"How does that work?" she questioned.

"Nothing—literally nothing—is insignificant. Every thought, every gesture, everything I say and do,
has an energy attached to it which is hopefully positive.
In the back of my head I am constantly aware that
harmony does exist, I mean, as a real energy, a resource
I can draw on. I am aware that everything has a reason
for happening. Also, I know that whatever good I can
do, whatever fun I can share, whatever contribution I
make, even if it's to say 'Good morning!' to someone,

will, somewhere, sometime, come back to me. It's not a matter of making Brownie points. It just feels a whole hell of a lot better in *me*. It gives me a kind of feeling of living in a universal *now*. Every *now* second becomes important. In fact, I think I might be seeing in a—what—a *whole* way, that the past, present and future are interdependent, are really what amounts to the same thing."

"And you're not going to opt out and go away and meditate in a hut?"

I laughed. "No, I promise you, no. I had to stay away while I searched out this stuff. It *has* taken me years to get to this point. But now, well—it's an added dimension, a tremendous joy, a well of energy for me. It means I can be more fully involved than before. But now I don't see life as a battlefield. On the contrary, I believe it can be a paradise, and what's more, we should *expect* it to be. That is reality to me now. Dwelling on the negative simply contributes to its power."

"But my darling, the negative exists. It has to be dealt with, doesn't it?"

"Sure. What I'm saying is that a lot of it exists because we make it so. We *need* to believe in a positive reality right here on earth because the believing will help to make *it* so. That's the real power we have for change. Look, Bella. Use nature as a guidepost. There's no morality or judgment in nature. Sure, animals kill—for food, not because they hate, not for 'sport.' I don't see nature judging our destruction of it. It just disappears if we destroy it. But it comes back again, doesn't it? Maybe in another form? So the real lesson in all of this is that life is eternal regardless of how mindlessly we behave. And I believe that souls, invisible entities, are a part of the cyclical harmony of nature. None of it ever dies; it just changes form. If you want to think of it that way, it could be that *this* is science, not mysticism."

The waitress came with the check.

"Well," said Bella, "I guess you were never able to do anything by halves, were you?"

"Nope. I guess not. And I guess that what I'm

really getting at is to be whole. For the first time in my life I'm beginning to understand what being whole really means. Particularly when it involves the recognition of everything you've *ever* been, which leads you to the realization of whom you are now. I don't worry about the past and I don't worry about the future. I think, act, live for the present, which the past created, and which is creating the future. It's like Krishnamurti says—each person is a universe. If you know yourself, you know everything."

"Oh my God," said Bella. "Is that the way you get to be a Senator?"

"I don't know. Is being a Senator better than being you?"

"Are you judging me, Madame Nature?"

I took her hand and patted it. "Sorry. I'm still learning..."

❷ We walked out together into the clear Manhattan night. I looked up and searched the stars above us as we strolled together, hand in hand. Neither of us talked. We walked for a few blocks before Bella decided to hail a cab.

"Well, my darling," she said, "maybe there is a way to avoid disaster for the world..."

"Hey, Bella," I said, "do you know the etymology of the word 'disaster'?"

"Jesus," she said, "now what?"

"Well, it comes from the Latin word *disastrum* and the Greek word *disastrato*. Broken down, *dis* is defined as 'torn away from or apart from,' and *astrato* means 'the stars.' Therefore a person who is 'disastrato' has been separated from the heavenly bodies or, torn from the stars. He then experiences what the Latin language describes as *disastro*—a disaster."

Bella looked up into the sky, then back at me, and blinked. "I can't deal with it," she said. "Just so long as it's right for you." She kissed me and I watched her climb into a cab and barrel down Second Avenue.

I walked back to my apartment, looking up until I

found the North Star, the Big Dipper, and then the
Little Dipper. Then I looked for the Pleiades, the
Seven Sisters. I remembered reading about the Pleiades
in the Book of Job. I remembered the Pleiadean connections in the research I had done that seemed to indicate
a relationship with the Great Pyramid, the Incas, the
Mayans, the Greeks, the American Indians, and the
East Indians. I stopped again to look up to the Pleiades
cluster and tried to imagine, in terms I could understand,
how far away those stars really were. Scientists said it
was impossible to cross such distances, that one would
die of old age before getting there. But wasn't thought
faster than the speed of light? Would it ever be possible
to travel by the projection of one's own thought? Could
thought control and propel physical matter? Maybe
that, in the end, would be the connection between the
spiritual mind and technology—making the discovery
that the power of the spiritual mind is the highest
power of all. Learning to work with it would develop an
even higher technology. In other words, if we learned
to raise our spiritual thought, perhaps we could locate
our bodies wherever we desired them to be.

I walked on toward my apartment, thinking of all
the human beings who had been so much a part of my
new way of thinking. I thought of Bella and what she
meant to me with her combustible, challenging personality, so consistently and determinedly intent on making
the world a better place.

I thought of Mike and his good-hearted skepticism,
of Gerry and his humanitarian political solutions, of
Kevin and his shining pure faith, of Cat and Anne
Marie and my friends in Sweden who had helped show
me another world of reality. Then I thought of David
and wondered if I would ever see him again.

Watching the crosstown bus chug to a stop at the
corner of my apartment building, I saw a taxi careen
around in front of it, running the red light. And I
laughed at the insane, sweet chaos that is Manhattan.

I took a final look at the stars, went upstairs, and
found the stones that David had delivered to me from
the Masai tribesman years before: stones which I had

had set in a pyramidal shape, long before that held any significance for me, long before David meant anything to me or I even knew who he was. I cradled the pyramidal shape in my hand.

Then I sat down and began to draft a book. I wrote until five o'clock the next morning.

Maybe one day I would take a trip to the Pleiades and see what was on the other side. Would it be as full of wonder as the inner journey I was just beginning?

ABOUT THE AUTHOR

Shirley MacLaine was born and raised in Virginia. She began her career as a Broadway dancer and singer, then progressed to feature performer and award-winning actress of television and films. She traveled extensively on her own all over the world. Her experiences in Africa, India, the Far East, and Hollywood formed the basis for her first book, *"Don't Fall Off the Mountain,"* which became a national bestseller, as did her subsequent books, *You Can Get There From Here*, *Out on a Limb*, and *Dancing in the Light*.

Special Offer
Buy a Bantam Book
for only 50¢.

Now you can have Bantam's catalog filled with hundreds
of titles plus take advantage of our unique and exciting
bonus book offer. A special offer which gives you the
opportunity to purchase a Bantam book for only 50¢.
Here's how!

By ordering any five books at the regular price per
order, you can also choose any other single book
listed (up to a $5.95 value) for just 50¢. Some
restrictions do apply, but for further details why not
send for Bantam's catalog of titles today!

Just send us your name and address and we will send
you a catalog!